The Grand Strategy
of the Soviet Union

Edward N. Luttwak

The Grand Strategy of the Soviet Union

With appendices by
Herbert Block and W. Seth Carus

St. Martin's Press
New York

Library of Congress Catalog Card Number 83-60410

ISBN 0-312-34260-8

First published in Great Britain by George Weidenfeld
and Nicolson Limited.

Contents

List of Tables   ix

Preface   xi

1 Introduction: What is the Soviet Union?   1
   The question of nationality   4

2 The Traditional Pattern of Soviet Strategy   13

3 The New Dynamics of the Soviet Empire:
   from Optimism to Pessimism   21

   Imperialism: the last stage of Soviet optimism   25
   The advent of pessimism   28
   Military optimism and its consequences   39

4 The Tools of Soviet Power   42

   The advent of operational confidence   55
   The decline of Soviet ideological influence   60

5 Soviet Imperialism and its Consequences   72

   The mechanics of expansion   75

6 The Future Scope of Soviet Imperial Expansion   81

   Expansion for political security   86
   Expansion for strategic security   89
   Expansion for regional security   107

7 In Conclusion: Soviet Grand Strategy and its Future   111

Notes   117

Contents

Appendix I: The Economic Basis of Soviet Power
by Herbert Block

Part One: the Present   119

Part Two: the Outlook for a Decade or Two   145

Notes   174

Appendix II: The Evolution of Soviet Military Power Since 1965 *by W. Seth Carus*

Strategic- and Theatre-nuclear Forces   176

Army   191

Air force   206

Navy   214

References   231

Index   235

*To David M. Abshire, in
small recompense for ten
years of patient friendship.*

List of Tables

1 Distribution of Soviet field divisions: current and contingent   84

2 Average annual GNP growth rates (USSR, US, world)   137

3 Estimated Soviet GNP at factor cost, 1950–80, by sector of origin and by end use   169

4 GNP for important countries and groupings, 1950–80; population and per capita GNP 1980   170

5 Estimated rates of growth of Soviet GNP and its subdivisions, 1950–80, with an international comparison   171

6 Total population, working-age population and labour force in the USSR   172

7 Soviet foreign trade and its geographic distribution, 1955–80   173

8 Strategic nuclear weapons delivery systems   183

9 Theatre and strategic bombers   184

10 Ballistic missile submarines   185

11 Strategic ballistic missiles   186

12 Strategic defence forces   187

13 Air defence aircraft   188

14 Theatre-nuclear weapons delivery systems   189

15 Theatre ballistic missiles   190

16 Army divisions, by type and region   196

17 Divisional strength   197

18 Army weapons and equipment   198

19 Tanks   198

20 Light armoured vehicles   199

21 Artillery   200

22 Multiple rocket launchers   201

23 Mortars   201

24 Anti-tank guns   202

25 Anti-tank guided missiles   203

26 Land-based surface-to-air missiles   204

27 Anti-aircraft guns   205

28 Air force   211

29 Tactical combat aircraft   211

List of Tables

30	Air-to-surface missiles	212
31	Air-to-air missiles	213
32	Transport aircraft	213
33	Naval vessels	221
34	Cruise missile submarines	222
35	Torpedo attack submarines	223
36	Aircraft carriers and aviation cruisers	223
37	Cruisers	224
38	Destroyers	225
39	Frigates	226
40	Small combatants	227
41	Ship-borne anti-ship missiles	228
42	Ship-borne surface-to-air missiles	229
43	Naval aviation	229
44	Naval aircraft	230

Tables 8–44 refer to Soviet forces

Preface

The worst fears and the best of hopes conspire to distort our understanding of the Soviet Union and its strategy. Certainly our welfare and possibly our survival may depend on our ability to make a true judgement of the Soviet Union; but as we strive to assay its power, as we seek to uncover the intent of its leaders, our view is obscured by the clash of rival opinions, each very categorical and none wholly persuasive.

Some persist in believing that the Soviet Union is essentially peaceful, or at least that its aims are strictly defensive. They evoke the record of Russian history to show that the Tsars conquered the largest empire ever made on earth not by aggression, but merely by holding their winnings each time they successfully resisted invasion. The leaders of the Soviet Union, they argue, conform to this pattern, so that while some modest effort to maintain Western strength may be justified, the current preponderance of Soviet military power over any feasible Western coalition should be accepted with equanimity. The Soviet Union, they assert, is no more inclined to start wars than the Tsars were, and indeed much less, given the nuclear sanction of our age.

In a more technical vein, some of those who belong to this school of thought argue that the military power of the Soviet Union is greatly overestimated; they insist that with an industry so backward its weapons cannot possibly be advanced; that as an empire of many nations its armed forces cannot have sufficient cohesion to risk a major war. Images of the clumsy Russian linger in their view to sustain a particular opinion about the nature of Soviet military power: very strong no doubt on the defensive, but fundamentally incapable of launching powerful offensives of swift and precise execution, to circumvent nuclear deterrence by a quick victory. Until the spectacular seizure of Kabul in December 1979 by airborne assault, this view had much to support it, including the Soviet performance in Czechoslovakia in 1968, when a great and disordered mass of forces flooded into that country only to suffer logistic breakdowns which would have made them quite vulnerable had the Czechs resisted.

Certainly the optimistic view of a Soviet Union fundamentally unaggressive and the adjunct opinion that discounts its military power suggest that our safety is easily assured, and with only the smallest sacrifice for the upkeep of Western defences. Only one thing spoils the happy prospect: our great difficulty in believing that it is really all so easy. And our doubts must be greatly stimulated by a peculiar contradiction: it is precisely those who belong to this school of thought who are most insistent in pressing for policies of accommodation towards the Soviet Union. If there is so little to fear, why strive so urgently to assuage Soviet hostility?

At the opposite extreme, there is the opinion that the Soviet Union is simply the Nazi Germany of our days, and just as aggressive – not this time because of a maniacal leading spirit but rather because a military empire is expansionist by its very nature. This is a Soviet Union that is bent on war, being now delayed only by some unfulfilled programme of military preparation. There are indeed some obvious parallels, including dictatorship and militarism, and then the fact that the Soviet Union seems to be oppressing those very same groups that the Nazis at first oppressed, and then tried to exterminate. It is perhaps more fruitful to contemplate the implications of the analogy than to examine its dubious merits, for this opinion of the Soviet Union does draw our attention to the undoubted fact that there has been no adequate Western response to the wholly unprecedented accumulation of military power which the Kremlin has achieved.

Those who belong to this school of thought can legitimately compare the present conduct of the West with the British and French failure to maintain forces sufficient to deter Hitler from his aggressions. And more parallels may be drawn between the emotional and intellectual atmosphere of our day and the 'culture of appeasement' of the 1930s – with an equally paralysing fear of conflict now being sustained by the terror of nuclear war in place of the imagined gas-filled bombs that seemed so terrifying in 1938. One notes the eagerness with which the Kremlin's most transparently manipulative disarmament offers are received in the West, and one notes also the ill-tempered and suspicious impatience that awaits each American call for a strengthening of the Atlantic Alliance. The very words nowadays heard in Bonn and The Hague forcefully recall the fretful anxiety of Paris and London for one another in Hitler's day, when each feared that the other might not be sufficiently feeble in its conduct to preserve Hitler's peace. But even if all this is persuasive it serves only to confirm the analogy between our present and our own past; the comparison between today's Soviet Union and yesterday's Nazi Germany on the other hand remains without much meaning or value: it does not enlighten us.

It is between these extremes that we must find the reality of the Soviet Union.

One

Introduction: What is the Soviet Union?

Unless we accept the Soviet claim that Lenin's *coup d'état* gave birth to an entirely new state, and indeed to a new era in the history of mankind, we must recognize in today's Soviet Union the old empire of the Russians – the only European empire that still survives. In a Darwinian vein, it might be said that when nationalism came to dominate the political attitudes of mankind, in Europe first and in the whole world later, the Russian empire survived and prospered because Lenin and the Bolsheviks imposed upon it a transnational ideology, at a time when all the other empires were going into dissolution for want of a similar remedy.

Lenin can therefore be seen as the only logical successor of the Tsars. Constitutional democrats, social democrats and all manner of others including even the Tsars might still rule the Russians themselves, but in the new era of nationalism, only a transnational dictatorship could preserve the empire. By accepting national sentiments as legitimate, but only within cultural bounds, after first decisively subordinating all ethnic priorities to the worldwide class struggle, the ideology that Lenin brought to power could justify the refusal to grant independence to each of the many nations of the empire; and this was a refusal that an efficient dictatorship could forcefully impose, as it still does. The largest empire known in history is thus preserved almost intact till this day while only memories and the smallest fragments remain of the Hapsburg, British, French, Dutch, Spanish and Portuguese empires which ruled much of the world in the days when Lenin came to power.

But of course the true successor of the Tsars was Stalin rather than Lenin, because during Lenin's tenure transnational communism remained the true ideology – which meant of course that the Russians and their power were supposed to serve the interests of worldwide communism. It was Stalin who turned the proposition right around by first establishing a clear priority for Soviet state interests over the worldwide revolutionary cause ('Socialism in one country'), and then going on to exploit for all they were worth the powerful loyalties that transnational communism could attract, to serve the interests of the empire of the Russians. By so doing, Stalin became the prudent keeper and successful aggrandizer of the Tsars' inheritance, as his successors remain till this day – a fact of great consequence in setting limits to the attractions of dissidence inside the Soviet Union as far as the Russians themselves are concerned.

Of the role of ideology as one of the instruments of Soviet strategy more will be said below, but in view of the unfortunate persistence of our sterile debates on the matter, it is immediately necessary to confront the issue of ideological motives in Soviet conduct. It is not illegitimate to draw a direct comparison between transnational communism and the Soviet empire on the one hand, and missionary Christianity and the Byzantine empire on the other. We know that the rulers of Constantinople exploited the gains of missionary Christianity to promote the interests of their empire whenever and wherever they could, even while being perfectly sincere in their own devotion to the creed. That men can both truly believe in an ideology and yet seek to use it to enhance their own temporal power seems paradoxical only to outsiders. To the protagonists themselves there is no contradiction: their solid justification is that the greater their power, the greater is their ability to protect and disseminate the true faith.

Certainly the Byzantine record suggests that it is unprofitable to speculate on the personal devotion of the rulers who so assiduously promoted the faith, and that it is quite futile to try to distinguish between ideological and state-political motives in their policies. Every religious act was meant to strengthen the state against its temporal enemies, internal or external, and every political act was meant to sustain the true faith in a world filled with unbelievers and heretics. The same, incidentally, was true of Tsarist Russia. Thus, for example, during the later nineteenth century the Tsars assiduously promoted the proselytizing of the Russian Orthodox Church inside the Ottoman empire and especially in Palestine (where it grew greatly, but only at the expense of Greek Orthodoxy). Was this effort motivated by religious considerations alone, or was the Russian missionary church an arm of Russian foreign policy in the competition with the British, French and Germans for influence in the Levant? To show that the Byzantines or the Russians under the Tsars would frequently ignore the religious aspect of things in their dealings with foreign unbelievers or heretics proves nothing, because the emperors could validly claim that it was a question of survival for them to do so – and the state that would thus survive was the only guarantor of the safety of the true church in the first place. To show by documentary evidence that it was the court that financed Byzantine missionaries, or that the Tsar's foreign ministry paid for the churches, monasteries, hospitals and schools that were built in such great numbers in Ottoman Palestine, again proves nothing, because the emperor was the head of the Byzantine church just as the Tsar's foreign ministry belonged to a government which was itself the official protector of the Russian Orthodox faith.

Similarly, in our own days, the Soviet Union loudly protested against the imprisonment of Egyptian communists under Nasser and the executions of Sudanese communists under Numeiri. It might seem that a purely state-motivated diplomacy would have refrained from such intrusive protests. But in both cases it can also be argued persuasively that it was precisely for diplomatic reasons and not because of any pure ideological solidarity that the complaints were made – for in both cases the protest was most convenient: in Nasser's regard forcefully to remind him of his debt to the Soviet Union, and with the Sudanese much later to provide justification for the Soviet liaison with Libya. Especially revealing is the record of Soviet relations with Iraq, whose successive dictators have had close connections with Moscow even while persecuting and indeed exterminating Iraqi communists from time to time. Ever since the overthrow of the monarchy in July 1958, the Soviet Union, under a variety of agreements, has supplied Iraq with arms, including large numbers of 'high-profile' weapons such as battle tanks and combat aircraft of modern design. Over the years, the Soviet Union and Iraq have cooperated in a variety of military joint ventures, and the formal agreements signed between the two countries include the fifteen-year Treaty of Friendship and Co-operation of April 1972. And yet, during the same period, the attitude of Iraq's rulers to their local communists has alternated

3

from a grudging toleration up to their inclusion in the government at cabinet level, all the way down to outright massacre – and no obvious correlation can be established at all between the ups and downs in Soviet-Iraqi relations and the abrupt changes in the government's treatment of the Iraqi Communist Party. When the sufferings of their Iraqi comrades were brought to the attention of Soviet leaders by French and Italian communists, the Kremlin's self-justification was identical to the Byzantine argument: namely that the worldwide enhancement of the faith sometimes imposes the cruel necessity of disregarding the welfare of some of its immediate representatives. And of course, the Kremlin would no more accept a distinction between the interests of the state, and those of the faith which the state upholds, than the rulers of Byzantium would have done.

The question of nationality

Lenin and his party seized power over the Soviet state by an act of force, and their Bolshevik regime immediately had to struggle against domestic and foreign foes by brutal repression and war; nevertheless it was the firm belief of the early leaders that once tranquillity was restored, education widely promoted, and a modest prosperity achieved, their ideology and rule would find genuine acceptance throughout the lands that Moscow controlled. Had that hope been realized, today's Soviet state would be a consensual union of nationalities linked by a common ideology, even if the dictatorship of each (national) communist party would have to continue till the advanced stage of communism is finally achieved – when the state structure itself will wither away. In other words, the Soviet state was supposed to evolve into a voluntary confeder-ation. The independence willingly conceded to Finland, and rather less willingly to the three Baltic states, was a tangible manifestation of this early attitude; and indeed the nominal right of each national 'republic' to become independent has been reaffirmed in successive Soviet constitutions, if only to remain a dead letter, like so much else in those documents:

It was neither Lenin's terror nor Stalin's that precluded the emergence of a genuine transnational state, but rather the primacy gradually accorded to the Russian nationality within the Soviet Union. Lenin had consistently treated Russian nationalism as the chief domestic antagonist of his creation; it was not by accident (as *Pravda* might say) that the most sensitive positions – in charge of internal security, propaganda and war – were at first filled by Estonians, Poles, Jews, Finns, Georgians and so on. It was only natural, after all, that small and weak nationalities would be especially responsive to a transnational creed that would place all on an equal footing. Russian nationalism, on the other hand, was inseparable from Tsardom and the church, and indeed it had shaped the world-view of the official class of the old regime.

But once the Bolshevik state was duly organized with a large and growing bureaucracy, its economic apparatus and its state services military and social, it was inevitable that the more educated peoples within the USSR should lead the less advanced in the implementation of 'socialism' in the economy, in education and in the entire structure of the new totalitarian state – and once the Finns, Estonians, Lithuanians and Latvians all became independent, it was the Russians themselves who remained as the most 'advanced' nationality of any size inside the Soviet Union.

In the beginning, therefore, the primacy of the Russian people within the Soviet Union was the unavoidable reflection of the achievements and qualifications of individual Russians, and thus unchallengeable; the mass of teachers and managers, bureaucrats and soldiers, Party leaders and publicists could obviously be supplied only by the educated class, which happened to be predominantly Russian. Since Russian nationalism as such was still very much in disfavour, and since 'cultured' elements from all other nationalities could and did share fully in this primacy, which was then still a professional rather than a national phenomenon, there was no contradiction between the transnational ideology and the clear predominance of ethnic Russians in all leading roles.

It was under Stalin that the transformation of a professional primacy into a national supremacy took place. Well before the German invasion of June 1941, Stalin began to appeal – if only in a carefully controlled degree – to the loyalties that Russian nationalism could still evoke for the ruler who held the Kremlin, whether Tsar or commissar. When the German war began, it became clear almost immediately that the Red Army was disastrously outclassed;

all restraints were then removed and everything possible was done to identify the regime with the Russian motherland. To do so was a necessity of war – or at least it must have seemed so at the time – for Stalin could scarcely have foreseen that the Germans would themselves provide the most ample incentives for a fierce resistance by soldiers and partisans, Russian and non-Russian alike, by their immense brutalities.

For the revolutionary Soviet state, the abrupt reversion to the symbols, language and emotions of Russian nationalism was itself revolutionary. Once repudiated as class enemies and imperialists, the successful fighting figures of the Russian past were quite suddenly restored to heroic status and greatly celebrated in print, on film and in that characteristic Bolshevik medium, the large wall-poster. The Russian motherland became once again a fitting subject of veneration, as a mystic entity rather than one merely geographic, and even the Russian Orthodox Church was accorded a new and much higher status, not as a spiritual institution of course but at least as a national one. Moscow, it seems, was worth a good many liturgies, and also the several seminaries reopened and the many churches restored to churchly use.

The great military leaders and greater Tsars of the Russian past, Suvorov and Kutuzov, Ivan the Terrible and Peter the Great, Alexander Nevsky and Ivan Kalita were powerful but dangerous allies for Stalin and the Party. Those names and all that went with them by implication, namely the empire-building of the Russians, could be just as irritating to the sensitivities of non-Russians as they were a source of pride and loyalty for the ethnic Russians themselves. It is one thing to speak of Cromwell or Kitchener among the English; quite another to remember their names in the company of Irishmen or Afrikaners. Historians of the Second World War have generally seen fit to praise Stalin's restoration of Russian nationalism to official favour, giving him credit for 'flexibility' and guile, especially since the man who thus restored to the Russians their history and national pride was himself a Georgian. Above all, it is taken for granted that the nationalist restoration was necessary to sustain the Soviet war effort.

But since it is now known that in virtually every non-Russian ethnic group in the USSR that came under German occupation there was a very widespread willingness to collaborate with the new power in the land (and among the Russians too, at first), it is difficult to say whether Stalin's manoeuvre was truly successful. If it is reasonable to believe that the Russians fought better for their own ethnic motherland than for the abstract entity of the Soviet Union, it is just as likely that the non-Russians were alienated by the nationalist restoration, which inevitably made them into less than first-class citizens. Certainly the fact that the German army reached most of the non-Russians only in the summer of 1942 (by which time the new nationalist propaganda was going full blast), and that the Germans found many willing collaborators among them – including tens of thousands of volunteers for the Waffen SS – is a matter of historical record. As for the true impact of the nationalist campaign on the fighting morale of the Russians themselves, that too is difficult to judge because German atrocities must have had a far more powerful impact than any number of nationalist articles and books, films or posters.

But if the necessity and net value of the nationalist restoration must remain in doubt, what is perfectly clear is that it was an admission of failure. In spite of twenty years of consolidation and pervasive propaganda, the Soviet state had failed to attract enough loyalty to be defended for what it was, or so at least its leader believed. Faced with the crisis of the German invasion and the enormous defeats of the summer of 1941, the Soviet state had to assume the protective disguise of the Russian motherland. In view of what has happened since then, it might rather be said that the original transnational Soviet Union was in fact defeated in 1941, and that it surrendered to Mother Russia in preference to surrendering to the Germans. That clearly was the better alternative, but it was a surrender all the same.

Just as nationalism is normally a cohesive force in nation-states, it must be divisive in states that contain many different nationalities. The nationalist restoration that pleased so many Russians in 1941, and pleases them still, must have been just as displeasing to non-Russians, and it still is. Ideologically, a powerful contradiction was engendered between the official transnational creed and the Kremlin's elevation of the Russian people to a quasi-official supremacy over all other nationalities. Politically, a fundamental tension was created between the multinational composition of the state and the primacy accorded to just one of the nationalities.

Having triumphantly survived the advent of the National Idea[1] by issuing the promissory note of a transnational future, the Soviet

Union thus began to default on the payments in 1941. Given the circumstances of the time, however, the creditors could do little to press their claims. For one thing, ethnic Russians (with the largely assimilated Byelorussians) then still accounted for a good majority of the total population of the USSR,[2] and many other people of diverse ethnic origins – notably many Jews and the educated, Westernized elements among the more backward nationalities – also identified with the Russians. In any case the Muslim peoples of Soviet Central Asia and the Caucasus were then still so backward that their identity was defined by family, tribe, clan and religion rather than nationality; in other words, they were in a prenationalist stage. Finally, the more advanced nationalities in today's Soviet Union, the Estonians, Latvians and Lithuanians of the Baltic states and the Poles, Ruthenians and Ukrainians of the 'western' Ukraine, were not in the Kremlin's keeping at all, until after the reoccupation and annexations that came at the end of the Second World War.

In the latest (1979) census by contrast, ethnic Russians accounted for no more than 52.4 per cent of the population and even if one adds the heavily assimilated Byelorussians the proportion is still only 56 per cent. In the meantime, the general betterment of their circumstances has brought all the peoples of Soviet Central Asia and the Caucasus to the stage of national consciousness, and, by a coincidence most unfortunate for their rulers, this has happened at a time when Islam has once again become a very militant political phenomenon.

What census returns cannot measure is the apparently wide-spread reversion of non-Russian elites from the more backward nationalities to their own distinct national consciousness. It is known that the more educated among the Turkic peoples (Uzbeks, Tartars, Kazakhs, Azeris, Turkmens, Kirgiz and Bashkirs) and the Iranian peoples (Tadzhik, Ossetians and Kurds), as well as many smaller ethnic groups, were quite voluntarily becoming Russified during the 1920s and 1930s. The small minority of educated men and the few educated women of those nationalities were pulled towards the Russian language and 'Soviet' culture by all the attractions of joining the leading nationality, and a modern culture, and they were being pushed in the same direction by the fact that their own communities offered little scope for men of modern outlook, while being mostly hostile to emancipated women. At the same time, with transnationalism still dominant in the Kremlin,

8

many elite Armenians, Georgians and Jews were also becoming self-Russified – if only because a Russian cultural identity was seen as the gateway to high career advancements. To put it crudely, many hoped to emulate the spectacular careers of the Armenian Mikoyan, the Georgian Beria (not to speak of Stalin himself) and such Kremlin Jews as Kaganovich.

In, say, 1930 it would have been reasonable to expect that the better educated among the non-Russians would become thoroughly assimilated into a synthetic 'Soviet' identity by, say, 1980. This obviously has not happened. On the contrary, a process has been under way that can only be described by the clumsy word 'disaffiliation'. Instead of becoming 'new Soviet men' of Russified outlook it seems that most Turkic, Iranian and other minority intellectuals have instead chosen to lead the national consciousness movements of their own peoples; and even the unbelievers among them share in the cultural, if not spiritual, revival of Islam. As for the elite Armenians, Georgians and Jews who were so eager to Russify themselves in the 1930s, their reversal has been spectacular. Once the leading advocates of transnationalism, the three groups are now equally prominent in the new movement of national reaffirmation (in the case of the Jews to the point of seeking emigration in very large numbers; some 250,000 actually left the USSR between 1967 and 1981). And then finally the peoples absent till 1945, the Estonians, Latvians, Lithuanians, Poles, Ruthenians, 'western' Ukrainians and the Moldavians (or Romanians) of annexed Bessarabia are all now pressing their national claims loudly enough to be heard in the West from time to time.

Larger than any of these, the Ukrainian nationality has also maintained itself as distinct in spite of both centrally imposed Russification and a degree of continuing self-Russification. It is impossible to determine to what extent disaffiliation is under way and to what extent voluntary self-Russification still continues, but it is obvious that if Ukrainians were to reaffirm their distinct national consciousness in the same degree as the Armenians, Georgians and Jews have done, that would be disastrous from the viewpoint of the rulers in the Kremlin.

A worldwide trend of ethnic reaffirmation is now obviously in evidence, but it is impossible to avoid the judgement that elite self-Russification has given way to 'disaffiliation', because non-Russians feel themselves to be much less than equals in the highest ranks of the Soviet power elite. Among ordinary folk as well, nationalist reversion has been given a most powerful impetus by the nationalist restoration of the Russians themselves. Obviously, non-Russians could scarcely take part in the glorification of the Russian people and their achievements. Moreover, their elevation in status as the Soviet Union's 'leading nationality' has given the Russians some licence for the expression of a sense of superiority over all other nationalities, and this in turn has caused the latter to fall back on their own ethnic identity. In the case of the Jews, it is known that a process of assimilation already well advanced was interrupted and then undone by the revival of Russian antisemitism and indeed its official sanction during the last years of Stalin and again after 1967. Ultimately, it was inevitable that the public reassertion of Russian national pride would evoke competitive reaction by all other nationalities; a vicious circle has been engendered in which non-Russian hostility stimulates Russian assertiveness, which in turn causes resentment.

Stalin had been the Party's expert on nationality questions before he rose to supreme power and became the Party's expert on all things. He must have been fully aware of the danger that the Russian nationalism he unleashed would become powerfully divisive in peacetime; and in fact even before Berlin fell to his armies, Stalin tried to restore the primacy of class over nationality. He ordered an end to the anti-German campaign and revived the pre-1941 distinction between Hitlerites and the good working people of Germany, and a serious effort was made to force the Russian nationalist genie back into the bottle. But an increasingly decrepit Stalin could not accomplish that most difficult task, and his successors have lacked the capacity or perhaps the will to do so. It is one thing to recall chauvinistic books and films from distribution or to cover up Russian nationalist posters with new ones on class-struggle themes, and quite another to restore a consistently transnational attitude throughout a predominantly Russian bureaucracy of immense size. Once the Soviet regime lifted the transnational mask to reveal the features of Russian supremacism, the consequences could not be undone by merely lowering the mask once again. Certainly the memory must have been indelible among those non-Russians who had truly believed in the transnational promise that Lenin had issued. Besides, the Russians themselves had by then learned a new repertoire of words and attitudes formally compatible with the official transnationalism but nationalist and indeed supremacist in tone and substance.

But there is also a far more fundamental cause for the perpetuation of the nationalist restoration: the Soviet Union's economic failure. Even as late as the early 1960s, Soviet leaders were in the habit of uttering rather specific promises of high living standards to come in the near future. Soviet citizens were then being told that they would live far better in, say, 1980 than their West European or American counterparts. Had the Soviet economy developed as the Kremlin leaders (and a good many others) had expected, including those Western economists who were forever comparing high Soviet growth rates with the much more modest growth of the United States during the 1950s, the Soviet Union would now be in a position to attract the economically motivated loyalty of Russians and non-Russians alike. Though living standards have certainly improved, especially for the more backward Central Asian and Caucasian populations, today's Soviet Union cannot possibly present itself as the flag-bearer of economic advancement – and for the Russians themselves least of all. They are as well informed of Western standards of living as the advanced Baltic nationalities and the enterprising Armenians, Georgians and Jews, while at the same time their own standard of living is distinctly inferior. In the absence of bread, circuses must be offered instead, and the most seductive circus of all is the stimulation of Russian national pride.

There is an even simpler explanation for the toleration and indeed encouragement of Russian nationalism by the authorities: today's Soviet rulers are themselves almost all Russians (or Byelorussians), in sharp contrast to the truly transnational leadership of Stalin's day, when in the highest echelons of the Kremlin the Russians were merely one nationality among several.

Since the promise of a voluntary transnational confederation has not been realized, and since it obviously cannot be a nation-state, today's Soviet Union must be an empire – that is, a state in which one nationality dominates the homelands of many. In fact, the Soviet Union is the only remaining multinational empire of any consequence, except for the People's Republic of China – where, however, the non-Han nationalities are demographically insignificant (even if their homelands account for a large part of the entire territory).

Moreover, since Russification and voluntary self-Russification have been aborted, the Soviet empire is not, and will not become, a Russian empire in the way that the Tsars' empire truly was, or the Roman became. In the days of the Tsars, the non-Russian nationalities mattered so much less in the political realm than in today's Soviet Union. In the Roman case, on the other hand, the political cement of elite Romanization followed very quickly in the wake of territorial conquest. By that process the empire of the Romans, or more specifically the empire created by the leaders of the city of Rome, became an empire that was Roman only in its public culture, in which elites of diverse ethnic origin could rise to the highest levels of power in all branches of the state. Plainly that is not the case in today's Soviet Union where, to the contrary, a multinational revolutionary elite has given way to a Russian bureaucratic elite. With Lenin's promissory note now in default, the Soviet Union finds itself confronted by the very force that dissolved all the other empires that loomed so large in Lenin's day: the National Idea – and this time it cannot be fought by any means except for repression pure and simple.

Two

The Traditional Pattern of Soviet Strategy

The empire of the Russians of our own days is by far the largest of all empires known to history. But it is worth recalling that this great expansion took place largely in the void, or at least at the expense of weak powers. Except for Peter the Great's encounters with the Ottoman empire, it was only in 1812 and again in 1941–5 that the Russians waged successful war against an enemy that was unambiguously a first-class power. In both cases the Russians did not prevail alone, and it is most doubtful that they could have done so. In both cases, moreover, their victories were won on the counter-offensive, after their enemies had first exhausted themselves by stretching their forces and supply lines to invade deep into the vast space of Russian lands.

With these exceptions, the centuries of successful expansion under the Tsars saw Russian colonists moving east into Siberia and north into Karelia against the feeble opposition of small tribes, while Russian armies fought against Lithuanian, Polish and Swedish kingdoms that were never first-class powers, against the Tatar Khanates and the Ottoman empire in decay, against the Chinese empire's weak outer peripheries, and against Caucasian tribes and central Asian emirates lacking the modern weapons of the day. In spite of the many victories in the record of Russian imperial expansion, we thus find not one case of successful war deliberately launched against a first-class power. Ever since Peter the Great, the Tsars could have great confidence in their eventual ability to defeat an enemy – any enemy – that would first deplete its strength by invading deeply into their immense territories. But the Tsars had good reason to doubt their ability to use military power in a deliberate fashion, to launch successful offensive warfare against a first-class power.

It is, of course, a commonplace of military theory that the defence is stronger than the offence strategically as well as tactically, but in the Russian case there was an unusually great disparity between the very great defensive strength of the country and its far smaller capacity to wage war offensively against serious opposition. Two compelling reasons immediately present themselves to explain the contrast: the fragility of autocratic rule, and military backwardness – at least as compared to Western powers, which were the only first-class powers in contact with Russia after the eclipse of the Mongols and the decline of the Ottoman empire.

The throne of the Tsars offered unlimited powers to its holder but it did not offer security of tenure. Until the nineteenth century, the succession was neither firmly dynastic nor elective but only 'occupative'. The Tsar who went campaigning in foreign lands at the head of his troops would risk losing the Kremlin to a rival claimant unless the outcome was swiftly successful; and an autocracy knew no substitute for the ruler himself when it came to an undertaking as great as an offensive war against a major power. In defending Russian lands against foreign invaders, by contrast, the problem of legitimacy was greatly alleviated, since the Tsar could remain in the Kremlin. Besides, all sound nations will rally around their ruler when home and country must be protected against the foreigner.

For Russia, military backwardness obviously did not mean weakness either in the seventeenth century or the twentieth, and of this backwardness the purely technical part was in any case the least important. That Russian weapons might not be quite so well designed, and would certainly be more crudely built than those of the most advanced Western nations, scarcely counts for much even in our own times of most rapid technical advancement, and certainly the difference counted for much less in centuries past, when it might take sixty years for the use of the bayonet to spread across Europe, and a century or more before a new musket-firing mechanism was generally employed.

Superior numbers *and* a military doctrine that recognizes technical inferiority and specifically seeks to circumvent it can easily obliterate even quite large differences in the quality of weapons. Just as the clumsiest matchlocks could do very nicely even against the smartest flintlocks when the former were being fired by vast numbers from behind the shelter of redoubts, while the latter were in the hands of outnumbered troops advancing fully exposed to attack, so also the standard Soviet battle tanks in service in the 1960s could fight well by the dozen against outnumbered Western tanks, even if the latter had better guns and more sophisticated ancillaries. Western tanks could have a superior lethal range and a faster rate of engagement due to their fire-control electronics, but Soviet armoured forces could overcome both by closing rapidly to eliminate the advantage of range, and then firing en masse to nullify the higher rate of engagement of Western tanks. In the seventeenth century as in the twentieth, the purely technical backwardness of the Russian armies counted for little, since numbers and the right tactics could easily nullify the differences in weapon performance.

It is, incidentally, interesting to note how readily Westerners explain Russian military successes as the result of sheer numerical advantage, and how reluctantly they recognize the virtues of Russian military thought. And yet before there was a Pushkin to be admired for his poetry, Suvorov had already proved the originality of Russian military strategy, and of Russian tactics and operational methods. What Suvorov taught should have been of great interest to all the armies of his day, but it was most specifically useful for the Russians themselves – for whom his doctrine offered a way of compensating for technical weakness by exploiting their numerical strength and the tenacity and excellent fieldcraft of the Russian soldier.

Far more consequential was another sort of backwardness that might most loosely be described as 'managerial'. In an economy always comparatively primitive, in a society where the rulers and the state have always loomed so large that all ordinary men are small, the techniques, talents and subtle arts of running large-scale organizations well enough to compete with other well-run organiz-ations were much less developed than in the greater and richer nations of the West.

In a defensive war waged inside Russia, simple orders enforced by drastic punishment, improvisations more or less disorderly, and all the expedients that come so readily to a people greatly familiar with shortages could suffice to deploy large armies in the field and keep them supplied. Even less was needed to sustain the peasants-in-arms who would wage petty warfare against the stragglers and outposts of an invading army. To mount large-scale offensive operations, on the other hand, the advance of the armies must be concerted by advance planning and by central command thereafter, and supplies must be organized to follow closely in their wake, move by move and step by step. One talented commander-in-chief, or even several skilled and cunning generals, cannot suffice to direct the whole complex operation; it takes organizers and 'managers' by the hundred to do that. And where in the old pre-industrial Russia would such men be found? Not among the bailiffs of lethargic estates, nor the old-style rural traders or small shopkeepers of the towns, and least of all could they be drawn from the state bureaucracy, where the deadening safety of procedure and the arrogance of petty power combined to strangle managerial talent.

When Tsarist Russia did belatedly industrialize, and in a fairly big way, there was more need and more scope for management of good quality, and for all manner of organizational talent. But even then, an economy whose labour and many of whose basic resources were (and are) cheap, and whose products did not have to meet the test of the free market, would not demand high standards of efficiency.

Russian backwardness in management was by no means unique – it was and is the common lot of traditional societies. But it was the sheer geographic extent of the empire, and its landlocked continental nature (which imposed overland deployment and supply) that made the 'managerial' disadvantage so telling. It was the combination of the empire's geography and the defects of Russian society that crippled the potentially great military power of Moscow's rulers when they set out to wage offensive war on a large scale against serious enemies. Since the lands already theirs were so vast, great distances had to be covered by their armies merely to reach the enemy frontier, and this would place a great burden on supply lines, poorly managed to begin with.

Moreover, the quality of junior officers is more important on the offence than on the defence. Since an advancing army must discover the placing and stance of the enemy as it moves forward, initiative is required down to the junior levels if the many small fighting decisions of each unit are to be made swiftly. That in turn obviously calls for a great number of officers willing to act by their own independent judgement and on their own responsibility. These qualities are to be sure of great importance in resisting invasion as well as in invading. But on the defensive, just to stand and fight is of value, and to strike at the enemy wherever he might be is of cumulative value also. On the offensive, that is not enough: specific lines of advance must be followed – and yet not so rigidly that units will attack frontal positions which may be safely bypassed, or that units will move straight across difficult terrain that might have been more easily circumvented. And of course the action must be purposefully concentrated on the offensive: to pursue any of the enemy whenever and wherever seen would only scatter an army into many feeble fragments.

For these reasons, the quality of junior officers' leadership and specifically their readiness to act on their own initiative count for much more on the offensive than on the defensive. It was in this regard that the Russians were at a great disadvantage. In a society rigidly hierarchical, in which a most strict conformity to rules and orders is imposed by draconian sanctions upon a people by no means as naturally disciplined as some, the habit is easily formed of passing all decisions to superior authority whenever it is at all decent to do so. Certainly the will to take action on one's own responsibility is more likely to be suppressed than in a more tolerant and liberal society. In Tsarist days, and till quite recently, the tactical rigidity that resulted from overcentralization greatly diminished the offensive power of Russian armies, while having much less effect on their defensive strength.

When the poverty of Russian management, tactical rigidity and the vast distances that had to be crossed to come to grips with an enemy are taken together, the great disparity between Russia's strength in defeating invasion and her own weakness in offensive operations is sufficiently explained. There is a clear continuity between the debacles of the Russo-Japanese war, the catastrophic defeats of 1914 under the last of the Tsars, the Bolshevik failure of August 1920 in fighting the Poles, and the weakness of Stalin's forces in the 1939–40 Winter War against the Finns. In each case, logistic inadequacy, a lack of tactical flexibility for want of junior-level initiative, and an unfavourable geography played their varied roles in defeating Russian aims. And then one may consider how poorly the Japanese or Finns would have done in invading central Russia in 1904 or 1939, respectively, or the poor showing of the Poles in 1920. Two of those nations held back; others less prudent did not. On the defensive, Russia would always ultimately defeat her enemy – then advance to drive the invader out, and finally to invade in turn, making easy conquests against armies already defeated.

The pattern of defensive-offensive warfare that created the greatest empire on earth under the Tsars was reproduced very faithfully in the Second World War – or Great Patriotic War, as it is most significantly called in the Soviet Union. It is the enemy that attacks first, and very successfully in this case. German forces invade Russia so deeply that all three great cities are affected, with Leningrad besieged, Moscow threatened and Kiev occupied. Soviet war plans turn out to be grossly inappropriate, and extraordinary incompetence is revealed at all levels of command, with absurd and self-destructive orders being nevertheless obeyed. Huge losses of men and of territory are the result. But then the enemy army finds itself thinned out along the front, since Russia's width increases from West to East as the Baltic and the Black Seas curve outwards. The enemy's lines of supply are more and more stretched, and it is harder and harder for his stock of vehicles to resupply the receding front. The few highways and railways are widely separated, and the vast tracts of country between them cannot truly be dominated. Local resisters and stranded soldiers can thus combine safely to form many little armies that begin to wage guerrilla war on the long and thin lines of supply. Their attacks and their sabotage add to the breakdowns that bad roads and over-use inflict, so that fewer and fewer vehicles remain to feed a front that is still becoming wider and is still receding.[3] Thus the enemy's offensive momentum is exhausted; German forces can still win their battles at the front, but that front can no longer advance.

Meanwhile new Russian armies are created, with new junior officers tested in battle, new generals of harsh realism, and new methods mostly learned from the enemy. Manned by the many recruits that even the remaining half of unoccupied Russia has to offer, equipped by the industry that was already in remote safety or which was there evacuated, the new armies find their schooling in combat and begin to resist better, and then to counter-attack. The enemy who has triumphantly advanced is now captured by his conquests – everywhere he is weak and his whole array is overextended. Only two choices remain to him: the abrupt withdrawal that would be inexplicable back home, where the vast territory won is seen as proof of strength rather than as the true cause of weakness it is; or else to stand fast to hold a defensive front under the constant threat of penetrations and encirclements. In such circumstances there are no longer any good seasons for combat in Russia: if spring, there is the deep mud that traps vehicles and exhausts marching men; if summer, there is the surprising heat, with no relief in a flat country which soon becomes dusty and insect-ridden; if autumn, mud again; if winter, there is the snow and ice, but mainly the cold that reaches spectacular extremes. In his weakness, the enemy is driven back step by step, so that he is too exhausted to defend his own initial frontiers when these are reached in retreat; or, if he stands, his armies are surrounded and destroyed, and some units may simply disperse, to be rounded up by Russian soldiers if they are lucky, or killed by outraged peasants if they are not.

Whatever the fate of the invading soldiers, that of the power that sent them is as bleak. Those new-made Russian armies will not simply go home once the invader is beaten and the war is won. Some net gain of territory or political control must ensue. It was by the accumulation of such gains rather than by original aggressions that the Tsars' empire was expanded in the West, and in 1945 Stalin added to their legacy by winning a war that he did not start, except in the Far East where a Japan already beaten was swiftly dislodged from Manchuria.

But even in the wake of the large and successful offensives of the latter years of the Second World War (and the invasion of Manchuria was technically the most successful of all), the Soviet leaders still had good reason to lack confidence in the ability of their armed forces to mount offensive actions on a large scale and of precise and swift execution. Soviet forces could win battles large and small, but only when they had a net superiority in *matériel*, only when mass could be employed in place of quality, and only when time and space allowed scope for such brute-force methods.

To be sure, there was nothing crude about Soviet theatre-strategy after 1942, or about the operational methods for armoured warfare, which were fully developed by 1944. By then experienced command skills at the top (along with mass) could fully compensate for the still rigid and ponderous tactics of the single regiments and divisions. But this remaining disability meant that Soviet forces could still not be employed successfully to carry out swift operations of the sort that would require high levels of technical proficiency and qualities of command down to the junior level. The Soviet Union could have mounted a large-scale invasion of Western Europe, but its forces could not have carried out swift interventions or surprise aggressions where mass cannot be substituted for quality. This operational shortcoming obviously circumscribed the *nature* of the threat which the Soviet Union could present, even if the total quantum of its military power was already very great indeed.

Three

The New Dynamics of the Soviet Empire: from Optimism to Pessimism

From the day of its birth in Lenin's *coup d'état* of 6 November 1917 (October by the old calendar), and until very recently indeed, the Soviet regime has been fundamentally optimistic, albeit for reasons that have varied over time.

At first, the Bolsheviks were optimistic about the future even in the midst of famine and civil war, because they were quite certain that revolutions similar to their own would soon break out in Germany and the other industrialized countries. This expectation was reflected in the conduct of Lenin's new-made government towards the Central Powers, whose armies were pressing hard against a disintegrating Russian front at the time of the *coup d'état*. When a peace conference was convened in Brest-Litovsk on 3 December 1917, the Bolshevik delegation under Trotsky was ordered to employ delaying tactics with the Germans and Austro-Hungarians, in the belief that revolution would overtake those countries not just soon but actually in a matter of days or weeks. It was only at the end of February 1918, when the Germans resumed their advance to penetrate deeply into Russian territory, that Lenin decided to accept their terms. But this did not mean that the estimate of imminent revolution had been abandoned. On the contrary, Lenin's readiness to surrender huge territories including Poland, the Baltic provinces, much of the Ukraine, Finland and even the Caucasus – very much more than the Germans had actually conquered – was due to his belief that the loss would soon be restored by the emergence of a fraternal Bolshevik Germany (and indeed his concessions were reversed, but only by the Allied victory in November).

The Grand Strategy of the Soviet Union

During its first years, the Bolshevik regime could easily sustain belief in the imminence of world revolution. The mutinies and soldiers' 'Soviets' in the French army and the German navy (which were imitated briefly in other armies also, albeit on a smaller scale), the sharp rise in political agitation by trade unionists and assorted socialists and revolutionaries throughout Europe and beyond, and the actual Bolshevik uprisings in Germany and Hungary that briefly brought to power Soviet-style regimes, inspired the worldwide 'red scare' of 1919–20, and they could also inspire red hopes.

By the time this first reason for optimism had waned, another had come to take its place. If the political millennium would have to wait, an economic revolution could still be accomplished. Central planning would allow the Soviet Union to achieve rapid economic growth towards an unprecedented prosperity, thus eventually offering an irresistibly attractive model which all other countries would eventually have to copy. Not itself part of the Marxist inheritance, but rather the offspring of the systems of economic control invented in both Germany and Britain during the great war just ended (which had made possible the huge and indeed utterly improbable increases in war production of the two countries), the direction of the economy by central planning seemed an innovation of epic proportions to the Soviet leaders.

From the inauguration of the first five-year plan in 1928, the course seemed to be set for the achievement of high and sustained rates of growth that would eventually allow the Soviet Union to overtake every other economy and move far ahead. And this great result was to be achieved by a method remarkably simple: the state would appropriate all production, allowing a minimum for personal consumption; the surplus would be used not to build factories and equip farms to produce consumer goods and food, but rather to expand the economy's energy supply, railways and other basic infrastructures, and above all to increase the output of 'producer' goods. By continuing to provide only a minimum of resources for immediate consumption while investing the maximum in machine-tools to make yet more machine-tools, the stage would eventually be reached when a greatly enlarged Soviet industry could turn to produce equipment to make consumer goods and farm machinery in great quantities; then the Soviet consumer would finally enjoy an unprecedented abundance.

Only three things were needed to ensure the success of the

scheme: the control of all capital by the state, so that the long-term growth priorities could be enforced; the enthusiasm of the public, or at least the willingness of all to work for very little while awaiting the great day; and peace.

The first requirement was so easily achieved in industry and commerce that its extension to agriculture seemed at least feasible if not easy. Factory owners and businessmen in general had either fled abroad or else they had been reduced to a frightened silence. The peasants, it is true, were very much in place and now the owners of the lands they tilled, but, just as the factories had been 'collectivized', the peasants too would have to give up their petty rights of ownership to form collectives. To do this was not a matter of ideology but rather an essential part of the whole scheme: the surplus production to be used for investment would largely have to come from the land, and the state bureaucracy could scarcely squeeze all there was from millions of independent farms. Hence the peasants would have to be organized into large units under Party control so that their production could be more easily extracted by the state. What followed, of course, were all the miseries and massacres of forced collectivization, which opened a wound which has turned out to be incurable.

The second requirement, maximum work for minimum immediate reward, was to be met by a combination of inspiring propaganda and police terror. Films, posters, books and songs explained the scheme and harnessed the enthusiasm of the young for the great projects that were the centrepieces of the plan; the competitive spirit was exploited in production 'races' between work-teams and factories; high achievers were given personal recognition in medals and publicity – in sum all the tricks of political progaganda and all the devices of commercial promotion were exploited in wave after wave of exhortation. As for the terror, that too was thoroughly done: shirkers were imprisoned, 'saboteurs' were shot and tens of millions of peasants were collectivized by brutal compulsion. Propaganda and police were in themselves diversions from the production effort; but to the extent that production could be enhanced and consumption squeezed further, the resources given to the secret police and the Agitprop would handsomely pay for themselves.

The third requirement, peace, was a function of international politics, which were beyond the exclusive control of the Kremlin leader who otherwise controlled so much; but Stalin did what he could. A major war would inevitably interrupt the Soviet Union's steady ascent to the centrally planned millennium – the key to its eventual worldwide political victory – and thus the Soviet Union followed a genuine peace policy, at least until 1939.

The prospect of an impending economic supremacy served to maintain the fundamental optimism of the Soviet leadership for several decades, perhaps until as late as the end of the 1960s. But then finally it must have been recognized in the Kremlin that the perpetuation of the central planning system, in effect a special kind of war economy, could not after all serve as the reliable highway to prosperity. Until the end of the 1960s, the ravages of the war – and before that the original poverty of the Russian empire – could serve as plausible excuses, not only for their propaganda, but for the rulers themselves. But after forty-odd years of central planning the great intellectual discovery was made, if only gradually and perhaps never completely: that central planning could indeed serve well in wartime to produce arms and ammunition in response to fixed specifications and quantity targets, but that it could not channel the right amounts of the right resources into the very many, very varied and always changing paths of peacetime economic development. In sector after sector, the Soviet system strives to produce more obsolescent goods even as radically new ones have already appeared on the world scene; it is not that too little is produced, but rather that the wrong things are produced: adding machines, even in the greatest number, cannot compete with digital computers any more than great quantities of cast iron can substitute for the right amounts of the right kinds of plastic. The very visible symptom of the Soviet economic failure was the slow rate of innovation, but the cause was the very structure of the system itself.

The other discovery of the late 1960s was equally sinister: in the wake of huge investments in agriculture, a fundamental structural malady was revealed there also. Under Stalin's policy, Soviet farming had been starved of machinery and fertilizers; it was natural therefore to presume that given great quantities of both, all would be well. But when Soviet agriculture did finally receive vast resources, it turned out that there was a far more intractable obstacle to an adequate productivity: the state of the peasantry, which collectivization had long before deprived of the will to work carefully and well. Soviet agriculture absorbs more than seven times as much investment as its American counterpart, but the return on that investment is spectacularly low: between 1950 and 1977 the capital stock of Soviet agriculture increased 11.9 times to yield an increase in output of 250 per cent. At present added investment yields almost nothing.

The world is full of dissatisfied consumers, and the prospect of an indefinite delay in delivering the long-promised abundance to the Soviet consumer was the least part of the regime's predicament. The decline in the rate of growth was far more serious, for in the Soviet case, uniquely, economic failure undermines the very legitimacy of the regime. The welfare of two entire generations had been ruthlessly sacrificed to the pursuit of economic supremacy, the declared goal of Soviet national strategy since 1928, and the consequences of disappointing long-stoked expectations were awesome. Palliatives such as the importation of Western technology, excuses old and new, and grim forecasts of an impending great depression in the capitalist world, could all serve to reduce the immediate political damage, but obviously the regime could no longer remain optimistic on economic grounds. Instead of overtaking the advanced economies, the Soviet economy was itself being overtaken.

Imperialism: the last stage of Soviet optimism

Once again the waning of one hope coincided with the birth of another, of a radically different sort. If the Soviet Union could no longer hope to conquer the world by the novel method of becoming its irresistibly successful economic and social model, it could instead pursue the lesser but still grandiose aim of becoming the world's leading military power. By sheer chance, the belated recognition of economic failure by the Soviet leaders at the end of the 1960s happened to coincide with the beginning of the abrupt and phenomenal decline of the United States as a military power. Already great in absolute terms, the decline was yet greater in comparison with the Soviet Union: while the armed strength of the United States was consumed both morally and materially in unsuccessful warfare, and was then further diminished by budgetary reductions year after year till at least 1976, the Soviet Union was steadily enhancing its capital of military equipment (in quality above all) and also of sound expertise.

During the same period, the authority of the United States on the world scene was relentlessly eroded by violent social disarray, by the perceptible loss of nerve of its policy elite, and by the public attack upon all the institutions of power. All this engendered a fatal lack of tenacity in American conduct overseas, which culminated in the outright abandonment of Cambodia, Laos and South Vietnam. The damage was then further compounded by a foreign policy of indecision, renunciation and outright retreat, which continued for several years after the final defeat suffered in Indochina. During that same period, the Soviet Union in contrast reaffirmed its strength and determination by forceful action in Czechoslovakia (which, it was soon noted, evoked no lasting sanction) and then proceeded to broaden the range of its influence; always a great power, it became for the first time a global power also. While American prestige was sinking, the Soviet Union was gaining in authority from the reliable if grim continuity of its policies. Moreover, as an inevitable consequence of the Strategic Arms Limitation negotiations, the Soviet Union received a full and formal recognition of its co-equal status as a superpower – also for the first time.

As a result of these sharply divergent trends, there could be no doubt in whose favour the global balance was shifting during the 1970s, and neither localized setbacks, such as the loss of Egypt as a client, nor all the varied consequences of Chinese hostility could alter the fundamental fact that the Soviet Union was emerging as the world's leading military power.

The Soviet Union thus found itself in the 1970s much more powerful and also distinctly poorer than its leaders could reasonably have predicted even a mere decade before. It was thus only natural that the goal of economic supremacy, which had become utterly unrealistic, should have given way to the pursuit of imperial power as the new dominant aim of Soviet national strategy.

This momentous change was of pervasive effect especially

because it converged with the other great transformation, the restoration of Russian nationalism. One must exercise great care in trying to understand such complicated matters and their yet more complicated implications, but one thing is immediately obvious: while the pursuit of economic supremacy was fully consistent with the aspirations of all the nationalities of the empire, and those of the client-states too, the pursuit of imperial primacy on the world scene could only be a source of genuine satisfaction to the Russians themselves. Had the Soviet Union become a voluntary confederation as Lenin had once hoped, all its nationalities might have shared in the psychological rewards of imperial status; to some extent this might have been true even if only the highest leadership itself had remained transnational, as in Stalin's day. But in a Soviet Union so clearly ruled by Russians, the members of all other nationalities must regard themselves as subjects, and they can hardly gain much satisfaction from the prospect of further expanding the imperial domain of the Russian people.

Actually the novel pursuit of imperial power may be a new cause of resentment to the non-Russians. When the Soviet Union was still giving its highest priority to industrialization and growth, the sacrifices imposed on the population would be less painful in the degree that they offered the prospect of a happy future for coming generations. Many Russians, and perhaps most, might still willingly accept economic sacrifice for the sake of increasing yet further the power of a Soviet state that has become so clearly a Russian empire. But that cannot be so for the other nationalities. For the non-Russians, the pursuit of external power, with all the military expense that it entails, and all the aid given to the menagerie of radical Third World states, must merely seem a cause of their poverty; many, no doubt, believe it to be the leading cause. All Soviet citizens, Russians and non-Russians alike, are certainly well aware of how greatly their standard of living has improved during the last thirty years or so. On the other hand, they also know that the peoples of all other industrialized countries (including their own client-states) enjoy a much higher standard of living than themselves. It is a fair guess that the non-Russians are much more likely to blame military expenditures, and the cost of supporting overseas dependencies such as Cuba, South Yemen and Vietnam, for the stringencies so vividly manifest in their daily lives.

There is one additional factor. While the restoration of Russian nationalism long preceded the advent of the new era of Soviet imperialism (and indeed it was virtually a precondition of the great change), the two phenomena reinforce one another. The success of the Soviet Union as a power on the world scene stimulates Russian national pride, and incidentally encourages all those manifestations of chauvinism that must unfailingly evoke the reactive nationalism of the non-Russians; on the other hand, Russian national pride further encourages the striving to globalize Soviet power. To the extent that the non-Russians do not in fact share in the psychological rewards of empire, the rise of Soviet power tends to antagonize the non-Russians, who pay their full share of the cost. Thus, for both economic and psychological reasons, the new primacy given to external aggrandizement intensifies ethnic tensions inside Soviet society. The failure to fulfil the original transnational promise is basic, but its consequences must be aggravated by the present direction of Soviet policy. This is the link between the last phase of optimism and the advent of pessimism.

The advent of pessimism

If the Soviet leaders estimated during the early 1970s that the United States was in sharp decline as a world power and perhaps that it was destined to revert to isolationism, theirs would have been a pardonable error. True, many social indicators – and the election of 1968 above all – proved conclusively that, for all the anti-war agitations and all the riots, the great majority of the American people remained firmly conservative and deeply patriotic. But such sentiments could only guarantee political stability at home. A foreign policy of substance and action requires much more: not just the vague approval of the general public, but rather the specific support of Congress and of the media and policy elites that influence Congressional dealings with foreign affairs. And such support can only be forthcoming if those elites are in turn confident of themselves and of the ability of the American government as a whole to act wisely overseas. And on both counts there was much evidence by the early 1970s to support the prediction that the United States would indeed retreat from the world scene, if only gradually.

While outright isolationism had never truly been the American stance and never would be by choice, in view of the retreat from globalism manifest by, say, 1972 it would have been reasonable to forecast that the perimeter of serious American concern would soon be restricted to Western Europe, Japan and possibly the Middle East, in addition to the western hemisphere. Similarly, while the United States would not of course disarm, the trends pointed to a great reduction in American military strength, particularly in regard to forces for distant intervention.

Had the United States been confronted by evidence of a sharply diminished Soviet military effort, a responsive decline in American defence expenditures would have been inevitable, since the procedures of Congressional budget-making for defence mean that every American military 'programme' must be cast as a response to some Soviet 'threat'; had the overall 'threat' diminished, the defence budget would have declined also. But all procedures aside, such an outcome would have been consistent with the implicit national strategy of the United States, in which the foreign policy instruments of choice are economic, technological and cultural, while military power is merely the instrument of necessity. The reaction of Soviet leaders to the great decline in American military power and foreign policy activism was naturally entirely different. For them, the accumulating evidence that America was in retreat could only be a powerful encouragement to yet more activism overseas, since now their efforts would no longer be countered, as in the past, by American reactions. Moreover, since military power must be the primary instrument of choice for the Soviet Union, lacking as it is in economic leverage, cultural influence and social appeal, the appropriate response to the decline of American military power was to increase the Soviet as much as possible. With the goal of achieving a clear primacy in military power at least within reach – as it could never be when the United States was seriously competing – the incentive to enhance the strength of the Soviet armed forces was very greatly increased. In the past, some Kremlin leaders could argue that the inevitable American response would soon deprive the Soviet Union of whatever advantage could be gained by additional military spending, but once it became clear that the Americans would not seriously respond, all had to agree that it was indeed worthwhile to make that extra effort.

If the broad implication of the forecast of American decline was that more Soviet military expenditure was warranted, the specific implication was that more effort should be devoted to the increase of long-range intervention capabilities, especially the Soviet surface navy as well as airlift capacity, both for direct Russian use and also to convey Cuban and other client forces usable overseas. The American retreat thus created a powerful added incentive to globalize Soviet power. So long as the United States still had almost one thousand warships, any Soviet flotilla sent far from Soviet shores would be dwarfed by American naval forces on the scene, but if a greatly diminished American navy was to be expected, an increased Soviet naval effort would become profitable, since in the future the Soviet navy would actually be able to outmatch its declining counterpart. What was true for the Soviet navy was valid for the Soviet military in general: once a goal previously beyond reach becomes attainable it is bound to evoke an added effort.

By the beginning of the 1970s, it seemed that the Soviet Union could indeed look forward to the day when it would become the world's greatest military power, and its only truly global power. A global reach for the Soviet Union would not of course mean global domination. Nor could the Soviet Union attain preclusive security, whereby its safety would be fully assured by the physical ability to defeat any attack before it could inflict any damage. Since the United States – and not only the United States – would still retain control of long-range nuclear weapons against which there is no fully reliable defence, the Soviet Union would still have to rely on deterrence. For Russians especially, deterrence is a most uncomfortable device, since its workings depend on others' calculations of risks and benefits. But certainly, even with such inevitable limitations, the achievement of a global primacy could justify for the Soviet leaders all the costs and all the risks of the pursuit of imperial power.

Matters did not turn out as so many, almost certainly including the Soviet leaders, had believed they would. By 1976, if not before, a net majority of the American public had clearly rejected the counsels of the media and foreign policy elites, which remained largely inimical to the restoration of an activist foreign policy, and to the rehabilitation of American military strength. But in faithful reflection of public opinion, Congress began to press with increasing success for higher defence spending, and by 1977 a President of contradictory impulses found himself compelled to spend more on defence than he might have wished, quite unable to proceed with his declared intent to disengage from Korea, and forced to maintain a greater American navy than he desired.

Strategy is made of paradox, irony and contradiction, and it was only natural in that unnatural realm that it was the Soviet attempt to exploit the favourable trend that caused its abrupt reversal. In more detached fashion, it can be said that a Soviet national strategy necessarily based on military power (in the absence of any other comparative advantage) evoked a competitive reaction from the United States, whose own national strategy would otherwise have given less weight to that particular instrument of policy, in which the United States has a comparative disadvantage.

By 1980 matters had evolved to the point where it was clear that the United States would soon be competing in full force, both in the building of armaments and in the activism of its foreign policy. Finally, by the beginning of 1981, the Soviet Union was presented with solid evidence of American determination to regain a global primacy in military power in the budget plans that a new administration unveiled and which Congress would obviously support in large measure. To be sure, no conceivable increase in American defence expenditures could gain any sort of superiority in continental land warfare forces, but for the strategic-nuclear and naval forces that was a perfectly feasible goal. Soviet ballistic missiles could not be usefully outmatched in quantity or even in quality, but they could be outclassed by the development of weapons of radically new form; and if Soviet submarines would still deny a true naval supremacy to the United States, its surface fleet at least could regain a clear ascendancy over the Soviet. As for continental land warfare, in which the combination of powerful Soviet ground forces, large anti-aircraft forces and less impressive tactical air forces would certainly remain stronger than the American combination of strong tactical airpower and weak ground forces, the overall strategic context made any direct comparisons irrelevant, since the United States would not confront the Soviet Union alone, but rather in alliance with many other countries in both Europe and East Asia. The exception – and it is one of great significance – is the region of the Persian Gulf, where the United States has vital interests but lacks allies of any genuine military capacity.

It is true, of course, that an optimistic Soviet observer could find good reasons to discount the strength of the countries which would be associated with the United States in a continental conflict. In Western Europe, such allies as have well-equipped armies are the most vulnerable and therefore the least resolute; other allies deploy forces which are mostly made up of ill-equipped infantry, and much larger in form than substance, and others still, who do have forces of high quality, are weakened by shortages of modern equipment. As for East Asia, Japan for all its industrial capacity is still quite unable to protect its vital sea lanes or even the country itself, while the People's Republic of China (PRC) for all its millions of militiamen and soldiers could not protect more than a part of its territory against Soviet invasion, and has no significant offensive strength. That fact, and the parallel inability of the European alliance to stage any serious offensive against the Soviet Union, mean that China and Western Europe could not assist one another if either were attacked.

But as against all these undoubted weaknesses and deficiencies in the array of American alliances there is the simple fact that the Soviet Union is now encircled by enemies. Some are possessed of real military strength, even if of limited dimensions; others have at least the economic potential to acquire great military power in the future; and three of the antagonists of the Soviet Union have nuclear weapons, in addition to the United States itself. Americans may judge the British, French and Chinese nuclear forces now aimed at the Soviet Union as technically weak in various ways and of insignificant size, but they would not treat them lightly if they were aimed at the United States. A classic paradox of strategy has been at work to the disadvantage of the Soviet Union: when a powerful country becomes yet more powerful, its strength may drive the very weakest of its neighbours into a frightened neutrality or outright client status, but neighbours marginally more secure will instead be stimulated to build up their own strength, and to cooperate with one another against the great antagonist that threatens them all. The Soviet Union is thus the true author of its own encirclement.

An optimism based on the hope of achieving an imperial primacy need not give way to regime pessimism merely because of the global reaction to the Soviet pursuit of global power – a reaction natural and inevitable and by no means sufficient in itself to deny the Soviet Union what it so assiduously seeks. As for the great reversal in the substance of American military policy manifest by 1981, that indeed was rather more abrupt and entailed a more powerful rearmament than could have been expected even a year earlier, but on the other hand, past experience and current economic forecasts both suggest that the upsurge in American military spending will not be sustained for more than a few years. That, to be sure, would suffice to deprive the Soviet Union of a great part of the gains it achieved in the military competition during the 1970s, but the relative position of the Soviet Union would still show a very great improvement as compared to, say, 1967.

Just as it did in the 1960s, when the United States was moving ahead in many areas of the military competition, the Soviet Union could now keep up its own armament effort, and rely on the superior tenacity of the long-lived Kremlin leaders to overcome eventually the effects of the temporary American upsurge. Similarly, the Soviet Union could count on the continuing growth of its power to dissolve the fragile alliances that were engendered by its past military growth. For the upkeep of alliances against a rising threat will only persist if that threat falls within a middle range. If the threat is small, there will obviously be no sufficient reason to overcome all the natural diversities that pull allies apart, but if the threat is so great that any attempt at a joint defence seems futile, then too the alliance will collapse. In that circumstance, diplomatic conciliation – that is appeasement – will seem the wiser choice, certainly less costly and perhaps less dangerous also.

Counting on the inconsistency of the great and ever-turbulent American democracy, and on its readiness to turn away from activism overseas to domestic concerns as soon as some foreign venture proves to be disappointing, the Kremlin leaders may persevere in their long-term military programme and in their foreign policy, which seeks, as always, to separate the United States from its allies, clients and friends.

By the classic paradox of strategy, the new American effort to restore a tolerable balance of military power which should eventually consolidate the alliance offers in the meantime great opportunities for Soviet diplomacy to divide the alliance. *If* the United States remains firm in its intent, and *if* it is successful in its major military programmes and *if* the alliances are kept together in the interim, then a reconstructed balance of power will emerge by the end of the 1980s, in which the Soviet advantage in land power will once again be offset by the strength on land of cohesive allies and by American (and allied) advantages in strategic-nuclear and naval capabilities. It was on that asymmetry that the overall military balance of the entire postwar era was based, and it was the decline of American strength at sea and in strategic-nuclear forces that destabilized the balance of military power during the 1970s.

The opportunity for Soviet diplomacy to divide the United States from its allies arises because allies made insecure by the diminished strength of their protector must now be exposed to all the stresses of the new policy of rearmament even while being still in the state of weakness created by the American policies of the recent past. So long as the Western Alliance was drifting gently into an increasing weakness, with Soviet-American arms control talks under way to relieve anxiety and offer hopes of a costless stability, the Alliance could be as comfortable as a patient drifting into a coma under heavy sedation. Now the patient is being told to rise and work, and all the unfelt wounds inflicted in the past begin to hurt.

In so far as the American rearmament is strategic-nuclear, it raises the fear that the Soviet Union will be tempted to exploit its present advantage to make permanent gains, before the advent of newly powerful American strategic-nuclear forces once again imposes the full restraints of deterrence upon Soviet conduct. In so far as the American rearmament is 'conventional', it must impose increased defence costs on the allies as well, since in some degree or other they each will have to make their gestures towards sharing the burden. As for rearmament in the middle category of forces – the battlefield nuclear weapons (mainly artillery shells and short-range missiles), tactical nuclear weapons (mainly bombs for fighter-bombers) and theatre weapons (mainly missiles of trans-European range) – that places a special stress on the politics of the European allies, because in being forced to think of those weapons they are confronted by the strategic predicament that they strive so greatly to forget: an alliance which relies for its protection more on deterrence than on defence obtains security more cheaply, but at a correspondingly greater risk of catastrophe. In due course, the fruits of the new American policy should greatly reassure European opinion, but in the meantime costs, risks and stresses all increase –

while the benefits of added security are not yet forthcoming.

If the Soviet leaders were still optimistic about the long-term future of their system they could therefore see advantageous prospects in Europe, and elsewhere too for that matter. In east Asia, the fundamental poverty of China guarantees an equally fundamental military weakness, and this in turn keeps open the possibility of forcing by threats a reversal of Chinese policy, from hostility to conciliation. Certainly there is no solid base of security for Chinese foreign policy, which constantly affronts and provokes the Soviet Union even while having no adequate shield of deterrence or defence. Chinese nuclear weapons, the dense population of the eastern rim, and the *de facto* American alliance can all provide some degree of security; but they cannot suffice to protect the vast and scarcely populated Chinese hinterland, where no serious guerrilla resistance would be feasible, which American conventional strength could hardly reach, and whose (non-nuclear) invasion could never warrant nuclear retaliation upon Soviet cities. In the meantime, the basic conditions that make Chinese politics so unstable will continue in being. Optimistic Soviet observers may thus calculate that sooner or later a leadership less ill-disposed to the Soviet Union will emerge in Beijing, if only because the present opening to the West entails cultural intrusions that must in some degree erode the very foundations of China's totalitarianism.

Soviet leaders who were still optimistic could also see ample opportunities in the rest of east Asia, for each country of that region is poor or insecure or internally unstable, or all of those things. Japan is the exception, but even in her case it is clear enough that the continued industrial evolution of that country on present lines is unlikely, for it would eventually lead to the elimination of the entire industry of the United States and Western Europe – a thing most unlikely to be tolerated. And it is only the Soviet Union that offers an alternative as a potential large-scale buyer of both consumer and producer goods, in exchange for raw materials, including perhaps oil and gas re-exported from the Middle East.

And so the survey could go on, from country to country and region to region, to find everywhere causes of weakness and disarray which afford scope for a Soviet diplomacy which offers security and support to its clients and which presents a many-sided threat to those who resist its offer.

But to sustain optimism about the long-term competition with the

United States and about the international scene more generally, the Soviet leadership must first remain optimistic about the future of its own system. Mankind has a great capacity to remain in a state of optimism even in circumstances most adverse, but it is difficult to see how Andropov or his proximate successor in the Kremlin (if there is one) can remain optimistic about the future of the regime. The Soviet economy is perceptibly falling behind, and the entire demographic base is changing in a way that is ultimately incompatible with the continued Russian domination.

The members of the gerontocracy who ruled the Soviet Union with Brezhnev at their head could be excused if they failed to see what lies ahead for the Soviet system. The old men of the Kremlin who could look back on the astonishing rise of Soviet fortunes must have found it very hard to see the future in a gloomy light. Their very long careers began during the grim terror of the purges; they survived the sinister tragedy of Hitler's war, in which the fortunate among the Soviet population survived in extreme misery and semi-starvation, while those less fortunate died by the million. Men who must have vividly remembered the phenomenal hardships of those years could hardly be greatly worried by the diminishing rate of increase in Soviet per-capita consumption.[4] Men who lived through the days when German guns could be heard in the streets of Moscow would scarcely be alarmed by the danger of some fractional increase in Belgian defence budgets, nor even by the greater fact that the Soviet Union now confronts the possibility of a Sino-American alliance in addition to the old Euro-American alliance. Nor would men who once solved nationality problems by deporting entire peoples see much to fear even in the relentless demographic change that is steadily increasing the proportion of the most intractable nationalities. Above all, old men who saw the Soviet economy recover from the devastation of a war unusually destructive to yield a modest prosperity, as well as a spectacular growth in armaments, were unlikely to be greatly alarmed by obscure phenomena such as the declining rate of growth of labour productivity. Although Andropov is scarcely much younger, he may have a different view – and may act upon it if he should survive in power.

In any case, harsh facts ignored do not disappear, and the ills of the Soviet economy and of Soviet society are becoming steadily more acute. As the products which the Soviet economy must produce become more varied and more complex, as innovation imposes change at an accelerating rate, central planning in the Soviet style accomplished by mandatory production quotas is less and less effective. That much was already publicly acknowledged by authorized Soviet economic experts as long as two decades ago; since then there have been many administrative reforms and all sorts of incentive schemes, but those efforts have failed, since the central planning mechanism ('Gosplan') remains the economy's controlling brain. Soviet economic experts certainly know full well by now that dynamic entrepreneurship and efficient management (the missing elements) cannot coexist with planning that specifies very exactly all output targets, and all prices. It is obvious enough that the system cannot provide a sufficient reward for the dynamic entrepreneur, or the efficient manager; it is the obedient administrator who lives best in the world that planning makes, and that is what the system gets.

We may therefore be sure that if the Gosplan's mandatory planning system has not been abolished it is for a very good reason, namely that the Party's power-structure requires its preservation. So long as the official ideology remained a strong force in Soviet life, the Party's mass of middle-ranking officials could be well employed as the keepers and teachers of the ideology. But in the modern Soviet Union the official ideology is no longer a live body of guiding ideas, in constant need of reinterpretation and propagation. Now fossilized, Marxism-Leninism has become instead an official religion, since its propositions have become dogmas; Soviet Marxism-Leninism now has its ceremonies, rituals and idols, chiefly the figure of Lenin himself – whose bust presides over all school-rooms, offices and places of public assembly. But if the ideology has become dogmatic religion, the Party could not likewise become a priesthood. The tens of thousands of officials who make up the base of the Party's power-structure could only retain their importance by finding non-ideological roles for themselves – and they have, as managers. It is they who are the directors of factories and farms, the managers of wholesale agencies and retail shops, the heads of service enterprises, design bureaux and research centres; and then of course they fill the ranks of the gigantic economic bureaucracy, with its double structure of 'all-Union' and republic ministries.

Some of those men and women are no doubt talented professionals, eager to emulate the best of Western standards, who would much prefer to be free to act on their own instead of being captive to the central planning process. But many more, inevitably, are essentially political hacks who have risen to managerial status because of their standing in the Party. For them, the plan is not an unwelcome straitjacket but rather the essential guarantee of their ability to cope. Since they lack the talents of the entrepreneur, since they could not possibly be efficient as managers, their professional survival depends on the preservation of the present system, which rewards the obedient administrator, gives only small incentives for efficiency, and offers no compensation for the risks that the true entrepreneur must face.

Since the entire power-structure of the Soviet Union is based on the allegiance of the mass of middle-ranking officials, it is the imperative priority of regime survival that prohibits any drastic economic reform. And yet without a liberalization true and wide, there can be no escape from the circumstances that result in the declining effectiveness of the Soviet economy. Actually superior to any free enterprise system in a warlike environment in which the goal is the supply of a few essentials for civilians and the maximum output of a fully specified range of products for the armed forces, and still able to sustain military innovation in all circumstances (the aviation design bureaux, for example, operate in a competitive fashion), the Soviet economy becomes less and less effective as its setting is further and further removed from that of a war economy.

There is therefore every reason to believe that the decline in the *relative* effectiveness of the Soviet economy will simply continue. It is not that its total output will decline or even fail to keep up with, say, the American GNP, but rather that its output will consist more and more of the wrong products, that is outdated products – a phenomenon long manifest in sectors of rapid innovation, such as computer technology or female fashions.

This being the case, the regime's increasing reliance on the appeal of Russian nationalism is politically the right course to follow – at least in the short term – because it is precisely the Russians who must feel the greatest sense of economic deprivation, since they compare themselves with West Europeans. The increasing proportion of Central Asians must by contrast feel the least sense of relative deprivation, since they compare themselves with their counterparts across the near borders in Turkey, Iran, Afghanistan and China. But in the long run it is inevitable that the licence given to Russian nationalism will stimulate the responsive self-assertion of the other nationalities, including the Central Asian nations, and that in turn must eventually erode the very basis of the Soviet order.

A more immediate link between the nationalities question and the economic problem is the increasing role of Central Asians in the labour force, which imposes a dilemma between bringing Central Asian workers into the established centres of industry – with the certainty of thereby increasing ethnic frictions – and the building of new industries in Central Asia, which would entail the greater long-run risk of increasing the economic power of the Asian republics. In fact, to channel new investments to Soviet Central Asia would assure the decline of the Russian-dominated centres of established industry, a course that must be politically unacceptable to a Russian-based regime.

The complex of internal problems facing the new Soviet leadership may seem deceptively similar to the economic and demographic problems now so vividly manifest in the West, namely slow growth, the 'guest-worker' problem of Europe, illegal immigration for the United States, and the decline of the traditional industries of the northeast United States, Belgium, northeast France, Britain and the Ruhr. The very great difference is that in the Soviet case the imperatives of regime survival deny 'natural' solutions which, however painfully, lead to a gradual adjustment of economy and society.

If Andropov or any other new leaders of the Soviet Union are already possessed of a whole battery of novel ideas until now concealed from us, or alternatively if they are willing to carry out a whole new revolution by disestablishing the Party from the economy, and restoring transnationalism in word and deed, they may remain optimistic. Otherwise, it is difficult to imagine how they can view the long-term future of the Soviet system with confidence.

Military optimism and its consequences

In what follows, the long-term pessimism of the Kremlin leadership is not assumed as fact but merely put forward as theory. Quite separately, it is argued that – also for the first time – Soviet leaders old and new have *operational confidence* in their armed forces, specifically that they now have good reason to believe that the Soviet armed forces can execute offensive operations with speed and precision, to win clean victories in short order against a variety of potential enemies in a variety of settings – so long as the risk of a nuclear reaction by the victim is low, and the Soviet forces themselves do not need to employ nuclear weapons to accomplish their goals. This great change alone suffices to increase the risk of war by choice, which is inherent in a great military empire that rightly sees itself as encircled by enemies, some of which are very vulnerable.

But to the extent that the notion of long-term Soviet pessimism is accepted, a correspondingly higher estimate must be made of the risks that the leaders of the Soviet Union might accept in their never-ending quest for total security. For it is notorious that the conjunction of a long-term regime pessimism with current military optimism is the classic condition that makes deliberate war more likely. Even in the presence of tempting opportunities, leaders optimistic about the long-term future of their regime will not willingly choose to go to war, because they expect that their strength will only become greater in the future. That of course was the condition of the Soviet Union until very recently. Again, leaders who lack confidence in the ability of their armed forces to carry out offensive operations reliably and well will not start wars either; rare indeed is the leader who in the end goes to war by deliberate choice fully expecting that the struggle will be costly, long and of uncertain result. But when leaders are pessimistic about the long-term future of their regimes and at the same time have high confidence in the strength and ability of their armed forces, then all that they know and all that they fear will conspire to induce them to use their military power while it still retains its presumed superiority. Only thus can today's strength be exploited to improve the prospects for a future which seems unfavourable. To convert a transitory military advantage into a permanent gain of security for the regime, there must be some profitable war in prospect. Profitable wars were rare even before the nuclear age, but once the urgency to act before it is too late is strongly felt, men will easily persuade themselves of the high likelihood of victory, of its small cost, and of its great benefits. It was under such a pressure that Germany accepted the Hapsburg call to go to war in 1914, and an unfavourable future was Hitler's best justification for going to war in 1939 – although character-istically it was his own mortality that Hitler invoked to explain the urgency of war. More seriously, it was the gloomy prospect of the loss of empire, in conjunction with high military confidence (and a fatal misreading of the American temper) that drove the Japanese to their Pearl Harbor decision in 1941.

Quite naturally, the opinions of most Western observers of Soviet conduct were based on the behaviour of a Soviet Union that was perhaps expansionist, but essentially non-aggressive and, above all, always prudent. That indeed was the conduct that could be expected from a regime that was both optimistic of its long-run future and also sceptical of its current military strength. It is understandable that this opinion should persist: to confuse pru-dence imposed by circumstances with restraint inherent in the very nature of the regime is easy enough, since the conditions that made the Soviet leaders greatly reluctant to accept risks persisted for so long, year after year, decade after decade. But if the theory of regime pessimism and the further claim that the Soviet leaders now have operational confidence in their armed forces are both accepted, it follows directly that a radically different pattern of Soviet external conduct is now unfolding before us – a pattern to which the invasion of Afghanistan already belongs.

Many intellectual reputations and much political capital are invested in the notion of a Soviet Union fundamentally non-aggressive. We must therefore suspect the eagerness with which many specialists invented *ad hoc* explanations to reconcile the invasion of Afghanistan with their model of a defensive and prudent Soviet Union. In the perspective of eternity such opinions may of course turn out to have been right – and not merely in the trivial sense that all expansion can always be explained away as prudential and defensive – but it is here argued that they are wrong, and indeed that the new phase of Soviet imperial strategy had emerged several years before the invasion of Afghanistan. The debate must con-tinue, but the possibility that Soviet conduct is being considered on the basis of outdated assumptions should at least be seriously examined.

Four

The Tools of Soviet Power

Over the last thirty years, we have witnessed great political and economic changes that should have resulted in the consolidation of a decisive Western military superiority over the Soviet Union: the dissolution of the Russo-Chinese alliance, the postwar recovery of Western Europe and Japan, and the emergence of a dozen newly successful industrial societies firmly in the American camp in a great arc from Norway to South Korea. While the Soviet Union lost the Chinese military alliance and has gained only Cuba as a satellite and Vietnam as an ally, as well as such lesser clients as South Yemen, the United States gained the effective alliance of West Germany, Italy and Japan, of a dozen smaller countries which had only token military forces thirty years ago, and most recently it has also gained a measure of Chinese cooperation.

But all these favourable changes have been offset by the spectacular growth of Soviet military power, the product of an armament effort of entirely unprecedented dimensions. As a result, the Soviet Union almost alone now presents a far more formidable threat to Western security than the 'Sino-Soviet' bloc of the 1950s ever did. Systematic and cumulative, the Soviet accumulation of military strength transcends by far in scope and duration the pre-war German mobilization, or for that matter the wartime build-ups of Britain and the United States. Hitler's preparations for war lasted for only five years, and the wartime German effort for only another six years after that; the British war mobilization did not truly begin until 1940, and the American was even shorter. The Soviet armaments programme has not of course been conducted at wartime levels of intensity, but on the other hand it has continued in one form or another for more than thirty years.

Between 1945 and 1950, while the United States and Britain were demobilizing troops, laying up warships and sending thousands of aircraft to the scrap yard while their military research-and-development barely kept going under minuscule budgets, the Soviet Union launched a crash nuclear weapon programme, several major rocket and missile projects, and laid the keels of many submarines and quite a few oceanic cruisers (the Sverdlov class).

From the outbreak of the Korean War in June 1950 until 1954, the steady Soviet programme was overtaken by the sudden upsurge of American (and British) military spending prompted by the war and by the fear that it was only a prelude to an attack upon Western Europe. But as soon as the pressure of the immediate crisis waned, the United States relaxed its efforts and returned to business as usual. Under Khrushchev, at least for a while, there was a definite relaxation in the overall Soviet military effort. This, however, was associated with a broad modernization of Soviet military power of which the world's first ballistic missiles were only the most prominent manifestation.

By 1959, the 'Missile-Gap' crisis, brought about by a combination of inadequate American intelligence and Soviet deception, had stimulated another brief American surge in spending, at first rather narrowly focused on strategic-nuclear weapons; but it did not last beyond 1964. Once again, the Soviet Union did not emulate the American upsurge, and once again it did not follow the American downturn. Instead, during a fifteen-year period in which American military resources were consumed by the Indochina War, and then drastically reduced by declining budgets, the Soviet Union continued to increase its net investment in military power at a steady rate.[5]

The most vividly manifest and quite incontrovertible result of these divergent trends in Soviet and American military investment is that the total stock of Soviet military equipment has grown to the point where it exceeds in quantity the combined inventories of the United States, the rest of NATO and the People's Republic of China in every category of armaments except for surface naval vessels, small arms and a few lesser items. Further, the once wide qualitative advantages of Western weapons over their Soviet counterparts have diminished to the point where they are of very small military significance, except for the weapons of air combat: Western fighter aircraft, or at any rate American fighters, are still clearly superior to their Soviet counterparts, and so are their associated avionics and missiles. But the spectacular Israeli victories over Soviet-equipped forces tell us more about Israeli skills than about the quality of Soviet equipment. The same air defences that fared so poorly in Lebanon against a most sophisticated electronic commando attack would be very formidable elsewhere, and the same Soviet T-72 tanks that were so easily defeated by the special munitions and remarkable tactics of the Israelis could scarcely have been penetrated, except at the closest ranges, by the tank ammunition which Western armies actually had at the time. Soviet weapons are always less advanced than the Western prototype, but if one compares what is actually in service at any one time it becomes clear that the Western advantage in research and development is overtaken by faster Soviet production cycles. Moreover, once the totality of the forces that would meet in battle is taken into account, any remaining differences in quality would be submerged by gross numerical disparities. Now that the habit of comparing the most advanced Western weapons, present only in sample quantities, with Soviet weapons already in mass deployment has finally fallen into disrepute, Soviet numerical superiorities must be accepted as superiorities *tout court*.

Less obvious and incapable of any numerical definition is the ultimately far more important change in the *nature* of Soviet military power which has been brought about by the great improvement in the competence of the Soviet officer corps. Since 1945 the expertise originally gained in combat by the survivors of an officer corps that had entered the war cruelly unprepared has been systematized and kept up to date by a most ambitious scheme of officer education. The Soviet armed forces operate 125 (*sic*) military colleges with five-year programmes, sixteen military academies which offer advanced courses, and there are seven specialized military institutes.[6]

The fact that young men gather in classrooms does not necessarily mean that they learn; and what can be learned in classrooms does not necessarily yield competence on the battlefield. And of course it is true that Soviet forces have not waged war on a large scale or against serious opponents since 1945. But our recent glimpses of the Soviet officer corps at work in Ethiopia and in Afghanistan suggest that the thirty-five years of concentrated Soviet effort have indeed produced results. Quite independently, we also have reason to believe that the political leaders at the summit of the Kremlin in hierarchy now have confidence in the ability of their armed forces to carry out complicated offensive operations swiftly and successfully. The invasion of Czechoslovakia was a heavy-handed mass operation in the old Russian style; but the high-speed seizure of Kabul in December 1979 was already a product of the new Soviet army.

Usually we focus our attention on the current state of the Soviet armed forces, and even more on their future evolution. But to try to understand the self-image and expectations of today's Soviet leaders, military as well as political, it is helpful to recall how drastic the advancement of their power has been over the last generation. If we take 1950 as our initial year of comparison, in that year the Soviet Union had no oceanic surface navy at all; it did have a considerable number of submarines but they could not hope to operate effectively astride the North Atlantic sea lanes of the Western alliance; and Soviet naval aviation had no long-range aircraft capable of strike missions. While the inventory of submarines was already large, it consisted mainly of small coastal defence boats, and the character of the Soviet surface fleet and naval air force was even more markedly defensive. As of this writing, Soviet naval power is incomparably greater: the Soviet submarine force can operate in all oceans of the world and its weapons are sufficiently powerful to threaten not only merchant shipping but even the strongest naval task-forces. The Soviet surface fleet can now fight offensively, so long as it remains under land-based air cover, but even with this limitation it can support submarine operations, by challenging American anti-submarine forces attempting to interdict the 'choke-points' through which Soviet submarines must pass. In addition, the Soviet surface fleet has also become an effective instrument of the Kremlin's foreign policy, serving as a 'presence' and suasion force active worldwide. Soviet naval aviation has also acquired a strategic reach, especially since the introduction of the naval version of the 'Backfire' bomber, which has both a long range and high speed.

Until the great transformation of Soviet naval power, the oceans of the world had been the safe rear of the American alliance system. While the continental allies of Europe and South Korea could be directly threatened by overland invasion, the 'islands', Britain, North America and Japan, as well as Australia, were immune from attack except for a still very small Soviet nuclear threat. The oceanic

45

connection between the American core and the allies on the rimlands of Europe and Asia was quite secure from Soviet naval interdiction. Now all that has changed. Quite apart from its nuclear delivery capacity of huge dimensions and global reach, the Soviet Union can now also threaten sea lanes of communication that link the Unites States to its rimland allies, and those which connect the sources of raw materials of the Middle East and Africa to both. The alliance thus no longer has a safe rear, and the possible interdiction of maritime communications undercuts the value of the American logistic base for the allies.

Even in 1950, the Soviet Union, China and the European satellite air forces had a large number of tactical combat aircraft, including several thousand jet fighters and several hundred light bombers. But the qualitative gap between Soviet and Western air forces was still very wide. Aside from superior aircraft and weapons, both the American and British air forces had the advantage of highly trained combat pilots with recent wartime experience; the Soviet air force had also fought in the recent world war but the quality of its pilots had remained very low till the end by the standards of the Luftwaffe. Western tactical air forces were capable of mounting powerful ground strike operations, both for close support and for interdiction. The Soviet air force did include good close support aircraft, but it lacked both the experience and the equipment to be effective in those missions; its higher quality aircraft were limited primarily to air combat. In other words, Soviet tactical airpower was largely defensive in character.

In 1950 Western tactical airpower had been the great compensating factor in the land warfare balance as a whole. In combat with Soviet forces, outnumbered Western ground troops could count on a virtual immunity from air attack and on much positive air support of high quality. That too has now changed. The Soviet air forces have greatly diminished the qualitative gap between the respective first-line forces. While Western air forces have a small number of the most advanced aircraft with a sharp advantage in quality over the mass of Soviet aircraft of the prior generation, the bulk of Western combat aircraft is much closer in quality to their Soviet counterparts. Although the West does retain an advantage in all the ancillaries critical to combat capability (missiles and other air ordnance, as well as avionics), the Soviet Union has also made much progress and the gap is narrowing steadily. Much the same applies to the infrastructure of airfields, maintenance support and ground-based radar and control systems. Only in *presumed* pilot quality is the West still ahead; obviously we cannot know how good pilots really are, but we do know that Soviet pilots fly much less and receive less varied training.

But the most important change in the balance of airpower is the decline in the *net value* of Western air-to-ground capabilities. The Soviet Union has developed and mass-produced a whole variety of air defence missiles from portable SAM-7s to high-altitude SAM-2s, with several low- and medium-altitude surface-to-air missiles mounted on cross-country vehicles in the middle of the spectrum. In addition, Soviet ground forces include large numbers of anti-aircraft guns, which are indeed the most reliable weapons of all.

In their sheer number, their overlapping coverage and their considerable technical sophistication, all these anti-aircraft weapons greatly reduce the ability of Western air forces to help in the ground battle. Quite aside from actual intercepts, the array of Soviet air defences on the battlefield would force Western aircraft to fly difficult evasion courses at low altitudes, would force them to employ costly and scarce air-to-ground missiles instead of cheaper bombs, and in general to devote so much effort to their own self-protection that the net capability available for attack is much reduced. Western ground forces can no longer expect to be immune to attack, and neither can they rely on prompt, accurate and heavy support from the air.

Of course, even in 1950 the ground forces of the Soviet Union greatly outnumbered those of the United States and its allies, while any East-West comparison that included the mass of infantry of the Chinese army would show a huge, though not very meaningful, imbalance. But the Soviet advantage on the ground was offset by the absolute advantage of US and British tactical airpower, and by the unchallenged superiority of the United States in nuclear weapon delivery. Now, by contrast, all the countervailing Western advantages have either disappeared or else have become of small import, while the Soviet army remains the superior force on the ground; it can effectively threaten NATO with invasion while the Soviet Union on the other hand is virtually immune from a NATO offensive on the ground.

Structured and deployed for the offensive, amply equipped with modern weapons of good quality, and trained in a realistic manner, the Soviet army also has a very great hidden advantage over its NATO counterparts: training, equipment and organization are all shaped by a coherent operational scheme for deep-penetration armoured warfare which is intended to cut through the NATO frontage, disrupt its defensive array and encircle the forces that have not retreated. This operational scheme exploits the full potential of the Pact's all-mechanized armies and it is fully consistent with the twin Soviet political goals of repressing Eastern Europe and intimidating Western Europe. The NATO ground forces by contrast have no coherent operational scheme for a defence-in-depth; instead they would form a thin linear deployment of the sort most easily defeated by concentrated 'mailed fist' armoured thrusts. From the Baltic to the Austrian frontier, NATO's front in Germany would amount to a cordon of German, Belgian, Dutch, British and American divisions deployed flank against flank just across the frontier. In Greece too there is no geographic depth, and the NATO front opposite Bulgaria would amount to a thin strip between the mountains and the sea. Only in Norway and Turkey does the NATO defence have some real geographic depth, and not by choice: it is simply that the Norwegian lands of the far north and the Turkish frontier in the Caucasus happen to be thinly populated and remote from the main centres of population.

The Soviet army of 1950 was already well equipped in the major weapons such as tanks, assault guns and towed artillery, but it was short of everything else, from trucks and jeeps to field radios. The major weapons were of excellent design for the time, even if crudely built, but other equipment, including small arms, was of poor quality. Thus the Soviet army of 1950 could only have fought then as it had during the Second World War itself, by combining set-piece artillery barrages (fired from great numbers of towed pieces laboriously assembled) with the thrusts of massed tanks, with the infantry following in turn to clear and occupy ground already won. Such means did defeat the Germans, but they could allow only a ponderous, step-by-step advance which was very costly in casualties, and which would have been dangerously slow against an enemy rich in airpower.

Nowadays, by contrast, it is precisely the Soviet army that has the fullest range of weapons and the model array of ancillary equipment for every need. Even the best-equipped of Western armies, that is the West German and the American, fall short of the Soviet standard, with the former lacking for example in chemical warfare equipment, while the latter is only now acquiring its first combat carriers for the infantry. And it is the Soviet army that now has the advantage of deploying complete families of weapons that offer overlapping capabilities in each category.[7]

In 1950, the Soviet infantry would have gone to the front on foot, on horse-carts or at best in commercial-type trucks; now it is equipped with armoured combat carriers of three different types, one wheeled and lightly armed for the motorized-rifle divisions, one heavily armed and fully tracked for the tank divisions, and a much lighter tracked vehicle for the airborne divisions. As for the ancillaries, Soviet tactical radios are now of Western quality and just as widely distributed, while chemical warfare weapons and defences are far more comprehensive than in any Western army. Soviet engineer equipment is notoriously superior and includes specialized items that are simply absent in Western armies, such as mobile automatic trench-diggers and ribbon-bridges. Until the mid-1970s the American army at least remained superior in one class of weapons: armed helicopters. By now, however, even this one remaining advantage has waned.

What all this tells us, quite simply, is that today's Soviet army is as different from the brute-force army of 1950 as the latter differed in turn from the bewildered troops which the Germans defeated by the million in 1941 and 1942. Continuously supported by self-propelled artillery and accompanied by armoured infantry, Soviet tank assaults would no longer need to stop after each successful thrust to allow the infantry and the towed artillery to catch up. Instead of ponderous step-by-step offensives, separated by weeks and months of laborious preparation, the Soviet army can now mount a continuous offensive that would persist by day and by night till its goal is reached. Instead of 'steamroller' offensives on pre-planned lines of advance, whose rigidity was no less pronounced than their mass, the Soviet army is now capable of fluid manoeuvre, so that an enemy's tactical success in stopping this or that thrust of advance would merely result in his subsequent encirclement. It is this formidable combination of 'Russian' mass and 'German' operational quality that characterizes today's Soviet army.

Along with its greatly enhanced capacity for continental warfare on a large scale, today's Soviet army has also acquired intervention

49

capabilities wholly absent in the past. In conjunction with long-range air transport, KGB operatives and the forces of Soviet clients such as Cuba, the airborne divisions and special air-assault brigades of the Soviet army are now equipped and trained to mount a wide spectrum of special operations, from the infiltration of small diversionary units to full-scale airborne *coup de main* assaults that can encompass an entire country. Such fine-tuned operations would have been quite beyond the capacity of the Soviet army of 1950, or 1960 for that matter, since one cannot rely on massed firepower and large numbers when surprise and stealth are absolute requirements.

We have to assess the abilities of the Soviet army in continental warfare from what we know of Soviet doctrine, exercises, field manoeuvres, officer training and equipment; but in recent years we have been afforded several opportunities to estimate how well the Soviet army performs as an intervention force, and our estimate cannot be dismissive.

For all its shortcomings, even in 1950 the Soviet army could have defeated any enemy it could then encounter in continental warfare, albeit at a high cost in casualties if opposed by American (and British) airpower. But this potential superiority in ground warfare did not offer any practical war-making opportunities to the leaders of the Soviet Union even if they had been so inclined, because America's superiority in 'strategic' air bombardment could then nullify any Soviet victories on the ground. When Stalin imposed his land blockade upon West Berlin, the deadly embrace of the Soviet army around the city was sufficient to force the suspension of all overland communications. But when the United States and Britain responded by mounting the airlift, the Soviet Union did not feel free to risk an air war by intercepting their aircraft. The great superiority of the United States in strategic air bombardment and nuclear weapons could not avert the crisis, nor decide its outcome all by itself, but it did set the rules of the encounter by providing an invisible but fully effective mantle of protection for all those heavily loaded transports that flew unharmed into West Berlin right over the Soviet anti-aircraft guns that ringed the city.

The Soviet Union was already a nuclear power in 1950, our year of comparison: it had both fission bombs and a long-range bomber (the Tu-4, a Soviet copy of the wartime American B-29). In fact the Soviet air force had several hundred Tu-4s which in theory could reach targets in the continental United States from bases in the

Soviet arctic. For the United States, too, the sole means of nuclear delivery was then the manned bomber. Ostensibly, American and Soviet bomber forces were thus roughly comparable. The Strategic Air Command of the US air force relied on B-50s which were modernized B-29s just like the Tu-4, as well as on B-36 bombers (larger but not much more effective); only a few B-47 jet bombers were already operational. But the similarity between Soviet and American bomber forces was entirely deceptive: the American force had the training and the on-board electronics to fly to the Soviet Union, find its targets, bomb them with tolerable accuracy, and survive against Soviet fighter-interceptors along the way. It had been the discovery of the early years of the Second World War that bombers were almost entirely useless without special skills and equipment for navigation and aiming. In 1950 the Soviet air force still lacked those attributes, and Tu-4s flying in American airspace in search of worthwhile targets would probably have run out of fuel or fallen victims to interception before reaching any American cities to drop their bombs.

By the early 1980s, on the other hand, the United States had lost the strategic-nuclear advantage that the superior economic, scientific and technological abilities of American society should naturally have assured. Outnumbered in every category of 'strategic' weapon except bombers, and outmatched in every conceivable index of capability except in the number of warheads (a rapidly waning advantage), American strategic-nuclear forces have much less delivery capacity as of this writing than the Soviet, unless theoretical bomber bomb-loads are misleadingly treated on a par with actual missile throw-weights (maximum bomber weapon-loads are only attainable at the shortest ranges; fuel almost always displaces bomb-loads to diminish greatly the usable payload; this does not apply to missile throw-weights). The long-standing American advantage in missile accuracies had to a large extent also disappeared. Uniquely, the outcome of the strategic-nuclear competition was not determined by the usual asymmetry between a steady Soviet effort and American inconstancy. It was by deliberate policy that the United States allowed its once great advantage to wane, and this policy was not dictated by budgetary stringencies but was rather the result of a pervasively influential and dogmatic belief in the theory of 'assured destruction'. This held that no advantage could be gained by any level of strategic-nuclear capability in excess of what was needed to destroy reliably a certain proportion of Soviet population unless and until the much higher level required for a fully disarming counterforce strike was reached – but that was a level universally deemed to be unattainable in practice. (To be 'fully disarming', a counterforce strike – that is, an attack against strategic weapons rather than cities or industry – would have to destroy *all* land-based ballistic missiles, long-range nuclear-capable bombers, and missile submarines; and, moreover, all these weapons would have to be destroyed simultaneously, to prevent retaliation.)

The theory of 'mutual deterrence' which guided American strategic-nuclear policy during fifteen years of unilateral restraint is ingenious and intellectually appealing. But what made it irresistible was that it offered a low-cost and low-risk solution to the great competition for power and influence with the Soviet Union. Thus the Soviet Union was allowed to acquire margins of advantage in one dimension of strategic-nuclear capability after another, and the balance of military power ineluctably changed, since the adverse trend in those forces was not offset by compensating changes in naval, tactical-air or ground-force capabilities. And the change in the balance of military power was just as inevitably reflected in the real-world political balance of access and influence. For all the intellectual plausibility of the American theory of deterrence, the Soviet Union showed that the universal rule of strategy still applies: one may not unilaterally quit the competition without penalty, and there is no such thing as cost-free competition.

While the West is weak in military power, the Soviet empire remains weak in economic achievement. It is sometimes claimed that in this divergence there is an overall balance. In fact, during the years when the military position of the United States and its allies continued to deteriorate, those who opposed a corrective build-up would stress the importance of 'economic power' and technical superiority, arguing in effect that the two are effective substitutes for military strength. But it is only in a *protracted* war that economic resources and technical abilities can in fact be substituted by the mobilization of economy and society. Given a long enough war, the United States and its allies could no doubt eventually muster superior military forces and thus achieve a superior overall power – if, that is, populations and industries survived until then.

But in the presence of thermonuclear weapons the potential military power that economic power can eventually provide is worth very much less than forces in being, actually deployed. Potential military power is useful for fighting wars, if they are long enough; but military forces actually deployed can *prevent* war, by deterrence. To be sure, the capacity to fight *protracted* war, which derives from economic power, can also deter, but only if the forces actually ready to fight are already so strong that they can hold off the enemy during the years which must pass before civilian economic capacity can be converted for military purposes. Elaborate preparations can greatly reduce this mobilization interval, and thus enhance the strategic value of economic power; but it will still be no deterrent at all if the enemy can be confident of defeating the military forces actually ready, before the mobilization of the economy can yield its results. It follows that reliance on 'economic power' implies a war-fighting strategy, while a war-avoidance strategy by contrast requires deployed military forces.

Of course the relative importance of economic and military power must also be evaluated in terms of their diplomatic worth, in the absence of war or the imminence of war. Some argue that the awesome destructive capacity of nuclear weapons inhibits the use of military power to such a great extent that even a large superiority cannot yield worthwhile gains; they therefore claim that military power itself is of declining importance in the affairs of mankind. In the same vein, it is argued that in a world that has made development and growth a universal religion, economic power is a highly flexible diplomatic instrument – altogether more useful than military force in providing influence over the course of international politics. The argument is plausible but it rests on a basic misconception, since armed strength need not be manifest in actual warfare to yield effective power.

As the relative power of a state increases in the perceptions of the world's political leaders and opinion-makers, its sphere of action that others deem proper and legitimate increases also. When we are confronted by a rising military power whose growth we do not match, for fear of the risk of war, or because we want to evade the economic sacrifice, or perhaps because our own means are simply too small, we come to terms psychologically with its increasing power by persuading ourselves that it will never be actually used, or at least that any possible aggressions will not hurt us directly. In 1950, or for that matter in 1960, the Soviet intervention in Ethiopia or the invasion of Afghanistan would have been regarded as outrageous

53

intrusions. Most likely, the Soviet leaders themselves would not have allowed their military men to dream of such adventures. But once the great increase in the armed strength of the Soviet Union was accomplished, its accepted sphere of action was widened also, and many were the voices that eagerly offered justifications for its expansive conduct. Of the Ethiopian intrusion, it was said that the Soviet Union was merely helping a legitimate government to protect its internationally recognized frontiers; and this is an argument both factually true and legally sound. But had the Soviet leaders chosen instead to support the Somali invasion of the Ogaden and the rebellion in Eritrea, the very same voices would no doubt have reminded us that the Ogaden had a population largely made up of ethnic Somalis, while Eritrea is of course inhabited by Eritreans, and that both peoples had long been oppressed by the Amharic Ethiopian government. The Soviet Union, they would have said, was merely upholding the principle of self-determination by supporting Somalis and Eritreans – and this is a principle universally recognized, notably by the United States, ever since 1917. Similarly, in the case of Afghanistan a suitably expanded principle of self-defence has been invoked on behalf of the Soviet Union: supposedly, there was a threat to Soviet control of the Muslim republics of the USSR; supposedly, this threat emanated from the example of the Afghan rebellion against the communist government in Kabul – hence to suppress that rebellion was mere self-defence.

It is thus that power conditions the minds of men. First comes the rising power and its use; later, after the fact, some principle or other can always be invoked to legitimize that which we did not dare to oppose. Economic leverage, real enough in single cases, has no such subtle and pervasive effect.

What others are so eager to legitimize, the Soviet leaders can obviously contemplate with equanimity. To discern the consequences of the great increase in the relative military power of the Soviet Union, we must therefore begin by estimating as best we can its impact upon the Soviet leaders themselves. Having made their career in the Party at a time when the Soviet Union was already a Great Power but lacked the attributes of *global* power, since its strategic reach did not go much beyond the frontiers of the Soviet Union itself, the Kremlin leaders now find themselves possessed of an oceanic navy, a powerful air force of intercontinental range, and of course large strategic-nuclear forces of global reach. Having graduated into the higher leadership at a time when the Soviet Union was already a greater power than all others except for the United States – but distinctly inferior to the latter – they now find themselves leading the most powerful of all nations. The possession of great power is not of course a novelty for the rulers of the Kremlin, which after all has been the seat of empire for centuries. Two things, however, are quite new. One is a matter of physical capabilities, concrete and incontrovertible, namely the achievement of extra-continental military strength of large dimensions; the other is neither concrete nor certain, namely the advent of a high degree of operational confidence in the skill of Soviet armed forces, and specifically in their ability to execute complex operations with elegant precision.

The advent of operational confidence

The claim here made is that the attitude of the Soviet leaders towards their own military power has undergone a crucial change which is likely to affect their entire conduct in international affairs. The evidence for this claim rests on the record of just two military operations, neither of them fought against serious enemies: the intervention in Ethiopia, in which Soviet combat units did not even take part, and the invasion of Afghanistan, entirely accomplished by Soviet forces. In neither case did the Soviet Union face a competent enemy, but then again in neither case could mass be employed to compensate for any qualitative shortcomings. Both operations were instead characterized by bold, self-confident execution of the sort not previously associated with the Russian style of warfare.

In the case of Ethiopia, the Soviet Union intervened to assist the new revolutionary rulers at a time when the territory they controlled had shrunk to little more than an enclave on the high plateau around the capital of Addis Ababa whose only overland links to the outside world were the railway lines to Assab and Djibouti – the former frequently interrupted by sabotage, and the latter actually cut by the Somali invasion. Formally begun on 2 September 1977, when a Soviet-Ethiopian arms supply agreement was signed, the intervention unambiguously placed Soviet prestige at risk in seemingly desperate circumstances: Eritrea was then largely in rebel hands, Somali troops and guerrillas had conquered most of the Ogaden (and cut the railway to Djibouti), and local rebellions had broken out in much of the rest of the country. A small Soviet command team headed by a lieutenant-general managed nevertheless swiftly to organize a series of successful counterstrokes which expelled the Somalis from the Ogaden by March 1978. Shortly thereafter, Eritrea was recovered also. By 20 November 1978, when the Ethiopian ruler Lieut.-Col. Mengistu Haile Mariam signed a twenty-year treaty of friendship and cooperation with the Soviet Union, his government was in full control of the entire territory of Ethiopia – a victory that would have seemed impossible when the Russians first arrived on the scene just one year before.

Before dismissing the significance of the episode on the grounds that the Somalis were weak and the Eritreans even more so, consider what the Soviet commander on the spot, Lieut.-Gen. V. I. Petrov, and his small staff had to achieve, and what obstacles they had to overcome. Petrov's victorious fighting force was made up of 15,000 Cuban troops, eight Ethiopian divisions and some 100,000 peasant militia with small arms and little training. For one thing, these disparate elements had to be coordinated in combat, across multiple language barriers. Second, the Ethiopians had never before used Soviet weapons, so that the 1,000 Soviet advisers had to train the troops and also give them some rudimentary maintenance skills while combat was actually under way. Petrov himself had to exercise overall control through a joint Soviet-Cuban-Ethiopian command, and his campaign had to begin in the midst of invasion and defeat.

The first obstacle was the unfavourable geography. The Russians were a long way from home, and the railway link to the sea was thin and insecure; even air transport was precariously dependent on the overflight of countries nominally opposed to the Soviet intervention. There was thus no possibility of redeeming failure by throwing in Soviet forces *en masse*. Second, the Russians sent to Ethiopia had to act decisively in the face of urgent danger without having any prior familiarity with the terrain and cultural milieu, in a country as different as could be from the realm of Russian experience.

The fact that the Soviet Union's political leaders were willing to make a clear and unambiguous commitment to the defence of revolutionary Ethiopia in circumstances so adverse, and with logistic links so precarious, is proof of a very high degree of confidence in the professional quality and versatility of their military men. Equally obvious is the bold self-confidence of the new kind of Russian military leader. Others less bold might have insisted on a prudent step-by-step campaign, which would start with the consolidation of the Ethiopian enclave around the one available port at Assab, to be followed by counter-guerrilla clearing operations to secure the railway line to Addis Ababa before launching any major counter-offensive. Instead Petrov launched the counter-stroke first, and left the reconquest of Eritrea till later. Others might have demanded much time to equip, train and reorganize Ethiopian forces before counter-attacking, but the Russians did all those things concurrently. Others would have required the prior gathering of vast stocks of supplies and all sorts of elaborate logistic arrangements before mounting serious offensive operations, but the Russians were willing to supply Ethiopian forces going into action straight from the ships and aircraft as they arrived, improvising all the way. This clearly was warfare in the style of Rommel rather than Oblomov, in the manner of the Germans at their best rather than of the Soviet army as we knew it, or for that matter of the American army in southeast Asia.

Too little is known of the actual fighting that goes on in Afghanistan as of this writing to make a serious estimate of the Soviet performance in that colonial war; and of course the final outcome of the conflict must remain in doubt. But the initial Soviet invasion is quite sufficient to confirm the judgement that one must make on the basis of the Ethiopian intervention. The Soviet invasion was spearheaded by four 'motorized rifle' divisions (actually, mechanized divisions). In fast concurrent drives, the 360th and 201st reached Kabul by way of the Termez and Kunduz roads, while the 66th and 357th moved down the Kushka-Herat road. The forces moving on each axis continued to advance until they converged on Kandahar, in a classic pincer movement. One more formation, the 15th tank division, followed the advance on the Herat road, possibly to act as an operational reserve for the Soviet area command, which was apparently provided by the 40th Army Headquarters (moved from Samarkand to Termez *before* the invasion).

By itself, the overland advance could not have seized Kabul swiftly enough to prevent some attempt at organized resistance. The Afghan leader, President Hafizullah Amin, could have tried to mount some sort of defence with such loyal troops as he had, possibly including the armed militia of his Khalq faction; he could certainly have called on the people at large to resist the invader; and, more dangerously for the Russians, he could have appealed for foreign assistance. Although none of these things could actually have stopped the Soviet army, each would have added to the political price of the invasion. But Amin could do nothing because the first move of the Soviet invasion was an airborne *coup de main*[8] which suppressed any attempt at resistance.

On the night of 27 December 1979, elite Soviet airborne troops along with special assault detachments moved into Kabul from the airport, sabotaged the central telephone exchange (to cut off international calls), and seized the radio and television station as well as the presidential palace and other major government buildings. At the same time, the Darulaman palace, where Amin had recently taken refuge with a guard of loyal troops, was attacked. After a short fight all resistance was defeated, and Amin was killed. On the next day, 28 December 1979, a new leader was given to the Afghans. He was Babrak Karmal, a former deputy prime minister delivered to Kabul in the baggage of the Soviet army.

The Afghan government and much of the military structure had of course been thoroughly subverted by the Russians long before the invasion. Years of penetration by Soviet-aligned Afghan communists and outright Soviet agents were compounded by last-minute seizures and sabotage carried out by KGB operatives and Soviet military advisers (several hundred were serving with Afghan forces and at major installations, including Kabul airport). In any case, one would not expect much effective resistance to a surprise high-speed action from the fierce but primitive and chaotic Afghans. Nevertheless, in examining the details of the Soviet *coup de main* one is reminded not of past Soviet actions, but rather of German operations such as Otto Skorzeny's 'Margarethe', in which Hungary's ruler, Admiral Horthy (who was by then eager for an armistice with the Russians), was overthrown and arrested on 16 October 1944, to be replaced with a German nominee after the successful seizure of the key centres of Budapest in circumstances very similar to those of the Kabul operation on 27 December 1979. Easy as such operations may appear in retrospect, the record of others in circumstances just as favourable tells us how easy it is to fail, and how hard it is to do a clean job. All the frictions of warfare are most strongly manifest when every move must be made swiftly, when specific buildings and even specific rooms must be found and seized in a surprise action tightly coordinated in time and space. In Kabul in December 1979, as in Budapest in October 1944, small teams of soldiers had to find their way, and quickly, in a strange city and at night. Only the most careful training and the most precise control can prevent accidental encounters with hostile elements, or even fratricidal fighting; only timing exactly coordinated can preserve surprise as the assault teams go for their separate targets all over the city.

To do such things quickly and well was not in the Soviet repertoire until quite recently. Even the 1968 *coup de main* mounted from Prague airport at the beginning of the invasion of Czechoslovakia was not of the quality shown in Kabul a decade later. The Czechs did not mount any fighting resistance at all, and yet the Soviet assault teams in Prague failed to carry out their plan. Refugees later told stories of Russians wandering around the city in a state of confusion, with lists of addresses in their hands. And it is proven fact that the Soviet teams failed to arrest key figures, and could not locate the emergency radio stations of the Czech civil defence, which came on the air almost immediately.

Although the Afghan armed forces could never have done much against an enemy so formidable as the Soviet, and although desertions and widespread Soviet subversion had further reduced what powers of resistance they might have had, the fact remains that the Soviet airborne troops sent on their own into Kabul airport could easily have been defeated, had the Afghan tank division deployed nearby intervened early enough, if only with a company or two. Had Afghan tanks reached the airport while the Soviet troops were still being flown in, a massacre could have ensued. Similarly, even very small forces could have blocked the Termez and Kunduz roads leading to Kabul, at least for a day or two, since the terrain greatly favours ambushes and sabotage; and any such delay in the overland link-up would have been very dangerous for the lightly armed airborne troops. Refugees have reported that KGB and Soviet military men already in place had neutralized the Afghan tank division by sabotage and subversion just before the *coup de main*. If true, this means that the Soviet high command ordered the daring airborne entry on the basis of a promise that undercover work would avert all danger. A more cautious military leadership would not have been so easily satisfied. Others in their place might have called for massive air strikes on the tank division's base before being willing to send lightly armed airborne troops into the depths of Afghanistan.

We are therefore confronted by clear evidence of an utterly novel boldness on the part of Soviet military leaders, and of an equally new confidence on the part of the Kremlin leaders in the professional competence of their military colleagues. The prudence that many observers recognized in the Soviet Union's conduct of the past owed much to the scant self-confidence of the Soviet military, and perhaps even more to the sceptical reserve of the Kremlin towards its own armed forces and their claims. Now that boldness and an elegant economy of means characterize Soviet military operations, it is natural that a more confident and far less prudent external policy should also be in evidence.

The decline of Soviet ideological influence

Ever since the October revolution the Soviet Union has been able to count on the support of some foreigners who are willing to serve its interests because of their personal faith in the rightness of communist ideology, and their acceptance of the Soviet government as the leader and supreme embodiment of the world communist movement. Thus, in addition to the usual military and economic instruments of statecraft, the Soviet Union has also had a further instrument that most other powers lack in its ability to manipulate the doings of communists abroad on behalf of its own policy purposes.

It is obvious, however, that Soviet ideological influence has greatly declined since Stalin's day, and especially over the last two decades. A sharp *relative* decline in the importance of the ideological instrument was the inevitable consequence of the increasing power of the Soviet state, and of its military strength above all. In

1919, the British intervention in support of the anti-Bolshevik White forces in the Civil War encountered the fierce resistance of some British trade unions and of left-wing opinion in general; at a time when the fragments of a navy which the Bolsheviks had could do nothing to oppose British deliveries of arms and troops to Russian ports under White control, the help of British dockers – who refused to load the supply ships – was very useful indeed for Lenin's regime. Nowadays, the Soviet Union would scarcely need to rely on the support of British trade unionists against the Royal Navy.

But there has also been a very great absolute decline in the appeal of communism as an ideology, and even more in the ability of the Soviet government to use foreign communists for its own purposes. A generation ago, communist parties directly controlled from Moscow could still attract the devoted loyalty of many intellectuals and trade union leaders throughout the industrialized world; in some countries, moreover, the local communist parties also had a mass following. In practice, it was only in France and Italy that parliamentary communist parties could actually influence public policy in important ways under Soviet direction, but Moscow had a far more widespread reach through the individual intellectuals, opinion-makers and trade unionists who were personally loyal to the Party as members or 'fellow-travellers'. The ostensibly non-communist trade union headed by communists overtly declared or not was a common phenomenon, and practical politicians were reconciled to the disproportionate leverage of the Party over labour unions, schools of higher education and the intelligentsia at large.

By way of the local communist parties and their networks of militants and fellow-travellers, the Soviet leaders could thus have a say in the policy of many industrialized countries in the Western camp; although they could only very rarely actually dominate government decisions, their influence could not be ignored. Moscow also had a more direct but narrower influence by way of the various transnational bodies it controlled – the 'world federations' which grouped trade unions, student groups and professional associations. More directly still, the Kremlin was served by the actual agents of the Comintern whose motives were ideological rather than career-oriented as in the other intelligence organizations – and Comintern agents were of a quality much superior on the whole. Communists who served as outright agents could of course be ordered to do whatever Moscow wanted done; the common run of Party members and fellow-travellers could never be so tightly controlled, but their support amounted to a much more powerful if less versatile tool for Soviet policy. To be sure, such ideological support could only be mobilized to serve Moscow's purposes when ideological proprieties and legality could both be maintained; further, it would take time to activate the mass of followers, many of whom were not actual Party members and thus did not belong to the chain of command that ultimately links the Soviet Politburo with the handful of members of each Party cell in the most remote of places. Finally, the network of foreign supporters could only be really effective when the issues which presented themselves were sufficiently dramatic to allow the local Party leadership to enlist the active help of the fellow-travellers first and then, with their cooperation, to mobilize in turn mass support from outside the Party. But when all of these conditions could be satisfied, the results could be impressive indeed, as for example in the worldwide campaign against the American war in Korea (when one widely exploited issue was the accusation that the Americans had resorted to 'germ warfare'). It is symptomatic of the decline of Soviet ideological influence that the worldwide agitation against America's role in the Vietnam War owed much more to the inspiration of the American anti-war movement than to Moscow's leadership and coordination.

This is not the place for a sustained analysis of the varied and complex causes of the decline of communism as an ideology, and of the further decline in the Kremlin's ability to exploit such ideological support as it still has. In no particular order of importance, one may mention the division in the worldwide movement caused by the emergence of a rival centre of the faith in Beijing; the shift in focus of the alienated intelligentsia from the problems of society to the problems of the self, so that a fascination with collectivism has given way to a fragmented faith in psychoanalysis, sexology, self-awareness cults and still more dubious pursuits; and the gradual discovery that the Soviet Union was a state much more bureaucratic than socialist, devoted more to the policeman than the worker, and more of a vehicle for Russian imperialism than for transnational socialism. In some quarters it was the belated recognition of the Soviet Union as yet another manifestation of Western culture, as one more 'White' power structurally opposed to the claims of the

'Third World', that destroyed its appeal. But perhaps above all it was the transformation of the Soviet Union from an embattled revolutionary underdog to the world's leading military power that made it seem less deserving of support. Certainly those who are systematically inclined to favour the weak and who identify military power itself with the source of all evil in this world can scarcely retain much affection for a Soviet Union so plainly strong, and so clearly militaristic.

The Soviet Union has not of course lost all its ideological supporters in the industrialized world. There are still firm loyalists, and in large numbers, in both France and Italy and also in Greece and Spain; and there are still communist parties affiliated to Moscow all over the world, each with its disciplined leaders, loyal members and active fellow-travellers. But the depth of the remaining support for Soviet purposes, its intensity, and the degree to which the Party networks can be used to mobilize mass opinion have all greatly declined throughout the world.

It is obvious enough that the decline of Moscow's ideological influence in the industrialized world diminishes the overall power of the Soviet Union. But this is not a phenomenon entirely favourable for Western security, because in the past the Soviet Union's desire to preserve the loyalty of its foreign supporters did in some degree inhibit its conduct. However perverted, a residue of humanism remains in the foundations of Marxism-Leninism, and even though Moscow could conceal much of the evil that it was doing, especially from loyalists all too willing to avert their eyes, and although the Kremlin's propaganda could successfully misrepresent much more, its need to preserve some outward ideological conformity long remained a moderating influence on Soviet conduct even in Stalin's day. Some specific inhibitions arose from the Soviet desire to preserve ideological support in countries where the communist party was particularly strong. Thus, for example, it is reasonable to estimate that one reason why Stalin did not use force against Tito's errant Yugoslavia in 1948 was the catastrophic damage that an invasion would have inflicted on the Italian Communist Party, then as now the largest party outside the Soviet bloc.

Another adverse consequence of the decline of communism in the industrialized world has been the shift in Soviet efforts, from the cultivation of broad social and political action by mass movements to the sponsorship of terrorism and guerrilla warfare, not only in

Latin America, Africa and Asia, but also in Europe and Japan. It is important to recall that for important organizational and ideological reasons the Soviet Union and the communist parties it controlled used to be strongly opposed to terrorism. Communist parties are supposed to organize the masses, while terrorist groups are by nature unlikely to inspire mass activity. Violence was to be sure very much in order to bring about the revolution, but the Leninist prescription called for mass insurrection rather than individual acts of terrorism. Above all, terrorist bands were viewed with disfavour by Moscow because they could not be controlled by a disciplined centralized leadership which would fit into the world-wide chain of command that runs from the Soviet Politburo to the national Party leaders.

It was only when it became clear that the Soviet Union was ineluctably losing the support of the trade unions and left-wing mass movements of the West that the Soviet leaders began to accept terrorists as useful allies; with the Leninist programme of revolution by the working classes finally exposed as totally unrealistic, the Soviet Union began to arm and pay small bands of violent extremists in many parts of the world. Given the inherent obscurity of links that are by nature most secretive, it is difficult to prove the direct Soviet sponsorship of all the revolutionary terrorism that plagues the world. But by now a mass of irrefutable evidence has emerged which proves that it is the Soviet Union which provides directly or indirectly the weapons, training and money which terrorists need in order to be effective. It is not by accident, as *Pravda* might say, that the typical terrorist has characteristically spent some time in training camps in the Soviet Union, East Germany or Bulgaria, or in such client-states as Cuba or South Yemen. When we catch a glimpse of terrorists in action, we usually see them armed with AK-47s, RPG rocket-propelled grenades or other such Soviet artefacts. And it is not by accident either that the great upsurge of terrorism in evidence since the mid-1960s followed closely the great decline in the Soviet Union's ideological influence. Always inspired by some local circumstance, so often greatly enhanced by Soviet support, terrorism has become the second-best substitute for the broad social, political and syndicalist action which the Soviet Union can no longer manipulate.

Given the fundamental causes of the decline of Soviet-oriented communism in the industrial democracies – the only countries where the phenomenon can actually be observed – it is reasonable to believe that the ideology is also in decline in the Soviet Union and in Eastern Europe as well. In Eastern Europe, to be sure, there was not much to decline from: there were only a few communists in Bulgaria, Romania and Hungary when the Soviet army arrived in 1944, and it took energetic pressure and much subversion to make mass parties out of nothing. In Czechoslovakia the Communist Party was also small before the Second World War, although it did have a base in mining and industrial areas; as for the much larger German and Polish Communist Parties, their mass following was decimated by the Nazis, while their leaders, who had haplessly taken refuge in Stalin's Soviet Union, were mostly killed during the purges. Quite a few German communists were handed over to the Gestapo in 1939, after the signature of the Nazi-Soviet pact.

Once the 'People's Democracies' of Eastern Europe were established, largely by Soviet police terror and the subversion of the remaining non-communist parties, there was of course a great expansion in Party membership. Along with purely opportunistic careerists, there were also a good many genuine converts, especially among the intelligentsia and the industrial working classes, where communist influence had been manifest before the war, if only in a small way. But the client regimes of Eastern Europe were destined to disappoint both the old militants who had survived to see the great day and the new believers. Their failure was both moral and material, both social and national. It is symptomatic that by 1968, when the closed doors of censorship were suddenly opened, the world discovered that there were very few communists left in Czechoslovakia. (The slogan of the Prague Spring, 'Communism with a human face', was a mere euphemism for social democracy, as the Soviet leaders pointed out.) Especially striking was the virtual absence of communist influence among the young, wholly educated in the schools of the regime, and supposedly indoctrinated from birth.

That communism has not 'taken' in Eastern Europe, that the Soviet Union has perpetuated all the old anti-Russian sentiments while creating new ones (Czechs and Slovaks had once been well-disposed to their fellow-Slavs of the East), means of course that there is no 'organic union' – as the celebrated phrase goes – between the Soviet Union and its European satellites, except possibly for Bulgaria, the one country backward enough to have been uplifted by the Soviet Union, and where pro-Russian sentiments were certainly very strong in the past.

Once again the otherwise welcome failure of communist ideology has an unfavourable consequence: it imposes the role of policeman and occupier upon the Soviet Union, thus further reinforcing the institutions of repression inside Soviet society itself.

It is notoriously difficult to estimate the true status of the official Leninist ideology inside the closed society of the Soviet Union. Almost certainly, it is not any one reality that eludes us but rather a wide variety of conditions. At one extreme, communism may still be a liberating faith to younger minds seeking to escape the tight bonds of the surviving traditional and Islamic societies of Central Asia and the Caucasus; at the same time, Marxism-Leninism may be thoroughly obsolete and unworthy of serious concern for the more sophisticated of the Russian intelligentsia who are nowadays responsive to the flux of Western ideas. At the opposite extreme, the ideology may simply be seen as part of the hateful baggage of imperial domination by many in the non-Russian republics. For many Russians, on the other hand, it may have become the accepted ritual faith ('Lenin-worship'), especially for that part of the population that has lost its roots and traditions in the upheavals of war, industrialization and the migration to the cities. Among the great mass of urban white-collar workers, that is the clerks of the bureaucracy, Marxism-Leninism is no doubt widely present as a strictly *pro forma* creed, largely ignored when not cynically play-acted; but then again, many low-level bureaucrats may have absorbed its dogmas as a set of pieties and conventions, much as their predecessors once believed in Tsar and church. And finally, in rural Russia especially, there may remain even now a widespread resistance to the ideology as a 'modern' and alien creed, both from genuine traditionalists still living the village life in remote corners of the country, and from nostalgics among the urban intellectuals. Some, we know, have become fond of evoking the mythic purities of Old Russia and have demonstratively returned to Orthodox Christianity – so as better to condemn the alienation and corruption of modern Soviet society. Very powerfully represented in exile, this form of specifically Russian anti-communism may also be strong in the Soviet Union itself.

One thing that may count for a great deal in all this uncertain diversity, at least for our present purpose, is the state of the ideology among those Soviet citizens who happen to be closest to the Kremlin leaders, whose attitudes are most directly manifest to them. It is a fair guess that what they say and do has a disproportionate impact on the perceptions of the most senior leaders, who are otherwise cut off from all personal contact with the populace. Evidence of continued devotion to the faith would naturally enhance the confidence of the leaders in the future prospects of the regime, while contrary information would naturally reinforce the pessimistic view – and thus intensify the urgencies for action that such pessimism must breed. Who is in most intimate contact with the Kremlin leaders? First of course, their own families – that is their children, by now middle-aged, and their grandchildren, who are themselves already adults – then the bureaucrats and plain servants around them, the 'consulting intelligentsia' retained for duty around the Politburo to play the expert role, and finally the literary and 'entertainment' intelligentsia of writers, poets and performers of various kinds, whose attitudes can be made fully manifest even in the absence of personal contact.

It is enough to draw up the list to answer the question: whatever we know of the new privileged class of the sons and daughters suggests that the assiduous study of the writings of Marx, Engels and Lenin would not fascinate them nearly as much as the pursuit of privilege; as for the *jeunesse dorée* of the third generation, it seems that among them an attitude of ideological indifference is a social norm and at least fashion, and even loud contempt is not rare. The body servants of the Kremlin might almost certainly manifest a very different attitude – if only because they want to keep their jobs – and besides, the moral economy of the servant requires a degree of respect for the master, and for his ostensible beliefs. But then again, the demigods of the Politburo are unlikely to be much impressed by the ideological conformity of their maids and valets, their waiters and chauffeurs. Nor is the consulting intelligentsia likely to be a great repository of the pure faith, if only because of all Soviet citizens they are the ones with the widest access to the West and its artefacts; one wonders how persuasive is their stance as rigid believers. Finally, the literary and 'entertainment' intelligentsia has in recent years voted with its feet to an unprecedented degree: a significant slice of Russian culture is now already to be found in exile. The writers, poets and entertainers still living in the Soviet Union must conform or at least remain silent, but the exiles speak for them: their *diversity* as well as their sheer numbers should be a sufficient indication to the leaders of the prevailing attitude of that class as a whole.

Among the elite and the masses alike, among both Russians and non-Russians, the decay of the official ideology of the Soviet Union, both in its role as a philosophical system to guide the elite and inspire the masses, and as a 'bonding' faith for a large and highly heterogeneous society, is in a state already advanced. Since the peoples of the Soviet Union lack any other basis of solidarity, and indeed are divided by deep ethnic resentments, the decline of Marxism-Leninism forces the regime to rely more and more on material incentives, or repression, to make up for the ideological cohesion that is plainly diminishing. To maintain the political equilibrium of Soviet society, the decline of the faith must be compensated by some increase in the standard of living, or some increase in police coercion, or a combination of both.

After Stalin's death, the role of repression in the mix was greatly reduced by the conscious and deliberate decision of the Kremlin leaders, who acted thus for their own political reasons (one cannot have an all-powerful police without having all-powerful policemen also). Since the ideology was already in decline, the great increase in consumer welfare that Khrushchev inaugurated was a necessary substitute for the sharp reduction in the intensity of police coercion.

Khrushchev's successors have followed in his path, but with increasing difficulty. Khrushchev had the great advantage of starting from a very low base, but even today's modest levels of consumption have established a new minimum standard, from which further increases demand more and more in the way of resources. Second, while the Soviet economy continues to grow, its rate of growth is diminishing. Finally, the great increase in military expenditures that started in the last years of Khrushchev's rule seems to have become institutionalized. The military budget appears to be increasing at a steady rate year after year, even as the growth of the economy is slowing down to very little. Since the supply of food and better products must also increase steadily if consumer satisfaction is to serve as a basis of political support for the regime, the Khrushchev formula could only work so long as economic growth could be rapid. And yet if the Soviet Union had remained on the path of Khrushchev's policy, it is precisely growth that would have suffered, since investment had to be sacrificed to pay for increases in both consumer and military spending. Obviously a decline in investment must reduce the further growth of the Soviet economy, thus making it still more difficult to satisfy both the Soviet consumer and the relentless appetite for more military spending of the 'metal eaters' (Khrushchev's own term for the Soviet military-industrial complex).

The partial reversion to 'Stalinist' police coercion that we have witnessed since the fall of Khrushchev is therefore both logical and necessary: since the rate of increase in the flow of goods to the consumer could not be kept up, repression had to increase to preserve the equilibrium of the system. The post-Khrushchev reversion to (mild) Stalinism could only have been avoided by somehow contriving to revive the ideology or by reducing military expenditures, or else by drastic economic liberalization to achieve high rates of growth once again. As compared to these alternatives, either quite impractical or unacceptable to the regime or both, the tightening of police control was obviously the safest and most practical course for Brezhnev and his men. The equally obvious necessity of increasing 'vigilance' during the years of detente, when Soviet society was inevitably becoming a little less impenetrable, worked to the same effect: repression and detente only seemed contradictory to outsiders; within the system they were perfectly complementary.

Without being too mechanistic about the whole thing, and always bearing in mind the great diversities of a very large empire of many nations, one may project the consequences of the combination of economic stagnation with the continued decline of the ideology as follows. First, an economic system that is becoming steadily less effective will require continued increases in investment just to maintain the present, very modest, rate of growth. Second, a Soviet Union in full pursuit of a global primacy in military power will have to spend more rather than less to maintain its current advantage, given the increased American defence effort and the emerging worldwide coalition that links the United States, NATO, the People's Republic of China and a dozen other countries, including Japan. Observers in the West must be a good deal more conscious of the weaknesses and disarray of the coalition than the Soviet leaders, who must estimate its potential strength prudently in the light of the great scope for increased military effort that theoretically remains possible in Europe and Japan. Third, now that increases in investment and military outlays jointly absorb most of the (slow) growth of the Soviet economy, very little room is left to provide the increase in living standards that the steady decline of ideological 'bonding' would call for. That being the case, it seems safe to predict a gradual stiffening of police coercion.

To be sure, today's Soviet Union is still a paradise of legality as compared to the worst years of Stalin's rule; there is pervasive repression but not the sheer terror of the midnight arrests and the Gulag. But as Khrushchev realized very clearly, the Soviet regime must either progress towards a genuine liberalization – if always under the Party's control – or else revert to the sinister tranquillity of the Stalinist order. It is obvious enough that the supreme bureaucrats who ruled in the Kremlin had their own good reasons to keep the policemen in their places, but the ideological decline and economic stagnation that were driving the regime towards increased oppression are far more powerful forces than the surviving hesitations, and political fears, of the Kremlin leadership. Every effort was no doubt made to ensure that the policemen did not come to dominate the Party leadership itself, but rather than risk a Polish-style collapse the police would undoubtedly be given all the unfettered powers it once had over the population at large. Now, with Andropov as the new chief, the police, that is the KGB, has attained power in some degree, at least for a while. All along it was the logical conclusion that either the policemen or the soldiers should come to dominate a once ideological state that had lost the true ideological impulse.

In theory, even with Andropov in charge, there is still the possibility of a drastic change of direction, whereby the political equilibrium of Soviet society would be preserved by reducing military expenditure and liberalizing the economy in order to realize its full potential for growth. Indeed there are those who loudly claim that Andropov's goal is precisely to liberalize the system. But it is the politically more prudent course of a tighter repression that seems far more probable. This need not in itself result in a more aggressive external policy by the regime. But an increase in police repression would definitely require a further intensification in both the 'threat propaganda' that justifies repression by pretending that it is aimed at a foreign threat, and in the controls that insulate Soviet society from the outside world. And it is these secondary and almost technical requirements that are likely to have an adverse impact on Soviet foreign policy, compounding all the other forces that are driving matters in the same direction.

Five

Soviet Imperialism and its Consequences

To show that the Soviet Union is now strong enough to expand by war does not suffice to predict that it will. To note the changes of political structure that have made of the Russians an imperial people once more does not necessarily mean that their imperialism will be expansive – even the Romans abandoned further conquest long before their power began to decline. To argue that the Soviet leaders of today have good reason to be pessimistic of the future of their regime does not in itself justify the prediction that they will seek salvation in further conquest in order to extend further their fringe of client-states.

To recognize that the power of the Soviet armed forces is now such that all weak countries directly adjacent are in peril, including both China and Iran, does not mean that the leaders of the Soviet Union will choose to avail themselves of the opportunity – since great risks and substantial costs must persist. To explain that the great increase in the professional expertise of the Soviet armed forces opens a whole new repertoire of swift and decisive operations in the German style does indeed establish that one more pre-condition of aggression is now in place, but proves nothing more. And finally, to observe that the decline of the ideology diminishes inhibitions while inducing a return to a society more closed, more martial and more fearful, does not prove that the path that leads to war will be taken.

The sceptics may therefore reject the view that the Soviet Union is now expansionist since no practical incentive to expansion has been proven. Few will deny that the Soviet Union is afflicted by structural maladies that are both incurable and destined to be fatal, but, since these dysfunctions are purely internal in both source and effect, why should the Soviet Union seek further conquests, which could do nothing to alleviate its fundamental problems and which indeed could make them worse?

To argue that the Soviet Union has already entered into an era of imperial expansion it may therefore seem necessary to prove that this or that conquest would yield some benefit that could directly alleviate the structural maladies. Why not for example show how greatly the Soviet Union might benefit from conquering the oil of the Persian Gulf? Or from imposing its power over Japan and its most industrious economy?

The attractions that such profitable ventures might have for the Kremlin cannot be entirely dismissed, but it would be wrong to offer them in support of the claim that the Soviet Union has now become a classic military empire in pursuit of expansion. For to do so would imply that the test itself is valid, i.e. that internal structural maladies only cause external aggressiveness when expansion promises to bring concrete relief for those maladies. But of course the test is utterly without merit. If it was not because of their internal structure why did the empires of the past ever arise? Was it for gold that the Romans conquered the Latium around their city, and then all Italy and then the entire Mediterranean world, and then more? Was it for silver that Athens built a navy of imperial dimensions, or was it not rather the very opposite that happened, with a silver mine accidentally found being used to pay for triremes very deliberately built? And what were the precious metals, raw materials or markets that persuaded the Hapsburgs to annex Bosnia and Hercegovina in October 1908, ten years before their fall?

To be sure, there must be sufficient profit in the empire to pay for its costs over the long run, but profit cannot motivate the quest for empire, even if costly and profitless expansion cannot long be sustained. The diversities of history will naturally offer contrary examples, but why should today's Soviet Union emulate exceptions such as the first, pre-Victorian British empire? After all, merchant-adventurers are not especially prominent in the Kremlin.

That nations set themselves on the course of imperial expansion merely because they can, since their neighbours are weak, is the normal pattern of history. That the actual force that drives them to expand is precisely their own internal structure, with all its strengths and disorders, is no more than a commonplace: given the power to

73

act, disequilibrium inside seeks relief on the outside. And of course the favoured justification for intruding on the lands of others is the defence of the lands already owned. That too is a thing entirely natural, because a regime openly and consciously amoral cannot evoke and preserve loyalty. But in truth all motives and all justifications are of small import: once the internal condition of society is in a state of disequilibrium, once its leaders acquire the physical capacity for conquest, once military institutions are created which have no sufficient role in self-defence strictly defined, all manner of reasons and all sorts of rationalizations will emerge to make expansion seem attractive and to make its costs and risks seem worthwhile. And the effect might now be compounded by the fact that the new ruler of the Soviet Union, seemingly lacking in support within the Party, has embraced the military leadership and invokes its backing. Unless Andropov (or some proximate successor) finds another basis for his power, a still greater expansion of Soviet military strength is therefore to be envisaged.

In the Soviet case the list of reasons and excuses for further imperial expansion may include any or all of the following: to arouse the national fervour of the ethnic Russians and enlist their enthusiasms to uphold the regime; to make the control of the non-Russians easier, by further enhancing the prestige of the empire to distract attention from a poor economy; to improve the boundaries of the empire and extend its protective glacis of client-states so as to strengthen it to meet the coming crisis; to weaken decisively a major antagonist, in order to allow a subsequent reduction in military efforts; or else to defeat a particular enemy deemed to be especially threatening over the long run. And so one may go on with the recitation of excuses good and bad, but to little purpose, for such justifications are easily invoked to explain deeds that are in fact caused by circumstances. And the circumstances of an empire already powerful and becoming more so drive its leaders to find employment for their armed forces – always supposedly to defend the conquests of the past by yet more expansion.

In this pattern, which is all too familiar in history, the justification of self-defence can easily be preserved: imperial territory is found to be in peril, or at least is disturbed by enemies based in lands that are beyond the limits of the empire, the security of the empire therefore requires that the frontier be moved outwards, to encompass and suppress the danger at its source. When that slice of expansion is duly achieved, by outright annexation or else by the creation of subservient client-states, it is soon discovered that the new frontier of the empire is also troubled from without – and thus the stage is set for more expansion which may again be explained away as defensive in intent. It is certainly more comfortable to think of one's wars as defensive rather than to admit an outright aggression, and besides, there will always be some foreigners who will find good reason to accept the claim of self-defence. After all, to recognize aggression for what it is imposes the necessity of confronting it, and that in turn demands courage and sacrifice. If by contrast one can persuade oneself that the empire remains 'essentially defensive' it can be claimed that resistance is unnecessary.

The mechanics of expansion

The aggressive nation-state is dangerous enough to civilization, but the aggressive empire is even more threatening because its growth – by definition – is not confined by the limits of a national homeland even if most ambitiously defined. Empires and nation-states can both expand but the former's growth is not bound by self-set limits of any sort. Some ultimate constraint is imposed all the same on the growth of empires, not so much by the quantum of their strength as by the *specific forms* of their instruments of power. In the Roman case, for example, the peculiar strength of the army was in the legions, whose troops were more combat engineers than (heavy) infantry. Thus the Roman army was strongest in lands where there were cities to besiege or defend, not mere agglomerations easily yielded and soon restored but cities that were vital centres, essential to the lives of the respective peoples. To be sure, if the land itself was suitable for arable farming of reasonable yield, conquest could be profitable anyway, and with a peaceful prosperity duly assured cities would grow naturally after the fact. But in the forests and swamp of Germany, peopled more by roaming slash-and-burn farmers, hunters and fishermen than a settled peasantry, in the steppe of the nomad horse shepherds and in the desert that could not be irrigated, the slow-moving Roman legion could neither get a grip on the elusive enemy, nor hold secure anything of value – except by long walls that would themselves mark the renunciation of further expansion.

Similarly in our own day, the military strength of the empire of the Russians is still most strongly felt on land, where there is direct territorial contiguity. By the first century AD, the Roman empire had reached its 'operational' limit, since expansion had everywhere come to an end in front of oceans, dense forest (with soil too heavy for the plough of those days), the desert and the steppe. The empire of the Russians is, by contrast, still far from its own operational limit of territorial contiguity; from the core of the Eurasian landmass that the Russians already control, they could still expand their power to the west, south and east without having to cross wide ocean waters.

If imperial expansion were only possible by outright annexation, another and more restrictive limit would soon be encountered: the ability to conquer does not guarantee the ability to rule – or not at any rate comfortably and at tolerable cost. When the new-won territory is densely inhabited by peoples which already have a political culture of their own, it can then be very much harder to rule than to conquer. In such circumstances, direct control would require an indefinite military occupation which, even if not greatly contested, must absorb some share of the forces of the empire, and diminish correspondingly its capacity for further expansion.

The Roman solution, like that of the Soviet Union, was to establish subservient client-states, nominally independent and charged with the administrative and political governance of lands effectively dominated by the empire but not annexed. The indispensable ingredient of indirect rule was and is a native political leadership able and willing to translate imperial desires into policy – without provoking in the process any more resentment than the client-state can handle by its own mixture of welfare, propaganda and repression. The Romans eventually absorbed virtually all their client-states to make them into ordinary provinces, but several generations intervened between the initial conquest and the final annexation, so that the population could be Romanized before becoming legally Roman. And it was not only the peoples of the client-states that were thus changed, but the empire too: while conquered peoples were gradually becoming Romanized, the empire itself was gradually becoming truly transnational. Until then, however, the client-rulers had to manage the difficult feat of mediating between nativism and the empire, local interests and imperial interests, and the Romans did what they could to help, by tactful conduct which concealed as much as possible their true subservience. But the method only worked when the political class of the client-states was already culturally assimilated, either in the Latin vein or the Greek, and when the mass of the population was not too far removed from a similar condition.[9]

To rule its client-states of Eastern Europe, the Soviet Union has a similar requirement: it must rely on a native communist elite that can build and operate a tolerable imitation of the Leninist state with a pervasive bureaucratic control over all spheres of public life (this being the state accurately described as totalitarian).

The Leninist client-states provide a desirable substitute for annexation and direct Soviet rule to the extent that they can satisfy an ascending hierarchy of imperial needs. In the first place they must of course deny the use of their own territory to any power hostile to the empire; this is a minimum condition and easily met – and not only by Leninist client-states (Finland comes to mind, unavoidably). Second, there are a variety of 'positive' services: diplomatic support, including bloc voting at the UN, intelligence collaboration and, above all, the deployment of subservient military forces – a service especially valuable if the client forces are also usable in part for imperial purposes elsewhere (Cuba is the prize exhibit). Not all the Leninist client-states provide all of these services, and the Soviet leaders have been satisfied with less than total support (Romania is the borderline case). Third, there are the economic services, achieved in the degree that the client's economy is integrated into Soviet planning, and to the extent that the Soviet Union can obtain valuable goods in exchange for exports that it can spare. Nowadays, few of the client-states fulfil the economic desiderata to any satisfactory extent, and Poland is not the only one which obtains valuable raw materials from the Soviet Union in exchange for shoddy goods unsaleable on the world market.

A final criterion is the degree of self-sufficiency in repression. The net value of the positive services and of the economic cooperation which the Soviet Union receives is diminished to the extent that the client's control over its own population requires the presence of Soviet forces. The Czechoslovak regime for example is very cooperative indeed in every way, but since it must be kept in power by large numbers of Soviets troops it may be less desirable as a client than the Romanian, which provides few positive services (aside from some espionage work) and which firmly refuses economic cooperation, but which also runs its own system of repression so well that it does not need any Soviet garrison at all. To be sure the five Soviet divisions in Czechoslovakia are part of the Soviet Union's general deployment on the 'western front', and would no doubt be maintained somewhere in the region anyway. But the fact that Soviet forces are actually tied down in Czechoslovakia since revolt could follow from their removal is a significant loss, since the Soviet high command cannot count on those divisions as part of its 'disposable' military capability available for expansion.

Whether fully satisfactory, as Bulgaria is, or only minimally adequate, like Romania, the Leninist client-states do for the empire of the Russians what their client-princes did for the Romans: they provide the security benefits of imperial expansion without the administrative and political burdens of direct rule. In the Roman case, the geographic scope of this device of empire was limited to the areas of Latin or Greek culture (and thus fully exhausted by the first century AD). In the Soviet case, by contrast, there is again much room for more expansion. Even though there may not be one state in the whole world whose citizens would willingly elect a Marxist-Leninist government, equally there is not one that does not have at least the nucleus of a communist party – which can instantly provide a Leninist client-regime upon the arrival of Soviet military power on the scene.

Even in a country as backward and fanatically Islamic as Afghanistan, with hardly a semblance of a 'working class' (as Marxists would define such things) and with only a tiny intelligentsia, the Soviet Union was able to find enough 'Marxist-Leninists' to form a government – even though their numbers and abilities turned out to be insufficient to secure control unaided by Soviet troops. One may doubt the ideological commitment of these Afghan clients, but in Moscow's eyes that has long ago ceased to be a virtue as important as plain obedience.

If the relative power of the Soviet Union were to increase in the future as it has done in the past, expansion might well follow. If so any further aggrandizement of the Soviet Union's territory would still remain most unlikely, and we would see instead the creation of new client-states at the periphery of the empire. Since a nominal independence can be preserved, and some licence given to expressions of nationalism, this classic device of empire is far better attuned to the temper of our times than outright annexation. Besides, the demographic equilibrium of the Soviet Union requires the exclusion of any more non-Russian nationalities.

Physical military facts still set hard limits to the scope of Soviet imperial expansion, but no inner limits are set by the requirement of political control: the Leninist formula, when fully supported by the technology of repression so well developed by the Soviet Union, has proved to be very exportable indeed. To be sure, nationalism is the hardy perennial of politics, but it can only threaten the client-regimes if they violate the Leninist formula by allowing truly independent institutions to survive. If that happens, it hardly matters what the institution is, for any institution left free in an otherwise controlled society will become a vehicle of nationalism – as indeed of all other anti-regime ideals. That obviously was the case in Poland, where the Catholic church has inherently served as the bastion of resistance to the communist state.

If the totalitarian state is true to its name and no independent institutions survive, the regime itself can harness national feelings for its own purposes. Where there is no shelter and nourishment for any more assertive nationalism, the client rulers can plausibly present themselves as the 'nationalist' alternative to direct Soviet rule. To some extent, all of the East European client-regimes attempt to play that role, with varying degrees of success. The Romanian regime can exploit nationalist feelings most easily because it has in truth a large measure of independence, to the point where its very status as a client-state is a matter of debate. The Czechoslovak regime brought to power by Russian soldiers in 1968 can scarcely benefit at all from its feeble nationalist pretensions. The East German regime is slightly better placed than the Czechoslovak, but matters are complicated by the hesitation with which any German government must approach nationalist themes. In the case of Bulgaria the traditional acceptance of the Russians as protectors makes things rather easy for the regime, while in Hungary the regime can make large use of the common perception that it stands as the only alternative to Soviet rule more directly applied.

The Soviet leaders continue to advertise their willingness to use force against popular revolt, or defection by the client-rulers themselves; but, with the growing confidence that comes from the sheer

79

experience of empire, and also from the rising power of the Soviet Union, indirect rule has become increasingly flexible and subtle. The nation-state which wages war upon the foreigner certainly fears defeat, but the empire that makes war on its own subjects must fear the costs of victory also, in the enduring bitterness and silent resistance that follows. The Soviet Union must prefer to avoid direct intervention, but in order to retain the deterrent benefit of its violent repressions of the past, in East Germany in 1953, of Hungary in 1956 and of Czechoslovakia in 1968, it must always remain poised to do the same again. In the case of Poland the credibility of a Soviet invasion was a most important factor in ensuring at least the temporary success of the martial law government inaugurated in December 1981.

In the Polish case, the rise of a free trade union movement exceeded the bounds of Soviet flexibility, but otherwise – so long as the essential security interests of the Soviet Union are duly protected – much may be tolerated in the client-states. Just as the Romans would collect tribute and recruits from some nations while being satisfied with recruits only elsewhere, or even with mere symbolic tokens of allegiance from still others, the contemporary Soviet empire tolerates the considerable liberties of Hungary, the deviant diplomacy of Romania and the long-standing abdication of the Polish regime from a proper Leninist monopoly of power. In 1948, by contrast, Stalin could not tolerate even the slightest nationalist deviation from an otherwise very Stalinist Tito, because the Soviet Union was then very weak, and her arts of indirect rule were still in embryo. A generation later, an immensely stronger Soviet Union much more experienced in the craft of empire can afford a much more relaxed attitude in dealing with the client-regimes. Certainly this new tolerance of diversity cannot be taken as a sign of weakness but must rather be recognized as evidence of a new self-confidence, based on strength.

Six

The Future Scope of Soviet Imperial Expansion

It is obvious that a great military empire will try to exploit such opportunities for aggrandizement as present themselves from time to time; and of course some states that are neither empires nor great will act just in the same way, if they have enough power for the deed. During the 1970s the Soviet Union thus engaged in successful ventures of penetration in both Ethiopia and Angola and otherwise made its presence felt wherever local circumstances created an inviting prospect, especially if American power was absent or else defeated, as notably in the case of Laos and Vietnam. More such opportunities will no doubt arise in the future (even though American passivity is no longer to be expected) and the Soviet Union will no doubt be tempted again, sometimes to meet with success and sometimes perhaps not.

But such things are not the proper business of empire, and would not offer proper employment for great and still increasing military power. Given the nature of the contemporary Soviet Union and its particular combination of strengths and weaknesses, it is not opportunities that will attract major attempts at expansion but rather threats. So it was for the Romans during their ascent and indeed for all other classic continental empires, including the British Raj in India – even if not for the maritime British empire as a whole.

Since even with Afghanistan in chronic revolt the Soviet Union has large and well-equipped forces that are fully deployable and not committed either to client-state garrisons or territorial defences, we may assume that the Soviet leaders are even now being pressed to use this disposable margin of strength to extend the reach of imperial control. In fact, we may take it for granted that competing war schemes of one sort or another, whose goals are to create more client-states, are now in circulation within the Soviet military and political hierarchy. Such schemes there must be, but they await the right circumstances, and perhaps the right leaders.

Needless to say, in Soviet circumstances, all such war schemes must be unfailingly 'defensive' in strategic intent; but that is merely ordinary procedure for an empire of rising power. So it was for the Romans, who had to conquer Latium to secure Rome itself, then Italian lands north and south to secure Latium, then Cisalpine Gaul and Sicily to secure the Italian core, then Gaul and Illyricum to protect Northern Italy – and so it went till finally the continental limits, or the economic limits of deep forest, swamp and steppe were duly reached. Even after that, Britain had to be subdued, officially to calm the dissidence of the far seashore of Gaul which the Druids of Britain were supposedly inspiring from across the Channel.

But aside from the usual dynamics of imperial power, there must also be a degree of urgency in the Soviet case (if the hypothesis of regime pessimism is accepted). It is not just a question of using uncommitted divisions (and all that goes with them) to expand the empire further, but rather of employing a transient military advantage before it is too late, to gain a permanent enhancement in the security of the empire. Having accumulated its surplus of disposable military strength by the great economic sacrifice imposed on the peoples of the empire, by a great tenacity of policy, by the professionalism of the military leaders and the wise economy of its military-industrial establishment, the Soviet Union cannot retain its advantage for long with a stagnating economy. During all the years when American strength was allowed to decline, and all the years when America's allies were failing to make the effort needed to offset the adverse change in the balance of power, the Soviet Union kept up its steady investment in military forces of all kinds. But inevitably Soviet planners must now foresee that the superiorities thus gained will evaporate during the 1990s. All the sacrifices and all the discipline will have been for naught – unless the power thus accumulated is wisely employed to achieve a permanent improvement in the security position of the Soviet Union.

There is to be sure the Soviet presence in Afghanistan, a most natural victim of the changed balance of power in which the buffer state of yesterday must now become another client, aspiring to autonomy at most, but certainly not to independence. But Afghanistan is too small a gain to satisfy a great empire, and too minor an entanglement to absorb its capacity for more expansion. The six or seven divisions in Afghanistan can hardly exhaust the disposable military strength of the Soviet Union. In spite of all the colourful prose of such journalists as venture into the Afghan war zones, the resistance is a small affair for the Soviet armed forces. One statistic suffices to prove the point: by the highest estimate, only 5 per cent of Soviet divisional troops were in Afghanistan in 1983. Measuring military power as the Russians would do, by counting divisions, we can estimate the magnitude of the Soviet Union's 'disposable' strength by a process of elimination. By the lowest estimate in 1983 the Soviet army had a total of 180 field divisions.[10] Of these, thirty are in Eastern Europe to secure its obedience and also to intimidate Western Europe. Another forty-six are deployed along the very long border with China and there are twenty-six divisions on the 'southern front', opposite Turkey and Iran, and also in Afghanistan. This leaves a minimum of seventy-eight uncommitted divisions, in theory a very large disposable force quite sufficient to carry out very ambitious war operations. But only a few of the uncommitted divisions are fully manned in peacetime; the rest would have to be filled with recalled reservists before they could fight. Moreover, war operations could not be mounted by the full number of disposable divisions since the Soviet leaders would insist on reinforcing other fronts as well, and they would also want to keep a central reserve in being. Thus the true magnitude of the Soviet Union's invasion potential on any front is defined by the present peacetime deployment and the additional reinforcement available upon mobilization, as illustrated in table 1.

The procedure followed in the table may seem antique, since military power is reckoned by ground force divisions much as an eighteenth-century marshal might count regiments of horse and foot. But it does correspond to the conditions of Soviet war planning. Strategic-nuclear, theatre-nuclear, and battlefield-nuclear forces are in place to deter others' attempts at deterrence, and the tactical-air and long-range aviation forces are more than adequate to support war operations whose scale and form are in fact defined by ground capabilities. For geographic reasons alone, the

Table I

Distribution of Soviet field divisions: current and contingent

	Western front	Southern front	Eastern front	Central reserve
Current deployments	30[a]	26[b]	46	78[c]
War in the West (NATO flanks or central front)	80–90[d]	26[e]	46–56[f]	18[g]
War in the East (Xinjiang or other in China)	46[h]	26[e]	90[i]	18[g]
War in the South (Iran, or Pakistan or Iran + Gulf)	70[j]	36[k]	46–56[f]	18–28[g]

[a] Forward-deployed only, in East Germany, Czechoslovakia and Hungary.

[b] Including six divisions (one airborne) in Afghanistan.

[c] Including many divisions actually earmarked for the western front.

[d] Even a limited-scope operation (e.g. to seize northern Norway) must imply the possibility of a wider conflict and requires in any case that potential NATO/US reinforcements be pinned down on the central front.

[e] Owing to its proximity and the weakness of the adjacent countries, no wartime reinforcements would be needed.

[f] Owing to the remoteness of much of this front, precautionary reinforcements might be necessary.

[g] It can be assumed that additional army divisions and KGB/MVD units would be formed as soon as the current forces were fully mobilized. As it is, 300,000 KGB border troops and 260,000 MVD security troops are available to augment the 18 divisions, at least for internal security and tactically-defensive purposes.

[h] The west would be reinforced not only as a precautionary measure but also to deter any transfer of military supplies to the PRC.

[i] Assumes that current basing infrastructures could accommodate two divisions in places where now only one is actually deployed.

[j] This would be a pinning-down reinforcement to deter US redeployments to the Persian Gulf.

[k] Infrastructure limits (especially the road net) and the weakness of the presumptive enemies would limit this deployment.

role of the Soviet navy in any non-nuclear war would be marginal at best. Thus the division count is a true indicator of the Soviet Union's war-making potential.

As we approach the core of the matter, the where and the when, we can diminish the range of possibilities to an important degree by removing from consideration all war schemes that would require the Soviet Union to use nuclear weapons and those which would entail any significant probability of a nuclear response by the victim. A war deliberate and calculated, started by a Soviet regime pessimistic about its future but certainly far removed from any desperate sense of immediate vulnerability, cannot possibly be a nuclear war by intent. Since the goal would be to capitalize on past efforts, to achieve a long-term enhancement of the already rather satisfactory security position of the Soviet Union, the atmosphere of decision would be far removed from the terrible urgencies that might make the resort to nuclear weapons acceptable. Moreover, given this context and this purpose we may take it for granted that the advocates of war in the Kremlin would have to persuade the supreme leaders that the entire operation could be brought to a satisfactory conclusion without any real danger that nuclear weapons would be used in retaliation by the victim.

Any decision to go to war entails risk, including the risk of having miscalculated the risk, but we may legitimately expect that the Soviet leaders will avoid the grossest kind of miscalculation, such as an attack on the NATO central front in Germany mounted in the belief that there would be no nuclear response by strategic, theatre or battlefield weapons – including weapons held under dual-key arrangements. However diminished the credibility of nuclear retaliation by the United States and NATO might be in peacetime, the Soviet leaders must be prudent in calculating how both might react amidst the unleashed terror and chaos of invasion.

A second limitation on the scope of any Soviet war scheme is that any territory to be seized in permanence from the enemy would have to be very thinly populated, or else its population must be politically suitable for the establishment of client-states. Thus, for example, northern Norway may be annexed, or at least kept indefinitely under some form of military administration, and the same would be true of China's remote and scarcely peopled border fringes, such as northwest Manchuria beyond the Khingan mountain range. On the other hand, no stable client-regime could be established in some part of a country whose population belongs to a larger ethnic or cultural community that would otherwise be left independent – and no doubt unreconciled to the loss. East Germany is exactly in that condition but scarcely offers a model to be emulated.

In practice, this limitation dictates that a new Soviet conquest must either embrace a country's entire territory (as with Afghanistan) or else it must coincide with the boundaries of a region which is ethnically distinct and thus has a prior inclination to separatism. In this way, the eventual client regime could seek popular support on a nationalist basis; moreover, the ultimate political cost of the Soviet invasion on the international scene could then be diminished by presenting the outcome as the successful liberation of a subject nationality. In due course, the new-made client-state could receive international recognition – just as the People's Republic of Mongolia has done.

To establish a list of all possible war schemes is easy enough, but it would not take us very far, since we cannot predict why or when any particular scheme might find favour with the Soviet leaders. It is useful on the other hand to group the various possibilities according to the *kind* of additional security which they would provide.

Expansion for political security

The pyramid of repression that begins with the rule of the supreme leaders over the Party (which in turn rules over the Russians, who collectively rule the non-Russians) and whose base is the Soviet Union's domination of the client-states can never be sufficiently secure to satisfy the leaders at the very top – especially if they stay on the present and difficult path whereby they retain totalitarian control while rejecting police terror in the Stalin style. The weakest part of the pyramid must be just above its base, where the client-state populations touch upon the non-Russian populations of the western USSR. The danger of course comes from further afield: so long as Western Europe remains provocatively independent and arrogantly free in expression – as the Russians would see it – the peoples of Eastern Europe will not accept the lot ordained for them by strategy and geography. And so long as the peoples of Eastern Europe remain chronically restive, the non-Russian western fringe of the Soviet Union itself must also remain vulnerable to nationalist dissidence. Lithuanians, Latvians, Estonians, some Byelorussians, all Moldavians and many Ukrainians remain unreconciled to the rule of Russians over them, and their stubborn refusal is sustained even by the dim light of self-determination that comes from the nearby client-states of Poland, Czechoslovakia, Hungary and Romania.

The radical solution would be to attack the ultimate source of the problem, namely the power of the United States which guarantees the independence of Western Europe. That being still impossibly dangerous at present, the second-best solution is to erode and if possible break the security nexus between the United States and Western Europe. To do so would establish the strategic order that would already have emerged in 1945 had it not been for the intrusion of American power embodied in NATO. The countries of Western Europe, collectively an appendage of the Soviet-dominated Eurasian landmass, would then quite naturally come under Soviet influence, certainly to an extent sufficient to nullify all dissidence in Eastern Europe.

The second-best solution is of course the central goal of the Kremlin's foreign policy, pursued ever since 1945 by the full range of instruments available to Soviet statecraft, from the softest kind of allusive diplomacy all the way to outright threats, from the general build-up of Soviet military power to the manipulation of trade links with Western Europe.

In this context, schemes for localized and limited war could serve two purposes, one broad and one narrow. If the Soviet Union could invade and hold some part of NATO territory without unleashing either a nuclear response *or* a wider conflict that would in turn inevitably entail large nuclear risks, it could hope to undermine the fundamental solidarity of the United States and its allies, thus accomplishing the broader purpose. To be successful, such an operation would have to result, swiftly, in some territorial gain which could be frozen by the familiar device of a quick armistice followed by protracted and inconclusive negotiations. The narrower purpose would be to seize territory of inherent strategic importance, such as the Baltic approaches, northern Norway, northeastern Turkey, and so on.

This of course is the most prosaic of war scenarios, already studied and debated ad nauseam. The fact remains that both the far north of Norway and the remote border region of northeast Turkey remain especially vulnerable to a Soviet *coup de main*. In Norway there are no nuclear weapons in place which might automatically deter by their very presence, and both areas are physically and psychologically remote from the centres of the alliance – including even Oslo and Ankara to some extent. As for the conventional balance, it is most unfavourable, and the prospects of successful resistance to a surprise attack are poor indeed. Of the two schemes, the seizure of northern Norway would rate somewhat higher in both incentive and risk because of the value of the territory as a basing area for the interdiction of US-European maritime communications.

So long as the Soviet Union continues to make such good progress towards its second-best goal of eroding the cohesion of the Alliance, by diplomacy, propaganda and the manipulation of trade, any war scheme against the outer flanks of NATO must remain almost as unattractive as an invasion of the German 'central front' itself. However localized and swift an operation might be, and even if Americans and Europeans were caught wholly unprepared psychologically and politically to make a deliberate nuclear response, the risk would still be great in the chain of events. Ironically the nuclear risk is only made greater by the very weakness of the non-nuclear forces of the Alliance: the prompt defeat of the local forces (which are small or ill-prepared in both northern Norway and eastern Turkey) is likely to be followed by a swift expeditionary response by mixed NATO forces, as now planned; that in turn is most likely to result in a debacle – if only because in all joint Alliance ventures symbolic forms utterly dominate the substance of true combat capability. Then, in the wake of a military defeat, tactical nuclear strikes upon the Soviet forces in place might suddenly seem unavoidably necessary, to redeem defeat, preserve the solidarity of the Alliance and restore its ability to deter further and more dangerous aggression against the more central regions of NATO.

This kind of localized operation is not therefore promising for the Soviet leaders, though of course it cannot altogether be ruled out. It is certainly inexcusable that the remote flanks of the Alliance should be so lacking in defences against a Soviet *coup de main* that would amount to a mere commando operation writ large: as it is, even a single Soviet division of good quality could seize the crucial terrain of the far north of Norway almost overnight, if well provided with helicopters.

Expansion for strategic security

This kind of war scheme must be of salient importance: political security protects against an erosion of control, regional security protects this or that periphery, but strategic security protects the empire itself. In the absence of any imminent threat, however, war waged to enhance the empire's strategic security is only conceivable if the theory of regime pessimism is accepted. Otherwise the great risk inherent in this kind of war scheme – of necessity directed against the greatest antagonist – cannot possibly be deemed acceptable. We begin by asking the classic question: what is the main enemy? What is the power whose future growth could eventually threaten the very existence of the empire?

Certainly two powers rise above all others, but the loose commonplace that would make the United States and the People's Republic of China similar to one another as the chief adversaries of the Soviet Union obscures the most fundamental of strategic questions: what is the role of each in Soviet strategy?

First and foremost, the United States is the great extra-continental European power that has intervened successfully ever since the Second World War to subtract Western Europe from the Soviet sphere of influence. In addition, the American intrusion has, as we have seen, an indirect effect yet more serious for the Kremlin, since it is the protected freedom of Western Europe that continuously undermines the stability of the client-states of Eastern Europe; and this in turn threatens not only the external security of the Soviet empire but also its own internal security. American power in Europe must thus amount to a basic security threat to the Soviet Union, quite independently of any military threat as such. It matters little, therefore, that the United States, its forces in Europe and NATO have no aggressive intent: the very existence of a powerful America active in Europe *is* an aggression from the Soviet point of view since by making Western Europe secure enough to retain its freedoms it subverts the machine of imperial control. Thus the Soviet leaders are merely being sincere when they claim that NATO is an 'aggressive' alliance, even if those in the West who actually believe them in a literal sense are merely fools.

Beyond Europe, the United States is not always the most serious antagonist that the Soviet Union encounters in its global quest for access and influence. Sometimes feeble or even absent from the scene, at other times highly energetic, thus inconsistent but always capable of very great sudden efforts, the United States has not been an easy opponent for Soviet policy, but neither has it been implacable in opposing Soviet aims. Certainly the Kremlin's quest for worldwide influence has had its setbacks, but having started with practically nothing in 1945 the Soviet Union can now count on quite a few clients and allies, well beyond the original continental limits of its power. It may be concluded, therefore, that the United States has been a manageable diplomatic adversary for the Soviet Union.

Second – and this is the quality that would have been first until quite recently – the United States is the world's second-greatest military power and the possessor of a great quantity of nuclear weapons of all kinds, including some nine thousand missile warheads and bombs continuously targeted on the cities, industrial centres, military installations and major infrastructures of the Soviet Union. The destructive capacity of the American nuclear arsenal is undoubted fact, and yet it is harder and harder to believe that it evokes any urgent sense of menace in Moscow. While no doubt much more sceptical of the reliability of 'mutual' deterrence than their American counterparts – some of whom seem to think that deterrence is a kind of machine, instead of a set of human expectations subject to all the vagaries of human emotion, and subject also to the cognitive distortions that flourish in crises – the leaders of the Soviet Union must certainly appreciate the high degree of safety which it provides, if only because the awesome threat of American nuclear bombardment is more than matched by their own ability to retaliate in kind.

Certainly for many years now the ultimate danger of a home-land-to-homeland 'strategic' nuclear war has lacked immediacy, and with the passage of time it has become less and less thinkable – except in the context of crisis 'scenarios' that must seem of diminishing plausibility even to the most pessimistic of Soviet leaders. The huge Soviet investment in non-nuclear forces proves conclusively that the belief of some that any major Soviet-initiated war would be nuclear from the start is not shared by the Soviet leaders themselves.

Chronic friction between the Soviet Union and the United States is inherent in the situation, and outright hostility must become the order of the day whenever Soviet policy is true to the character of an expanding military empire – and American policy chooses to recognize it as such. But in spite of all the crises and confrontations of the last three decades there is just too much sheer space between the two antagonists to allow the growth of the sort of lethal intimacy which is characteristic of enemies that are in direct territorial contact. Images of American forces invading Russian lands, there to occupy towns, burn villages and massacre innocent civilians, and likewise images of Soviet troops invading American soil, belong to the realm of paranoid fears, if not comic invention. For all the fundamental gravity of the clash of interests and values, the contentions of the two sides must be judged as ultimately peripheral, as compared to what is at stake when nations fight to protect their own homelands against one another.

Finally, the United States is by far the most important source of food, animal feed and technical knowhow for the Soviet economy. Sometimes sold directly on quite favourable commercial terms, and sometimes restricted by way of reprisal, what Americans export and invent is always in fact beneficial to the Soviet Union because these things flow into the global pool from which the Soviet Union also draws, directly or indirectly. No matter what restrictions are imposed on direct trade and technology transfer, the United States cannot avoid contributing to the welfare of the Soviet Union, either by way of the natural migration of technology or because American exports of products denied to the Soviet Union (e.g. grains) are still sold elsewhere, displacing third-party supplies, which are in turn sold to the Soviet Union.

Compare now the People's Republic of China by the same criteria. In the first place, there is the plain fact of territorial contiguity over several thousand miles of border – some of it disputed. Mere topographic complexities and even climatic instabilities (such as the variable floods and shifting mud islands of the Ussuri) can be sources of tension in themselves. More important, there is much scope for Chinese territorial revisionism hinged on historical boundaries – even if that means that the People's Republic of China has to assert the claims of an imperial dynasty that was Manchu and not ethnically Chinese, over lands never seriously settled by the Chinese people.

But to view the length, the complexities and the history of the border as the source of hostility between Moscow and Beijing is to confuse cause with effect. And the same is true of the ideological rivalry that supposedly divides the two sides. That the contentions between the vulgar-Marxists of Moscow and the vulgar-Marxists of Beijing cannot possibly be anything but the instruments of a hostility that has quite other causes is clearly proven by their mere persistence through the wildest gyrations in the official ideological line of the Chinese Communist Party.

Once we duly disregard such effects, the true cause, which is simple enough, stands revealed: the Soviet Union and the People's Republic are both Great Powers in a world that now counts only three, and they are adjacent, while the third is removed from both. The People's Republic and the Soviet Union both have some latitude in shaping their American policy but they are almost mechanically preordained to hostility towards each other. So much is true, obvious, and not particularly enlightening. But there is much more than that in the quarrel.

Clearly, the Soviet Union is no longer simply a Great Power but has now become a great continental military empire. As such it is engaged in the classic quest for total preclusive security. Russians *qua* Russians are said to have their own culturally ordained hostility towards the Chinese, supposedly by transfer from their historic experience of Mongol and Turkic domination (of which the Chinese were in fact fellow-victims). It is hard to say to what degree such misdirected folk memories and ancestral fears are live forces in the minds of Russians nowadays, though no doubt the 'Yellow Peril' theme offers much scope for propagandistic manipulation. There must be a 'Russian' element in the overall Soviet attitude towards the People's Republic of China, but that is surely conditioned much more importantly by the very character of the Soviet state as a military empire in search of preclusive security.

As we have seen, in the imperial scheme of things a belt of client-states must ideally begin where territory actually annexed comes to an end. Beyond the client-states, or in their place, states of small power and respectful conduct are also acceptable. What is quite intolerable is a neighbour directly adjacent that is both significantly powerful *and* defiantly independent. The People's Republic of China is both these things. In addition, it is also an ideological competitor. When the very large geographic dimensions, huge population and theoretical power-potential of the People's Republic are added to the scales, it becomes clear that for the Soviet empire its very existence as a power of growing strength is no more acceptable than a strong and prosperous Carthage was for Rome.

Two things served to moderate the Soviet attitude to China until 1977 or thereabouts: the so-called Cultural Revolution that began in 1966 and the continued primacy of Mao Tse-tung, its chief protagonist. So long as the predominant faction in Beijing was content to subordinate industrial growth and economic development in general to the pursuit of equality, so long as Red prevailed over Expert in all matters, and, above all, so long as the growth of Chinese military power almost ceased – partly to preserve a balance of sorts between well-armed militias under leftist command and well-trained but antiquated regular forces under professional control – the leaders of the Soviet Union could cheerfully defer all radical solutions to their Chinese problem. The balance of military strength, already very favourable, could only become more favourable still so long as the steady growth of Soviet military power continued year after year, while the Chinese armed forces remained stagnant. Moreover, the great scientific and industrial advantages of the Soviet Union would also become greater still with the mere passage of time.

In the West there has been some talk from time to time about a supposed 'point of no return' for Soviet military action against China, or more precisely against its nuclear arsenal. But in fact there was no such point in the past, though there may be one in the future. It is true that the number of Chinese nuclear weapons continued to increase, but only very slowly throughout the sixties and seventies. During the same period, on the other hand, the number, accuracy, presumptive reliability and controllability of Soviet long-range nuclear weapons increased very greatly indeed. Detailed comparisons between Soviet disarming counterforce capabilities (versus the number, hardness and stability of Chinese 'nuclear' targets) in, say, 1967 and then again in 1983 show that the Soviet Union could have accomplished what some are pleased to call a 'surgical' nuclear strike much more easily on the second of those dates. The reason is simple enough: in mid-1967 the Soviet Union reportedly had an inventory of roughly 460 intercontinental ballistic missiles (ICBMS), all single warhead types with median inaccuracies mostly worse than three-quarters of a nautical mile; by 1983 its ballistic missiles could deliver several thousand warheads, many of them with expected median inaccuracies of less than one-quarter of a nautical mile. As for ballistic missiles of less than intercontinental range, it is simply pointless to compare the ss-20s of 1980 with the weapons (ss-4s and ss-5s) available in 1967, since the latter were far too inaccurate and much too unreliable for any purpose more demanding than the bombardment of large cities. Similarly, against the background of Chinese air defences scarcely improved during the last decade and more, Soviet airpower achieved a very great enhancement in long-range strike capabilities with the introduction of the 'tactical' Su-24 and the 'strategic' Backfire. The Soviet ability to destroy Chinese missiles and bombers before they could be launched has increased much more than the resilience of the PRC's nuclear arsenal. Since 1967 the vulnerability of the Chinese nuclear forces has continued to increase, as the sequence of testing and calibration improves Soviet missile accuracies while the Soviet air force realizes its full strike potential with the newer fighter-bombers of the MiG-23 and Su-24 families. In fact the possibility of a *non-nuclear* Soviet attack – which could truly be 'surgical' – cannot now be excluded.

Thus a Soviet Union gaining steadily on the Chinese faced no crisis of decision. There was, moreover, a positive reason for waiting, or at least a plausible excuse for delay. While Mao still lived, the Chinese government could not possibly negotiate a *modus vivendi* acceptable to the Soviet Union. Such an arrangement would require Chinese recognition of the 'realities' of power as the Russians see them; in other words, it would call for a Chinese acknowledgement of Soviet predominance – symbolized by the Chinese Communist Party's formal acceptance of Moscow's ideological primacy. That Mao would never agree to any such accommodation was self-evident. To be sure, it was by no means probable that Mao's successors would agree either, but the Soviet leaders could always wait and hope. Their own strong ideological bias towards what they understand as 'realism' may well have inclined them to believe that post-Mao Chinese leaders would turn out to be reasonable men, willing – as Mao never was – to accept the imperatives of power.

There was, moreover, the American factor. Regardless of the formal diplomatic status of Washington-Beijing relations, American military power must play some role in any Soviet-Chinese conflict in ways both direct and indirect. While the immediate scale and actual usefulness of American military assistance given to a China under attack would depend on the specific form of Soviet military action, *some* sort of American initiative would have to be taken for certain. Whether significant in itself or not, the mere fact of American involvement would have two very important longer-term consequences: first it might serve to engage the United States in the conflict by slow stages; supplies of medical equipment might come first, and then weapons covertly supplied, and then more; naval protection of US ships at sea might give way to harbour defence and then more; unacknowledged air support could come next, and then more. Second, this process would almost certainly drive the United States towards a high degree of general rearmament. The hope of the first and the results of the second consequence would encourage the Chinese leaders to persevere in a conflict rather than to accept a Soviet victory as a *fait accompli*.

Even if the United States were to remain in a stance of strict neutrality its power would still loom large in the Kremlin's calculations because the Soviet Union would seek to maintain a favourable military balance with the United States while being engaged in a conflict with the Chinese. In that regard, it is worth noting that a Soviet disarming counterforce offensive against China's nuclear forces would have expended three-quarters of the Soviet force of intercontinental ballistic missiles in 1967, as much as one half of the more modern types as late as 1972, but would only require a small fraction (under 10 per cent) of the Soviet ICBM arsenal as of 1982. More generally, the relative growth of Soviet military power in all categories has greatly reduced the indirect constraint imposed by American military strength upon Soviet conduct towards the Chinese.

For all these reasons the Soviet leaders could easily defer any decisive action to solve their China problem. In the meantime, however, they launched a massive construction programme to transform the logistic and operational environment along the Chinese border. When the great increase in Soviet army deployments there took place between 1968 and 1972 (which doubled the number of divisions) the newly-sent Soviet forces found themselves at the end of very long, thinly stretched and highly insecure lines of supply. Far from being able to 'jump off' for deep penetration attacks in the normal manner of Soviet mechanized forces, many of the divisions sent to the more remote sectors on the Chinese border would have had a hard time in combat even if fighting in place. Their own motor transport could only link them to the nearest tract of the Trans-Siberian railway; it could not possibly have supplied the fast advance by armoured forces deep into Chinese territory.

The huge building effort that went into high gear during the 1970s changed the situation radically. Instead of huts and dirt roads, a full panoply of bases and communications has arisen. Well-built army camps are linked to the rear by rail lines that branch off from the Trans-Siberian railway as well as hard-surface roads usable in all weather conditions. Within the divisional bases, the troops now live in permanent barracks, sized to accommodate the fully mobilized strength of each formation. Command posts and communications centres are fortified. A network of supply depots and repair facilities has been provided, which could now sustain prolonged operations. As a result of this very great investment in construction, supply storage and ancillary equipment, Soviet mechanized forces could now move out to attack with their logistic potential fully available for exploitation in depth, like coiled springs fully compressed.

During those same years, the Soviet Union's ability to use air power against the Chinese was also greatly increased. In part this was due to the building of properly equipped air bases around the Chinese border in place of the bare landing strips of the past; in part it reflected the general improvement of the Soviet air force, and notably the extensive replacement of short-range interceptor fighters of the MiG-21 variety by heavier fighter/fighter-bombers of the MiG-23 family, as well as the deployment of long-range strike aircraft such as the Su-24 and the Backfire bomber.

These great changes in real ground and air combat capabilities, and in the highly important ancillaries, including the construction of the Baikal-Amur mainline railway (still unfinished), and also the Soviet civil defence programme – which is no doubt more seriously pursued in areas close to the border – have transformed the ability of the Soviet Union to wage large-scale (non-nuclear) war upon the Chinese. Any quantitative comparison between the true military balance of 1967 and that of 1983 would be pointless: the change that has taken place is of a momentous, qualitative order. At the earlier date, Soviet military capabilities against the Chinese were already very considerable, but only at the extreme ends of the spectrum of war: in border skirmishing on the one hand, and in the general nuclear bombardment of cities on the other. In between these extremes, the Soviet Union's actual ability to wage (non-nuclear) war upon China was quite small. By now the Soviet Union has acquired the capabilities needed to achieve *decisive* results in large-scale warfare; notably it could now mount fast-moving offensive operations to penetrate Chinese territory up to depths of hundreds of kilometres in order to encircle enemy forces, capture major installations and communication nodes, and thus cut off and seize large tracts of territory, in the classic Blitzkrieg style. Soviet airpower, after brushing aside Chinese air defences, could now deliver abundant air support, and mount heavy interdiction attacks as well. Moreover, the Soviet long-range air force could launch at the same time a full-scale bomber offensive against industrial and military targets throughout Chinese territory, including areas very remote from the actual theatres of war.

The new Soviet capacity to mount large conventional operations against China means that for the first time the Kremlin now has some realistic war options. Even the most restrained of 'surgical nuclear strikes' would entail horrific consequences and terrible risks for the Soviet Union. But non-nuclear war, even on a very large scale, is another matter. Border incidents can be easily staged to provide a plausible excuse for a wider attack, which can develop into a serious deep-penetration offensive; the strategic intent can thus be masked for a while in the guise of a reprisal action. To do so would prolong the effect of surprise, and also begin to engage the Chinese forces in a *non-nuclear* defensive reaction, thus setting the stage for a war in which the Soviet side refrains from using nuclear weapons because it does not need them, while the Chinese on the other hand would find themselves deterred by Soviet nuclear superiority because they would be *insufficiently provoked* at each stage of the conflict. (The assumption is that the Soviet invasion armies would stay well away from the major populated areas.)

All this does not of course mean that nuclear capabilities on both sides would play no role in the outcome of a war, far from it; but it does mean that their role must be contextual rather than decisive: nuclear capabilities would define the rules of the game, but it is the non-nuclear forces that would fight it out. The not-so-reliable Chinese strike-back capability against some Soviet cities can serve only to deter a Soviet attack upon Chinese cities, or rather to weaken the already weak Soviet ability to employ that particular threat to coerce the Chinese. By contrast, the entire panoply of

Soviet nuclear capabilities in battlefield, theatre and 'strategic' weapons should effectively deter the use of Chinese nuclear capabilities, except in two cases: the Chinese would still of course retaliate if their own cities were attacked, and they might take the risk of using nuclear weapons *in a tactical mode* against Soviet forces actually *inside* Chinese territory.

The real military worth of using the small and unsophisticated Chinese inventory of nuclear weapons against Soviet armour-mechanized forces is uncertain. The physical impact is likely to be small (it might take dozens of bombs to destroy a single division). In the circumstances of a Soviet offensive (without nuclear use) deep into their own territory, the Chinese leaders might calculate that nuclear strikes against Soviet invasion columns would cause a massive breakdown of morale among the enemy troops, and force an 'agonizing reappraisal' upon their leaders in Moscow if not on the military commanders in between. On the other hand, the Chinese might be inhibited from thus using nuclear weapons to 'shoot across the bows' (as the French, by the way, mean to use their Pluton missiles) by the further calculation that to do so could trigger a Soviet disarming counterforce offensive against *all* their remaining nuclear weapons. Nevertheless, this particular Chinese countermove, unlike the totally unpersuasive threat of a retaliatory strike against Soviet cities, would amount to a serious risk for the Soviet Union – especially since the difficulty of coping with large populations would in any case confine even an ambitious Soviet offensive to the thinly populated parts of the People's Republic, which is precisely where the Chinese use of nuclear weapons in a 'tactical' mode would be most acceptable to the Chinese leaders themselves.

Such considerations do undoubtedly limit the Soviet war-making potential against China. Nevertheless, the vast military investment made along the border has certainly changed the balance very greatly since the later 1960s, when the Soviet Union for all its claims to superpower status had very few military options against China, and none at all that were both of acceptable risk (and thus credible) and also of powerful effect.

The other dimension of Soviet strategy against China which provides further evidence of Beijing's new status as the 'main enemy' has a primarily diplomatic character – though even in the softer kind of Soviet diplomacy military instrumentalities must loom large. The goal of this stategic diplomacy has been to enrol as many of China's neighbours and near-neighbours as possible in a Moscow-centred alliance directed against Beijing. Not one country of east and southeast Asia has any natural affinity for things Soviet or Russian, but after decades of increasingly serious effort Soviet diplomacy has registered considerable success in building alliances of one sort or another around China. In (Outer) Mongolia, a poor and landlocked state whose very legitimacy is open to challenge by the Chinese, the Soviet Union has its most dependent of all client-states. In Vietnam, Hanoi's regime has become more reliant on Soviet support than geopolitics alone would have dictated because of its imperialism – although *any* Vietnamese regime must seek some kind of counterweight alliance given the imminent presence of China. In India, finally, the Soviet Union has found a genuine ally. The relationship between the two is not based on a transient amity between regimes, but rather on the pressure of strategic circumstances which will endure so long as the state of Pakistan continues to survive.

It is unfortunate for Moscow that although India is by far the greatest military power among its allies, it is not, however, a particularly useful ally precisely for military purposes. Specifically, India's military strength cannot significantly restrict the ability of the Chinese to deploy forces against the Soviet Union, simply because neither side can deploy large numbers of troops or much heavy equipment in the very high mountain terrain of the Sino-Indian border. Moreover, the Indian alliance has its costs for Moscow, since it ensures the diffidence of the lesser countries round about, including Bangla Desh, Burma and Ceylon; and of course it virtually guarantees the hostility of Pakistan.

In the case of Vietnam, by contrast, there being no impassable mountain barrier between the two, Hanoi's activism and dispro-portionate military strength oblige the Chinese to assign large forces to their Vietnamese front. This is especially useful for the Soviet Union, since that front happens to be exceptionally remote from the Sino-Russian borders. In this case, therefore, the classic purpose of military alliance is amply fulfilled. Mongolia for its part offers a most useful basing area for Soviet forces (its own strength is insignificant) and it also provides a potentially useful political instrument, since that country can compete for the ethnic loyalties of the Mongols living within the borders of the People's Republic in

Inner Mongolia. Elsewhere, Soviet diplomacy has been disappointed to varying degrees. North Korea continues to preserve its freedom of action by its successful and long-standing policy of equidistance between Moscow and Beijing; even though the Soviet Union is far more able to give aid and support, the North Koreans refuse to prejudice their independence by joining the Soviet camp. And in southeast Asia of course the Vietnamese connection denies any other alliance for Moscow, at least for now. In that part of the world, it is not the friendship of those who arm and support Vietnam that is now in demand, but rather the help of those who seek to contain the Vietnamese. In the longer term, if Chinese power does increase, Vietnamese strength will no doubt come to be appreciated as a shield against Chinese domination, but for now its alliance with Hanoi has earned Moscow two more indirect clients, the Vietnamese-controlled Cambodian and Laotian regimes, but also the hostility of the increasingly significant ASEAN nations, Indonesia, Malaysia, Thailand and Singapore.

There is a sharp and most significant contrast between the entire attitude of the Soviet Union towards the West and towards China. Moscow's diplomatic strategy in Europe is crafted out of blandishments on arms control and trade, while the element of coercion is tacit, always carefully controlled and mostly muted. The Kremlin's propaganda and diplomacy seek to persuade the governments and peoples of Western Europe that the United States is a reckless and thoroughly unreliable guarantor of their security while being a ruthless economic competitor – all this in contrast to a Soviet Union which is depicted as very willing to establish friendly relations if only American military power is first removed from the scene, and which offers in the meantime very profitable opportunities for trade. Soviet declarations aimed at the United States stress different themes at different times, but focus mainly on the denial of any real threat and explicitly denounce American claims that the Soviet Union is engaged in a quest for military superiority. Moscow's conciliatory diplomacy is perfectly consistent with its overriding strategic goal of dividing the Alliance. Any threat too overt, any brutal intimidation, would only undermine that strategy.

Moscow's strategy towards the Chinese is of a character altogether different. It amounts to a vast encirclement. Along the thousands of miles of the common border, Soviet land forces do not constitute a defensive perimeter; they amount, rather, to a ring of offensive deployments. Mongolia is for all practical purposes an integral part of the Soviet array, while on the far side of China, to the south and southwest, Vietnam and India watch a large part of the remaining land frontiers of China. In between, the Soviet navy's traffic around the coast of China amounts to a thin but increasing presence, potentially threatening. Owing to the great importance of coastal shipping for the Chinese economy, the Soviet navy's inability to mount significant amphibious operations does not mean that it could not intervene powerfully in the context of a general offensive. In contrast to all this, the 'soft' diplomacy which looms so large in Soviet dealing with the West is distinctly less prominent in Moscow's China policy. The recurrent attempts at border delimitation talks seem to be pursued with a distinct lack of conviction on the part of the Soviet Union.

All these reasons suggest that the People's Republic of China has now become the Soviet Union's 'main enemy', and therefore the most likely target of war schemes aimed at enhancing its strategic security. The growth of Soviet military strength vis-à-vis China need not however culminate in a war. An alternative outcome – just as likely – is that Beijing will belatedly recognize that some accommodation to the reality of Soviet power can no longer be avoided. We may be quite certain that the Soviet leaders retain that very hope. A disengagement of Chinese troops from the entire eastern and northern periphery that runs along the Soviet border, the suspension of Beijing's worldwide diplomatic campaign against the Soviet Union, and perhaps some gesture of ideological non-belligerence if not outright subordination to the CPSU might be the goals of Andropov's conciliatory diplomatic manoeuvre, which has the added virtue of frightening the Americans with the spectre of a full-scale reconciliation. But for the Soviet Union they have the very great defect of being reversible. The Kremlin leaders know that any favourable settlement negotiated with the Chinese in their present weakness would merely allow them time to build up their overall industrial strength, thus increasing their long-term military potential; then, in due course, all concessions would be withdrawn. Hence the superior attraction, one presumes, of permanent map-changing solutions to the China problem – solutions which must be costly and entail grave risk to be sure, but which would have the capital virtue of being irreversible, except by force.

This is not the place for any detailed military scenarios, but the various constraints reviewed above do in fact define quite closely the most probable form of Soviet military action.

At the level of grand strategy, any Soviet war scheme must start from two premises: that China is not destroyable, and that it cannot be occupied in its totality to be remade to order, *à la* Afghanistan or for that matter 1968 Czechoslovakia. This leaves only one feasible goal for a Soviet war: if an independent China of growing power can be neither tolerated nor destroyed, then it must be divided.

What Soviet military power can achieve directly is the conquest of territories which can then be turned into client-states; obviously this is only feasible where the population includes a large non-Chinese element. One model is the People's Republic of (Outer) Mongolia; another is Tuva, a Chinese dependency until 1914, a Russian protectorate thereafter, and a Soviet-made People's Republic (Tannu-Tuva) until annexed in 1944. And Soviet military power may also be used in the hope of achieving indirect political results: the Kremlin leaders may calculate that if the Chinese armies in the field are defeated swiftly and decisively, in humiliating fashion, this would undermine the prestige of the central government, and certainly diminish its powers of coercion, thus releasing the separatist tendencies that the profound diversities of China naturally breed.

As a purely practical matter, the provinces and especially those which are remote from Beijing would have to look after themselves if the central government is devastated by war; and in any case Beijing's authority is not what it used to be now that Chairman Mao is gone and the myth of higher-party infallibility has been very thoroughly exploded. In such circumstances, the important provinces of the south and southwest, Kwangtung (Guangdong in the now official Pinyin transcription) and Szechwan (Sichuan), of the coastal provinces to the south, Fukien (Fujian), dissident Shanghai, and others too might emerge as *de facto* independent; they would certainly have to cope with a conflict on their own. Some provinces would then naturally be drawn into relations with outside powers across the sea, while others might even orient themselves on the Soviet Union if only because of geographic imperatives. Since unity is no more a norm in Chinese history than fragmentation on provincial lines, the division of China may seem an attainable goal to the Soviet leaders. But of course this is not a goal that military power as such can assuredly achieve directly – and there is always the possibility that a Soviet attack could have the opposite result of inspiring a heightened sense of all-Chinese solidarity in the face of the enemy. Much would depend on the psychological circumstances of a war and Beijing's recent record of governance.

Nor can the two ways of dividing China be combined, since the loss of vast tracts of national territory to 'independent' states of non-Chinese character is most unlikely to encourage separatist tendencies among the Han Chinese themselves. For this reason, the Soviet Union must choose between a peripheral and a 'core' grand strategy, the former offering results more certain, the latter more far-reaching.

At the level of theatre-strategy, the Soviet offensive must in any case aim at swift penetrations, in great depth. At the operational level, moreover, the scheme of the Soviet action would of course seek to exploit the superior mobility of Soviet mechanized forces as well as the huge advantage in airpower. The goal would be to cut off large slices of territory while evading main enemy troop concentrations on the border itself, and the more elaborate of the defended zones which the Chinese have established, with fixed tank barriers, extensive minefields and protected gun positions. Chinese forces and positions thus bypassed would find themselves isolated and encircled once the Soviet penetration thrusts met deep in their rear. Until a few years ago, the Soviet Union would have been unable to execute such an ambitious theatre strategy. Advancing forces could not have been kept supplied to sustain thrusts of hundreds of miles, and neither could the Soviet air force have provided timely close support in large amounts, or mounted precision attacks deep inside Chinese territory. As of now, all these capabilities are in place.

But in one respect Soviet military power has not improved at all: for all its 180 divisions, the Soviet army does not have much infantry in its highly mechanized forces, and no real foot infantry at all.[11] It is therefore thoroughly unsuited for the control of large, densely populated areas, and for all manpower-intensive forms of combat, from street-fighting to rear-area security duties against large numbers of elusive guerrillas. With helicopters, even the small number of infantrymen in the all-mechanized divisions of the Soviet army can easily control guerrillas in open country that offers little cover, but elsewhere there is no substitute for large forces of infantry.

What emerges from this is that the densely-populated eastern rim of China and southern Manchuria is as inimical to the Soviet army as forest, steppe and desert were to the Romans. If the Soviet Union did invade the eastern provinces where most of the Chinese live, its armoured columns and modern airpower could control much territory, as they undoubtedly would in areas of open terrain and thin population. The invasion itself could no doubt be easily achieved, but the mobile columns of the Soviet army would become vulnerable to raids, sabotage and all forms of elusive warfare as soon as their forward movement came to an end. The Soviet army might thus achieve all its planned objectives, and easily, only to be bogged down in endless petty combat. It is hard to believe that the leaders of the Soviet Union would deliberately begin a protracted guerrilla war by invading areas of large population. If that possibility is therefore excluded, the sphere of possible Soviet warfare must be limited to the thinly populated West, that is Sinkiang (Xinjiang), Chinghai (Qinghai), northern Kansu (Gansu) and Inner Mongolia, as well as portions of Heilungkiang province (Heilongjiang) in the Manchurian north. Taken together, and adding Tibet – which must be lost to Beijing if the rest is lost – these provinces and 'autonomous regions' account for roughly 56 per cent of the total territory of the People's Republic but only some 6 per cent of the population, or not more than 60 million people in all. Moreover, at least one-third of them belong to non-Chinese nationalities, mostly very unhappy with the Han Chinese domination they now endure. Obviously, the geographic setting and the demography would preclude any serious guerrilla resistance in the aftermath of an invasion, especially since the entire 'West' is arid and offers little cover. At the same time, the local population offers a ready cultural basis for the creation of client-states which would have a genuine national claim to legitimacy internally, and also to some extent internationally. In a world that affirms the universality of the principle of self-determination, the 'liberation' of Beijing's subject nationalities would not be universally condemned.

Even if it cannot induce fragmentation on provincial lines, and even if territory is conquered and a client-state created only in Xinjiang amd Qinghai (e.g. a 'Turkestan People's Republic'), the Soviet Union could gain a number of important strategic advantages from the venture. First, the *de facto* military boundary would be shifted eastwards by a thousand miles or so, depriving Beijing of its territorial shield to the west, while adding that much interposed space to the Soviet security system. Second, since Tibet must also become independent once the major Sino-Tibetan overland routes are cut (the Sichuan route is much too tenuous a link), China would cease to be an all-Asian power, in contact with Afghanistan, Pakistan and India, and would be reduced in effect to an east Asian power only, with a correspondingly diminished role in world affairs. Third, important Chinese military and scientific facilities would be overrun (or forced to evacuate) by the Soviet advance, and many more could be destroyed in a concurrent (non-nuclear) 'strategic' bombing campaign. Finally, a swift elegant Soviet offensive culminating in the emergence of a 'liberated' Turkestan would expose the weakness of China's armed forces, and also the incapacity of the United States to save a *de facto* ally from crushing defeat. The credibility of Soviet military power to friends and prospective enemies alike would be enhanced in corresponding degree – perhaps thereby transforming some enemies into neutrals, and some neutrals into clients more or less subservient: to possess the physical attributes of military power is one thing, to demonstrate the ability of using such power effectively is quite another – and altogether more persuasive.

In these diverse ways, the strategic security of the Soviet Union could be enhanced by a limited but map-changing war upon China. There is no doubt that the Soviet armed forces could accomplish a 'Turkestan' offensive in short order, and it is hard to see what countervailing power could prevent a favourable outcome for the Soviet Union. Given the very great imbalance in the nuclear forces of the two sides and the fact that none of the core areas of Chinese life would be invaded, the Chinese could not rely on nuclear deterrence to protect the vast, remote territories that their regular forces cannot defend and in which there is little scope for guerrilla warfare. On the other hand, the small but real possibility of 'tactical' Chinese nuclear strikes upon Soviet forces inside Chinese territory cannot be entirely dismissed, and there must also be some residual possibility of 'irrational' Chinese nuclear retaliation upon one or two Soviet cities. But if NATO does not hold itself adequately secure, notwithstanding its great panoply of battlefield, theatre and strategic nuclear weapons, in addition to ground and air forces both large and rather well equipped, China can hardly expect to obtain a satisfactory degree of deterrence against a peripheral Soviet offensive from its much weaker non-nuclear forces and from its small and primitive nuclear arsenal.

Nevertheless, to make war upon China the Soviet leaders must obviously accept a large risk; some have persuasively argued that they will not act under any conceivable circumstances. That may be so, but the 'Turkestan' war scheme offers the most plausible way of converting the transitory military advantage of the Soviet Union into a permanent enhancement of the empire's security. Again, it can be argued that this scheme, or indeed any other such operation, would weaken rather than strengthen the long-term security of the Soviet Union since it would engender an implacable Chinese hostility that might be manifest in chronic warfare on the borders of the new client-state. First, in a technical vein, it will be noted that even if the new military frontier is set a thousand miles east of the present line it will still be running through terrain that virtually prohibits an effective guerrilla resistance, and which also happens to maximize the tactical advantages of Soviet air and mechanized forces against Chinese armies that must consist mainly of infantry. A petty border warfare of raids and skirmishes may long continue, but it is unlikely to detain more than a dozen Soviet divisions.

It will be recalled that the prospect of inaugurating warfare of long duration did not dissuade the Soviet Union from invading Afghanistan, where geographic circumstances and the nature of the population are so much more favourable to guerrilla war than would be the case in Xinjiang. Military power can seldom be employed in ideal circumstances – and yet it is still employed by all manner of states that are not even great military empires, and with some frequency. Any war that successfully changes the map must engender the long-term hostility of the loser, and yet attempts to change the map are still made by all manner of states. But to argue that the Kremlin would recoil from any war scheme for fear of provoking the implacable hostility of China implies a most fundamental misunderstanding of the essential nature of Soviet statecraft. The Soviet Union is not primarily in the 'goodwill' business; it is in the security business. It is not the voluntary goodwill of those who remain free to give or withhold that the Kremlin truly seeks, but rather the obedience of subjects and the deference of lesser powers. To be sure, where obedience is not yet a realistic goal, goodwill is most eagerly pursued, and where deference remains out of the question, mere respect is gladly accepted instead; but the Soviet Union will not give up the prospect of further enhancing its strategic strength for fear of increasing Chinese hostility because its leaders do not fundamentally believe that security can be obtained from the friendship of other nations. They believe only in preclusive security, the security that is assuredly provided by one's own strength quite independently of the goodwill of others. Besides, in the case at hand, it is a fair guess that the implacable hostility of China is already a basic assumption of Soviet policy – and there are no degrees in implacability. Nor can the Soviet calculation be fundamentally changed by any tactical diplomatic accommodation that Moscow and Beijing might negotiate; that might serve both rather well in increasing their respective leverage on Washington, but it will not affect the axiomatic incompatibility between an imperial Soviet Union and a China determined to remain truly independent.

Expansion for regional security

The desired pattern of imperial control that requires a belt of client-states in front of the Soviet border itself is largely achieved only in the West. Finland under its own special arrangements does duty for a client-state on the international scene without suffering any great loss of its domestic freedoms. Then south across the Baltic there is the double belt of East Germany and Poland; the latter of course must always be restive in some degree, but ultimately it is well-secured nevertheless, and not only by its own policemen backed by Soviet military power. Since today's Poland holds large tracts of land that Germans might reasonably claim as their own, a new partition in favour of East Germany cannot be altogether removed from the realm of possibilities; if Poland ever does acquire a government that seeks a genuine independence, that free Poland would still have to defer to the Soviet Union, for it would still need security – if only from East Germany. Then come Czechoslovakia, Hungary and Bulgaria, with Romania within that array and Yugoslavia outside, the first functioning more or less as a Finland in reserve, and the other as a true buffer state.

In none of these lands are the Russians loved or even accepted as fitting overlords, but, so long as the client regimes persist, none of their territory will be available to the enemies of the Soviet Union to serve as a basing ground for soldiers, or as the refuge of nationalist dissidence for the non-Russian populations inside the empire.

Beyond the limits of Europe the next land border, with Turkey in the Caucasus, neither has nor needs its client-state. For all military purposes the sector is well secured by Turkey's weakness and by the unsuitability of the terrain for any serious attack upon the empire. Politically, the sector is even better secured, since it is in the Caucasus just across the border that the empire has its Armenian population in concentrated form, and Turkey is the least likely of all countries to offer its territory to Armenian nationalist dissidence.

Further to the east the situation is by no means as satisfactory from the Soviet point of view. There is no client-state on the long border with Iran, and the need for one or more may be felt at any time – if only because this is an appetite that may be satisfied so easily. To be sure the Russians have little to fear from the Iran of the Ayatollahs. Of the many Muslims in the Soviet Union only a few are Shias, and, until a new Shah appears on the scene to restore order and resume the quest for material progress, Iran must also offer a most unattractive example to the consumer-minded among the Soviet Asians. But to a well ordered empire, the turbulence of a direct neighbour must be troublesome, and to an empire as powerful as the Soviet it must also be greatly tempting.

Perhaps it is true, as many claim, that the experience of Afghanistan will suffice to discourage the Kremlin from any further assumption of duties in the governance of Muslims. But one cannot be certain of the true meaning of that example. Where an impatient democracy might see a disastrous outcome and endless rebellion, an empire might view the same evidence differently, as a normal progression from initial conquest to a gradual pacification which will mature in due course. The Roman Senate allowed its legates two hundred years to make Spain a peaceful province, and even in these faster times the Politburo may choose to grant twenty years to the Soviet generals to pacify Afghanistan (more or less the time it took to bring a totalitarian peace to Soviet Central Asia, after the Revolution). In considering the Afghan example when deliberating over Iran, it will not escape the attention of the Politburo that, of all the peoples of Afghanistan, the ones that are Persian (or most closely resemble them) are also the least troublesome of the empire's new subjects. It seems that it is in the nature of the Persians, more than most peoples, to be fierce with those who present themselves as weak, and to be meek with the strong.

The real protection that Iran now has is Moscow's hope that if it refrains from taking the northern parts it might find itself with great influence over the whole. As the regime of the fanatics and the priests moves towards its appointed end, the Soviet Union has its own candidates for the inevitable succession. Their chances are indeterminable but must be improving as time passes. Should Iran fall under the control of left-wing elements inimical to the United States and the West in general, the Soviet Union might acquire some sort of Asiatic Finland on its borders. And the Kremlin leaders may hope for much more if the faithful Tudeh communists somehow come to power, though that is not a likely prospect.

Should the Soviet Union be disappointed by the political roulette in Tehran, it might then collect large winnings all the same, by creating one or more client-states in the predominantly non-Farsi areas of the Shah's former empire. The dominant population only in the central plateau, the Farsis or Persians proper are no more than a minority elsewhere – and all the agitations of recent years have greatly enhanced the consciousness of the non-Farsis.

The most obvious possibility is a recreation of the Azerbaijan client-state that was actually in being until 1946. As Turks, the Azeris have a well-defined national identity and their numbers are large enough (upwards of 11 million) to sustain a substantial state. Another possibility would be to form a Turkmenistan in the northeast of the country, a perfect match for the Turkmen SSR across the border. More ambitiously, a strategically much more valuable Baluch state might be formed in the southeast, to obtain a client-state corridor leading straight to the shores of the Persian Gulf. Finally, there would also be room for a Kurdistan that might eventually be aggrandized by expansion into Iraq if that were deemed desirable. The Soviet Union does not at present own the Kurdish independence movement as it once did, having sold out that long-held card to the Iraqis (at a time when Iraq was the Soviet Union's most favoured Arab ally). But the Kurds still want their own state, and the Soviet Union might see benefit in giving them one.

The dissolution of Iran into a number of separate states (including that of the Persians themselves) may well come about spontaneously, and regardless of Soviet desires. Given the fragmented ethnic composition of Iran, where diverse peoples of diverse culture and language are clustered into distinct regions, unity can only be contrived by a strong central government. In its absence, each ethnic region tends to follow local leaders in a natural drift towards *de facto* independence. And if ethnic states do emerge from the chaos of the Ayatollahs, those that are directly adjacent to the Soviet Union will quite naturally become its clients, not only out of weakness but also because their overland communications with the outside world will depend on Soviet goodwill if – as is highly likely – an unfriendly residual Iran denies safe and economic passage to the ports of the Gulf. For the Soviet Union it would be essential to ensure that any successor states did in fact become clients, for otherwise they would automatically become dangerous, given the fact that there are Soviet Azeris, Turkmens and even Kurds inside the empire, who also have their dissatisfied national sentiments.

Should the Soviet Union choose to force events, no major military operations would be needed to achieve the 'liberation' of the Azeris, Kurds, Turkmens and Baluchis of Iran. A quick entry by fast road columns that could only be feebly opposed by whatever small Iranian garrisons remain on the frontier would be preceded by air landings to secure the way, and followed immediately by ceremonial marches into the nascent states, culminating in the appointment of new-made governments, each with its contingent of Moscow's men. (Local communists aside, the Soviet Union has its own Azeris, Turkmens and Kurds in government service.)

Beyond Iran, Afghanistan is now being remade into its new status as a closely controlled client-state. The resistance continues, but the Soviet Union shows no sign of being inclined to give up the fight. It means to outlast the guerrillas and extinguish their strength by as much killing as that will take. The most striking aspect of the whole affair is not what is happening but rather what is not: there is no great American effort to sustain the resistance by a most generous supply of arms of the highest quality and right types; there is no outpouring of Muslim and 'Third World' support for the resistance, nor any move to give it international recognition on PLO lines; there is no worldwide tide of protests and demonstrations. It seems that the world has resigned itself to the Soviet Union's imperial will.

Seven

In Conclusion: Soviet Grand Strategy and its Future

The upkeep of the Soviet empire is an expensive proposition for its subjects. The armed forces themselves consume more than one-seventh of the total output of the economy, and then there is the internal army, of security troops, gendarmes, border guards, police uniformed and in plain clothes, full-time agents and part-time informers. This other army is known to include some 560,000 KGB and MVD border and security troops organized in military fashion, but the overall total is wholly unknown. It would be pointless, however, to try to calculate the cost of the empire's domestic control apparatus as such, since the entire structures of the state, the Party and the USSR's centrally planned economy should be considered as a single gigantic internal-security system. Naturally those vast bureaucracies have important social and economic functions as well, but the imperative of political control comes first. One would therefore have to estimate what the lands of the empire, its industry and its people could produce under a free-market system to be able to calculate just how great is the true cost of the present structure. And nowadays there is one more bill to be paid. The Soviet Union has long ago ceased to extract a net economic gain from its client-states and dependencies, and in recent years the cost of supporting Cuba, Vietnam, Ethiopia and other poor relations has been significant. The total cost of the empire to its subjects must therefore be estimated as very much higher than the 14 per cent or so of the total GNP which is formally assigned to the armed forces. More likely, to hazard a guess, the cost of empire is closer to the 50 per cent or so of a full-blown war economy than to the Western 4–6 per cent given over to military outlays. Unlike most other empires of history, the Soviet directly owns its economic base, so that no shadow army of tax collectors and enforcers is necessary. But this modest economy is dwarfed by the high expense of the largest empire in the history of man.

From the viewpoint of the Russians themselves, however, the empire is a much more economical proposition. Collectively, it is the Russians who really control the total array of Soviet, client-state and dependent power, both military and not, but they only pay for part of the upkeep since the non-Russians within the Soviet Union and in the wider imperial system are also forced to pay their share. Without the empire, the Russian nation might have the power of three or four Polands; with the empire, the Russians are the most powerful single nation on the planet. It is impossible to say how many Russians would voluntarily accept their present level of economic sacrifice for the sake of the psychological rewards of being part of an imperial nation, but the fact that the Russians themselves only pay the bill in part must have some influence on Russian attitudes towards the Soviet system.

In this century, the world has witnessed the voluntary renunciation of empire by the British, Belgians, French, Dutch and Portuguese as well as the Spanish – whose overseas possessions were left very small by their American war. In each case, the withdrawal from empire was voluntary, in the sense that the metropolitan power was not actually expelled from its possessions by direct force. But in each case, widespread civil unrest, outright revolt and even armed insurgence in some of the dependencies imposed large human and financial penalties on the imperial power, and created the fear that violence might soon spread to dependencies still at peace with their lot.

In the case of Britain, France and the Netherlands, the moral legitimacy of imperial rule over other nations was strongly challenged at home long before there was any serious violent resistance abroad: liberal democracies could not comfortably maintain illiberal colonial regimes. In the British case, the renunciation of empire was decidedly more voluntary than imposed, for it was there that the imperial idea was most widely and strongly rejected by liberals and socialists. When a Labour government came to power in 1945, the empire was doomed, but even under uninterrupted Tory rule it would not have lasted for much longer – for among the Tories too the belief had spread that the era of empire was over. In France the liberal predisposition to challenge the imperial idea was weaker, if only because the French empire was much less illiberal at least racially, and also because some colonies and especially Algeria were lands of French settlement seemingly on their way to assimilation. Moreover, as the power defeated in 1940, France was most reluctant to give up its last claim to greatness, as such things were then defined. Thus it took two costly wars finally to induce the renunciation. In the Dutch case, the challenge to imperial power in the East Indies came early, in 1945, and much too soon. After their own experience of defeat and occupation the Dutch were in no mood for a purely voluntary withdrawal; this was imposed in any case by the insurgency that was to create Indonesia with the support of Britain and the United States, otherwise friendly powers to the Dutch. In Portugal itself the liberal challenge to empire was insignificant. It took colonial warfare exceptionally prolonged and particularly costly for a poor nation to bring about decolonization – and it only came after the conservative dictatorship that ruled Portugal itself was overthrown.

None of these circumstances are present in the case of the Soviet empire. A totalitarian regime, unlike a liberal-democratic one, does not find itself placed in a contradictory stance when it imposes the same dictatorial rule on other nations too. Ultimately, it is only the quintessentially Western belief in the inherent worth of each and every human, and in the right of humans to define themselves in national groups of their own choosing, that stands against the practical notions that the strong can best order the affairs of the weak, and that the more advanced nationality can govern the less advanced better than they can govern themselves. The body of ideas that destroyed the legitimacy of the Western empires in their own homes, among their own elites, has never had a sturdy growth in the Russian political realm, nor even in Russian political thought. Even now these ideas seem to have much influence within a social group itself very narrow, the Westernizing urban elite. But of course one can make no certain judgement of such matters: it suffices to recall the sudden efflorescence of the Greek-Jewish-Christian ideal in Beijing itself, when the veil was briefly lifted, to wonder whether it is not the case that Western individualism as a moral concept has silently tunnelled its way into the consciousness of the whole world. In the meantime, the Soviet claim to trans-national legitimacy based on the supposed solidarity of the working classes of all nations is no doubt less and less persuasive to non-Russians, but it remains a useful delusion for such Russians as desire the imperial role – and who want to be spared from the moral discomfort of upholding a morally repugnant system.

But it would be false to see only ideas and ideals at work. Had the empires of Western Europe not encountered a rising tide of native resistance, it is doubtful if decolonization would have taken place; even if the intellectuals and the moralists wanted to surrender imperial power, some cost had to be felt before decolonization would receive popular support. And the native challenges to Soviet rule have been weak indeed: since 1945 we have seen only short-lived uprisings in East Germany and Hungary, the feeble and disarmed attempt at defection of the Czech regime, some unrest in Poland, and most recently the very remote insurgency of the newly conquered and most primitive Afghans, whose cause can elicit very little sympathy from Russians.

Thus the two great agencies that resulted in the dissolution of the Western empires are both weak in the Soviet case, there being neither much moral self-doubt among the master nationality, nor much unrest among the subjected peoples. There is on the other hand a political idea in circulation, at least in some Soviet circles, that is potentially corrosive of the will to empire: so long as their state is the prison house of peoples, the Russians themselves will be the least free and the most poor of all the nations of Europe. The imperial consciousness which the regime now deliberately encourages as a substitute for the waning ideological appeal of Marxism-Leninism entails a subtle danger: it attracts attention not only to the imperial role, but also to its cost. As with everything else that is not visible, concrete, stable and of classic form, and thus observable by photography from space, this Soviet phenomenon cannot be observed, let alone measured. We do not know the present importance of this idea, and cannot even begin to estimate its future impact. What we do know with certainty is that at present neither this nor any other cause of dissidence has been of sufficient weight to induce either a liberalizing accommodation by the Soviet regime, or the restoration of the Stalinist system of police terror.

An expensive proposition to its subjects as a whole, less expensive but still costly to the Russians themselves, the empire is on the other hand very efficient indeed as a producer of power for the Kremlin rulers. From their very special point of view, the empire may be seen as a 'power multiplier' of very great effectiveness. In 1913 the Tsar's Russia had a gross national product that amounted to roughly 40 per cent of the American GNP. In those days Russia was already of course a Great Power, but only as one among several; it was certainly not the leading European power. Nowadays, the Soviet-American GNP ratio is of the order of 50 per cent – thus only slightly improved, notwithstanding the inherent catch-up advantage of the more backward economy, and more than two generations of severe sacrifice that was supposed to yield very rapid economic growth. And yet the Soviet Union has so greatly increased its strength that it is now the world's leading military power.

Somewhat mechanistically, we may estimate the 'power-efficiency' of the Soviet empire by its ability to convert GNP into power. By that standard, we may say that the Soviet system is roughly five times as efficient as the alliance that embraces the United States, NATO Europe and Japan, since the combined GNPs of those countries are roughly five times as great as the Soviet, while their conjoint power is at best equal.

It will be recognized immediately that a power position so efficiently acquired must be correspondingly fragile, since it owes so much to what others refrain from doing, as opposed to what the Soviet Union itself does. Neither the United States nor any of its major allies convert anywhere near as much of their GNPs as the Soviet Union does, and this means that they could do much more – indeed they could submerge the entire Soviet military effort in a few years of defence budgets amounting to 10 per cent of the GNP (as opposed to the Soviet Union's 14–15 per cent). Neither the United States nor any of its allies emulate the vast Soviet effort in political warfare, based on the entire array of controlled communist parties, 'front' organizations, agents of influence, radio broadcasting 'white' and 'black', trade union operatives, newspaper and book publishing, overt and covert news agency operations and systematic disinformation. And there is no Western counterpart at all for the Soviet effort in covert operations, including the sponsorship of many terrorist organizations. In such things, the possibility of competition is more remote but the present feeble passivity scarcely defines the maximum potential of Western activity.

Western observers must regard the possibility of an all-out competition for power as totally unrealistic; they might fear that even the small effort now made will not be sustained. As it is, the Alliance is only preserved because the fears generated by the Soviet Union's military growth just barely overcome the natural tendencies that stand ready to undermine each country's effort for defence, and the cohesion of the whole. But the Kremlin rulers must consider matters more prudently, and they no doubt are very conscious of the vast untapped potential for military growth that the Alliance retains.

If Soviet military power continues to grow in relation to that of the United States and the Alliance, if Soviet blandishments and all manner of internal restraints overcome the defensive reflex that the very growth of Soviet power should otherwise stimulate, the Kremlin will eventually consolidate its power position, by forcing some members of the Alliance into a frightened neutrality. That danger is already imminent for the West, but until it actually materializes the fragility of the Soviet power position must persist. That is why it is only a Soviet leadership in any case pessimistic of the regime's future that will be tempted to exercise the option of expansionist war in a major fashion. For in the Soviet case in addition to all the classic risks of war, and in addition also to the new risks of the nuclear age, there is the peculiar further risk that more aggressive expansion will precipitate an Alliance-wide mobilization response which could quickly erode the Kremlin's power position down to a 'natural' level – a level, that is, where the power of the Soviet Union begins to approximate its economic capacity. That is the great deterrent, but as with all other deterrents its credibility must be actively sustained. It can hardly be argued that the Western reaction to the invasion of Afghanistan in December 1979 and to the Polish 'state of war' two years later did anything to sustain belief in the capacity of the Alliance to respond effectively to provocation. If in the Kremlin the fatal conjunction between regime pessimism and military confidence is indeed affected, and if at the same time it is also believed that the nations of Western Europe and Japan will simply refuse to respond seriously to anything short of a direct attack, thus undermining both the capacity and the incentive of an American response, the Soviet Union will be set on the road to war – a war neither Western nor nuclear but quite possibly catastrophic all the same. The pieces are even now on the board; the game could begin at any time.

Notes

1 'Nationalism', in its original meaning. In Tsarist Russia, as in the rest of Europe, 'nationalism' defined the demand that each language group ought to have its own independent state in order to safeguard its own language-culture, among other things. During the post-war era of decolonization, 'nationalism' was drastically redefined to express the demand that each colonial territory should become independent under the rule of local elites. Since hardly any of these territories consisted of a single linguistically defined nation, the so-called 'nationalists' were in fact 'statists', and indeed they soon found themselves in conflict with the nationalism (old definition) of the diverse language groups they had come to rule. Hence in writing of the Russian empire – or of today's Soviet Union – clarity demands that we avoid the distorted term 'nationalism'.

2 The 1926 Census of the USSR lists 52.9 per cent of all Soviets as 'Russians', the 1970 Census even 53.4 per cent. The percentages are probably exaggerated: persons not ethnic Great Russians but using the Russian language primarily may have preferred to call themselves 'Russians'. The figures are as follows:

	1926	1970	
Total population	147.028	241.720	(all figures in millions)
of which;			
Russians	77.791	129.015	
Ukrainians	31.195	40.753	
White Russians	4.739	9.052	

3 For a most interesting analysis see Van Creveld (1977), chapter 5.

4 Five per cent annual growth over 1966–70, but only 2.9 per cent in 1971–5 and less than that in the years since. *Soviet Economy in a Time of Change*, vol. 1 (1979), table 4, p. 768.

5 The amounts allocated in American defence budgets for investment (equipment purchases, research, development and testing, and military construction) declined steadily in absolute terms during the entire period from the mid-1960s until 1976. It was only then that the trend was reversed but only rather slowly: in real terms (deflated dollars) the 1964 level of military investment (roughly eighty US billion in 1983 dollars) was not attained again until 1983.

6 Odom (1981), p. 42.

7 For example, for anti-armour use: shoulder-fired RPGs, longer-ranged recoilless weapons and several types of portable and vehicular anti-tank missiles; for fire support: light, medium and heavy mortars in addition to howitzers, gun-howitzers and guns in medium and heavy calibres as well as mobile multiple rocket-launchers of varied range and warhead-weight; and for ground air defence: heavy machine-guns, radar-guided cannons and several classes of mobile AA missiles, some mounted on tracked launchers.

8 Carried out by the 105th Guards Airborne Division (with supporting elements from the 103rd and 104th Guards ABDs), whose troops were airlifted directly into

The Grand Strategy of the Soviet Union

Kabul International Airport in roughly 150 (AN-12 and AN-22) transport flights.

9 In places where such circumstances did not obtain, as in Judaea and the Bosporan state for example, endemic revolt made the client system quite unworkable; and when annexation followed, imperial rule was also violently challenged, and was thus made costly and difficult.

10 From *Soviet Military Power* (1981). There are 180 'field' divisions: forty-seven tank, seven airborne, and more than 126 'motorized rifle'. In addition, there are also at least fourteen artillery divisions, and a variety of special units, including eight elite helicopter-assault brigades. Not under army command but equipped on military lines, the 560,000 border and security units of the KGB and MVD would play a major role in any war deployment.

11 Excluding the seven elite airborne divisions and the helicopter-assault regiments, the total infantry of the Soviet army amounts to the dismount crews of the troop carriers of the motor-rifle divisions, and those of the combat carriers of the tank divisions.

Appendix I

The Economic Basis of Soviet Power
by Herbert Block

Part One: The Present
Economic development and foreign relations

Two questions define the subject. In what respect does the Soviet economy bolster or hamper the regime's aspirations in world affairs? And how does the Kremlin's foreign policy either promote or disturb Soviet economic interests?

The supporting role of the Soviet economy is not limited to supplies of goods or money. The economy also has an image which affects, positively or negatively, the mood and cohesion of the nation, the resolve of its leaders, and the opinions of the outside world. The world watches the economic goals which the USSR pursues, the methods of implementing them, and its success or failure in meeting those goals. What is perceived colours judgements of the Soviet Union as a partner in the world power game, and on the world markets. Quite often in the course of time the prestige of the Soviet economy and of the USSR as a whole has abruptly changed; the Soviet Union (like its Tsarist predecessor) has been prone to being over- or underrated. While every nation or government wants to be respected, the Soviet regime is uncommonly prestige-minded because it views its ideology, institutions and policies as models for other nations, developed and underdeveloped.

The Soviet economic system as a model abroad and a handicap at home

The model was and still is Stalinesque. Lenin's economic ideas were harebrained, and he had to retreat from their topsy-turvy implementation to a 'state monopoly capitalism', which combined nationalized 'commanding heights' in a market economy with small- and medium-sized private enterprises and farms. (This is now one option for a thorough reform of the Soviet economy with a Leninist imprimatur.) Stalin's command economy received its classic definition in 1957, when a renowned communist economist from Poland, the late Oskar Lange, said: 'I think that, essentially, it can be described as a *sui generis* war economy.' At a more primitive stage of development and in a real or imagined national emergency, if such a system is used with a judicious mixture of public enthusiasm and police terror, it can achieve great things, provided that human and material resources are recklessly spent. When it is applied under more complex modern conditions (and the zeal has evaporated), it becomes an obstacle to efficiency and innovation. The immutable Stalinist system is one of the basic reasons for the slowdown of Soviet economic progress. But it is dear to the leaders and their bureaucracies because it gives them power over every-body and everything at home, and much power abroad, through its commercial and monetary controls and through its military-industrial capabilities.

Changes in allocating resources

Great as the regime's power is, it has its share of discord among the leaders; it is from time to time exposed to popular unrest, affecting at least the labour morale; and it creates or reacts to international complications unforeseen by the planners. Such happenings alter the priorities in allocating resources. Changes of this nature have been a second reason for economic deceleration. Seweryn Bialer, citing Thane Gustafson, called imposing new priorities on old structures and processes the major dilemma of the Soviet system.[1] No doubt, one of the autocrats may use an impending or attempted change in priorities as a pretext to oust his dear colleague; administrators and managers may sabotage the change, or, what is equally counterproductive, overdo the policy. But priorities have frequently been changed for major categories and within categories. Stalin shifted from investment in steel and allied industries to military preparation as the Second World War drew closer. Faced with sagging labour morale, even the man of steel boosted (or considered boosting) consumer supplies at various times, both before and after the war. His successors first curbed then promoted military expenditures; throughout they improved allocations in favour of personal consumption. In the process, growth-inducing investment unavoidably decelerated. Since the system obstructed productivity gains, national product growth slowed down significantly.

For growthmanship addicts, investment acquires the dignity of a goal rather than being a means to an end; of Stalin, Abram Bergson remarked that he viewed steel as an end product, bread as a means to keep economic activities going. In so far as rapid economic growth redounds to a country's prestige, growth-promoting investment may indeed be considered a goal in itself. Be that as it may, the authorities of a command economy have to ensure that the required inputs are available in order to produce whatever goods their priorities demand. If they indulge in wishful planning, as the Kremlin so often does (the Yugoslav economist Alexander Bajt said: markets are imperfect, planners even more so), some priority will remain unobserved.

Foreign economic relations enter this picture because – quite apart from the welfare-promoting effects of a systematic division of international labour – they add to or detract from the resources available to the economy (and because they can alter the use pattern). Stalin, for instance, exported the grain of a famished nation to import machinery and raw materials. Brezhnev imported grain for livestock breeding to supplement the food supply while exporting industrial materials and arms – and contracting foreign debts.

Priorities and inputs

The capital goods that an economy is induced to manufacture in phase one (by limiting consumption) are then put to work in phase two; their productive services (measured by capital charge and amortization) are counted as an input. Consumer goods and services sustain the gainfully employed and their dependents, improve their performance and lift the collective ego; the hours they work are the labour input. The third input is derived from 'land', i.e., nature yielding its treasures when worked with labour and capital.

Each fragment of the three factors of production that supply the inputs starts its services in a given condition which may improve or deteriorate in the course of time. A copy of the same machine may be well maintained in one plant and poorly in another; it may be fully or badly utilized in different phases of the business cycle or in different societies. Land may become exhausted or new deposits may be discovered.

Labour may gain in quality on the job or lose quality. Such changes are reflected in the *output per unit of input*, which is the definition of productivity. Productivity gains or losses may be related only to the labour input or the capital input or – a minor factor – to the land. When the three factors of production are combined in an equation giving each its proper weight in line with real costs, we arrive at total factor productivity. It measures the high or low, increasing or decreasing output per unit of all inputs entering the formula.

Passing over the many conceptual and statistical difficulties of productivity research, we are on fairly safe ground in contemplating three countries as examples of different relations between output, inputs and productivity. The American economy progressed moderately fast in the postwar decades, once reconversion from war was achieved and until the oil price increases late in 1973. It offset a slow increase of the inputs (with investments on the low side) by high productivity gains, due in particular to managerial and technological progress (after 1973 productivity became a problem). Japan's expansion was sensational, fostered by large inputs (minimal defence outlays made large investments easier) and equally large productivity gains – Japan took over US advances and then developed them creatively. Soviet economic growth, respectable until recently, has always been achieved with a poor, if not dismal, performance in productivity; massive inputs of labour, capital and sometimes also of land did the trick.

Stalin's immediate successors faced a difficult situation which only a change of priorities could alleviate. Living and working conditions, though they had risen from the lower depths of the war years, were still miserable. The Soviet population was restive; the East European satellites were on the edge of revolt. Malenkov increased consumer supplies in a rush. Khrushchev, starting as a hardliner who changed his tune once he had overthrown his predecessor, grabbed the flag Malenkov had been forced to drop, and fled forward; he proclaimed that communist abundance was around the corner and that the Soviet Union would soon catch up with the richest country in the world, the United States, in per capita consumption. For 1960/61 he announced a meat output of 20–21 million tons (actual output in the early 1980s was officially reported at about 15 million tons!). Whether these promises of instant abundance calmed a populace with little faith in government pledges (with a high boiling point, though) is doubtful; at least they indicated that the new boss understood and cared, if only because he was afraid. Khrushchev's success in overcoming a potentially explosive state of mind and in improving labour morale can be attributed to slow but noticeable improvements in living and working conditions, to measures rectifying the highly unjust income distribution of Stalin's days, to de-Stalinization in general, to the absence of unemployment (the workers prefer the system's under-employment to joblessness), and here and there to some prestigious feat evoking patriotic pride, such as the first space flights.

Even within the ineffective system, Soviet consumption would have made greater strides if Stalin's successors had not embarked on a series of foreign adventures which provoked a new arms race, first from the end of the 1950s, and again currently. With a volume of output only half as large as the American, the USSR undermines the desideratum of rapid economic growth when it opts for increased military spending *and* improved consumption. Ever since the late 1950s the growth rate of investment has declined and then, with a time lag, the rates of capital stock, capital inputs and national product growth inevitably did too. Paul Holland and Seweryn Bialer credit the Kremlin with an astute 'management of expect-ation'.[2] The credit should rather go to a patient population. The Soviet leaders themselves have had difficulties managing their own expectations, otherwise they would not have predicated the success of each five-year plan on obviously unachievable productivity gains.

Allocating resources to national security

The Kremlin's appraisals of costs and benefits in the field of national defence are completely unknown outside its walls – quite a feat of concealment. The single budget figure that the USSR publishes once a year for planned as well as actual defence outlays has since 1968 been fixed at roughly 17 billion* roubles. As a share of the Soviet GNP, this nominal figure declined in the course of the 1970s from about 5 per cent to roughly 3 per cent – a fulsome

* US billion are used throughout.

understatement. Some additional information on 'science' is not helpful either. Only once, in 1974, did the Central Intelligence Agency receive a limited amount of (financial) inside information on 'defence' in a past year, namely 1970. Thereupon it doubled the estimated rouble value of Soviet security spending. The revision implied not that the Agency had discovered heretofore hidden men and their arms, nor that it had to raise its dollar calculations, but rather that military equipment, plant and operations were far costlier than had been supposed. The economic efficiency of the Soviet military-industrial establishment was – and presumably still is – as unsatisfactory as in the rest of the economy. The increase of the estimated defence figure betokens a Soviet weakness rather than a strength, a heavier burden on the population than had been believed. The CIA's previous calculations had been criticized both within the US government and by outside specialists, and the new data caused a great deal of further discussion, some opting for higher, others for lower figures. By now the controversy has died down from pure exhaustion. Everything that could be said has been said (several times over), and the debates must now wait until new evidence erupts or new thought eructs. Neither, when it occurs, need be correct.

The CIA's revision for the year 1970 raised the share of Soviet national security outlays in the GNP from 6.5 to 12 per cent. The estimated annual growth in defence expenditures in the 1970s was similarly increased from 3 to 4–5 per cent. This amounts to a real increase of 50–60 per cent in the course of a decade. We need not quibble about a couple of billions or a percentage point this way or that, since we find ourself in the realm of meta-Intelligence. If the figures just cited are near reality, they imply that in 1980, after ten years of average annual GNP growth of only 3.1 per cent, national security spending had reached 13–14 per cent of the national product. At 1970 rouble prices, which were by at least 10 per cent (probably 20 per cent) lower than 1980 prices, national security outlays may range from 67 to 75 billion roubles. The estimated GNP share contrasts sharply with the 1980 ratios of about 5.5 per cent in the US and 4.5 per cent in NATO as a whole, not to mention Japan's 0.9 per cent; in fact, the Soviet ratio appears to be by far higher than that of any other country not involved in acute conflict. The military burden on the Soviet population is the most obvious contribution of the economy to the Soviet power position in world affairs.

Appendix I: The Economic Basis of Soviet Power

The Western rouble estimates do not or cannot take into account several Soviet peculiarities which add to the real resource cost of the military establishment. There is, first, the actual rouble cost of maintaining the large number of armed forces personnel (close to 5 million men or 3.5 per cent of the labour force). The CIA still uses the *1970* outlay per man-year. Actually, the rouble expense has gone up, partly because of the (modest) inflation that afflicts the USSR, partly because, as consumption improved for the population as a whole, the upkeep of the military personnel was also upgraded. In so far as the CIA calculations are in 1970 roubles, purely monetary changes must indeed be deflated. But the higher cost of a better life should be imputed to all years after 1970, particularly since the 'output' of military as well as of government personnel is – for lack of better data – determined by their pay and maintenance. The 1980 costs of such improvements may be in the neighbourhood of 1 billion roubles, which in turn would increase the share of national security by, say, 0.2 of a percentage point. This is a very rough estimate and, while the figures are modest, they do increase the military outlay.

The second consideration does not affect the rouble costs but is nonetheless a burden on the Soviet economy and on the soldiery in particular: like conscripts practically everywhere, the lower ranks do not receive any opportunity pay. Volunteer personnel, of course, must be paid their opportunity cost – otherwise they would not offer themselves – and it is fully applied in the dollar calculation of Soviet defence outlays, which imputes American pay and maintenances to the Soviet armed forces. Soviet conscripts are greatly underpaid,[3] and their sacrifice actually reduces the Soviet GNP by the difference between military and civilian income.

There is little doubt that the military-industrial establishment can claim the choicest resources in management and technology, labour, equipment and materials. Nobody knows for sure whether the CIA defence totals in roubles are on the low side because they may include subsidized or otherwise reduced prices for such resources. If – to indulge in counterfactual history – the Brezhnev administration had seen fit to order less armament production, valuable inputs would have been channelled into the civilian economy. Here and there they would have upgraded not only the quantity but also the quality of civilian output – something not to be sneezed at under Soviet conditions. Since it now appears that the armament industries have only a technological but not an efficiency edge over most of the civilian economy, a transfer of managerial staff might not have improved the overall productivity of the civilian economy.

Post-Stalinist attention to mass consumption

Even Stalin had occasional fits when he imagined or pretended that life had or should become 'more joyous'. His successors, without exactly being welfarers, paid attention to the public mood, as reported through party echelons and by the police. The moods of masses as well as elites have favoured creature comforts. Among the leaders there are usually a few anti-consumerists who root for austerity (except for themselves), but they are rare; asceticism does not really fit into the ideology of communists, though it may appeal to the militarists and nationalists among them.

Calculations of the growth and structure of current Soviet consumption in comparison with the past or with other countries are beset by problems arising not only from the deficiencies of the USSR's statistics but also from the profound differences that exist in scarcity relations between the present time and the past and between East and West. There are now goods and services on the market that were hardly dreamed about in the past; urbanization has changed the requirements of the consumers; monetization has crowded out home-produced goods and services; the mix of personal and communal consumption differs from period to period and from country to country, as do quality, selection, novelty and repair services. Per capita consumption is also affected by demographic developments (e.g., had the Soviet population increased between 1913 and 1980 as much as the American, the USSR would now number more than 370 million inhabitants instead of 265.5 million (1980), with corresponding effects on labour supply, savings capabilities and investment requirements in the intervening decades).

In 1950 Soviet per capita consumption was hardly more adequate than in 1928 at the start of the five-year plans or, for that matter, in 1913. Consumption had deteriorated during the First World War and the civil disorders following it, during Stalin's Great Leap and during the Second World War. There were modest recoveries in the NEP period of the mid-1920s, in the mid-1930s and late in the 1940s. The ability and willingness of the population to bear harsh privations were most impressive and must be remembered in thinking about the future. Between 1950 and 1980 the average annual growth rate for personal consumption was about 4.6 per cent in toto and 3.2 per cent per capita. It differed greatly not only from year to year (chiefly as the result of good or bad crops) but also from period to period. The per capita rate went up by 2.6 per cent in each of the two years before Stalin's death (in March 1953) and by almost 4.5 per cent between 1953 and 1956. It dipped to 2 per cent in the six years up to 1964 (rearmament and economic policy blunders making themselves felt), rose again to 4.1 per cent in the first six years of the Brezhnev-Kosygin era, and fell to 2.2 per cent between 1970 and 1980. The decline of *total* consumption growth is still more pronounced because of the demographic deceleration: 6.2 per cent in 1953–8, 3.1 per cent in the 1970s (the rate of population increase declined from 1.75 per cent during the postwar baby boom of the 1950s to 0.8–0.9 per cent in the last decade).

Compared with the turbulent decades up to 1950, the better performance of the last thirty years does not require an explanation. But by international standards, that performance was not outstanding, particularly if we consider the low level at the beginning of the period. An otherwise fairly modern economy cannot in the long term operate with the nutrition and housing conditions of a wartime economy.

Between the early 1950s and the late 1970s the average annual rate of growth in per capita private consumption was 6.5 per cent in Japan, 4.6 per cent in West Germany, 3.9 per cent in France, 3.8 per cent in Italy, 2.4 per cent in the US (which did not suffer wartime destruction and deterioration), and 1.9 per cent in the UK (with great sacrifices during the war, the loss of all its colonies, and that mysterious *mal anglais*). The rate of increase was 3.9 per cent both in OECD Europe and in the OECD area as a whole, above the Soviet rate of 3.2 per cent.

There were times when the Soviet population grew restive either in view of Western affluence or in the presence of East European uprisings and disturbances over conditions which were actually superior to those in the USSR. This was particularly the case at the time of the Hungarian and Polish insurrections in 1956. Khrushchev's extravagant promises addressed themselves exactly to a bloc-wide discontent over glaring contrasts between living and working conditions in East and West. The Polish strikes of 1973,

1976 and 1980–1 provided the Kremlin with food not for sale but for thought; planned price increases for mass consumption items were postponed and purchases abroad stepped up. By and large, however, Soviet citizens, with their characteristic submissiveness, have been content to compare their present lot with that in previous years; they have found a little comfort in each little step forward. They have appreciated the absence of noticeable unemployment and have used the job opportunities available for as many bread-winners in the family as possible. With most women working and with housing space still quite limited, the Soviets have reduced the number of children to one or two per family, at least outside republics with large Muslim populations. For the time being, most Soviets would probably prefer better housing and a small car to a second or third child. The recently introduced cash bonuses and fringe benefits for mothers with many children (according to a report in the *Washington Post* of 4 June 1981) will have little effect.

Some relief in consumer supply for those with money is provided by extensive black and grey markets; many earn a living or supplement their income by working for them. These activities are bound up with 'diverting' collective property (or time paid for by the government) to private pursuits; it also entails much bribery and corruption. In an international comparison, the Soviet second economy is second to none. If in past decades the regime had done more to satisfy the needs of the population, there would be fewer extra and illegal dealings, perhaps also less absenteeism, alcoholism and crime – although these degradations have their roots not only in Soviet living and working conditions but in national traits and, above all, in the modern mass society. If, on the other hand, the regime had done less, order might have cracked or collapsed. That it did not – disregarding occasional disorders of a strictly local scope – shows that the Kremlin's stand-pattism in all matters deemed essential for preserving the system, in combination with concessions in resource distribution to 'satisfice' the consumers, has indeed worked – up to now. We will come back to the issue in the context of labour input and productivity in the past and future.

Capital formation under pressure

A price had to be paid, however, for this limited attention to consumer needs and, except for the short-lived restraint of the mid-1950s, rather lavish armament programmes. The chain of events has been as follows. First, the rate of growth for new fixed investments declined. It fell steadily from an annual 12.9 per cent in the first half of the 1950s to 3.5 per cent in the second half of the 1970s; the official plan for 1981–5 provides for an average annual increase of only 2.6 per cent.

Sooner or later a declining investment rate pulls down the increase in the existing stock of fixed capital. Its growth decelerated from 9.9 per cent per annum in 1951–5 to 6.8 per cent in1976–80. The capital stock would have levelled off more rapidly but for a long-standing Soviet policy of artificially prolonging the life of capital assets. In the United States and the West in general (though not without exceptions in old industries) obsolescent plant and, above all, equipment are quickly written off and replaced by modern capital goods. The USSR maintains outdated assets by repairing them on the premises – an inefficient method to preserve inefficient machinery. In other words, the Soviet capital stock has not only grown more slowly than previously but has also progressed less in quality than desirable for a modern economy.

This, in turn, has adversely affected the volume and efficiency of the capital services that are part of the inputs used to generate new national product. Soviet official statistics indicate that the 'produced net material product' grew between 1951 and 1955 by 11.4 per cent in the annual average; the rate declined to 5 per cent in 1976–80; the plan stipulates for 1981–5 a 3.7 per cent increase per annum. In terms of Western-style GNP and without Soviet over-statement, the growth developed from 5.8 per cent in 1951–5 to 2.6 per cent in 1976–80; it will be modest during the present five-year plan.

While investment *growth* decelerated, its rates still remained above GNP growth. (The current plan is meant to reverse investment and national income growth; more on this below, in Part Two.) As a result, new fixed investment as a share of GNP rose from 11.4 per cent in 1950 to 19.4 per cent in 1960, 21.6 per cent in 1970, and 25.4 per cent in1980. These ratios exclude changes in livestock capital (a minor and much fluctuating item in new fixed investment) and, by definition, inventory changes and capital repairs. (The latter have increased as a share of GNP from 2.8 per cent in 1950 to 6 per cent now.) *Total* fixed investment (including repairs and livestock but, of course, without inventory changes) increased from 14.8 per cent of GNP in 1950 to more than 31 per cent in 1980. This is an unusually high share. In the OECD area as a whole the ratio between gross fixed capital formation and gross domestic product (GDP) moved from 19.7 per cent in 1960 past a 23 per cent peak in the boom year 1973 to 21.7 per cent in 1979; *the OECD members achieved the same average annual growth of the total product (4.3 per cent) as the USSR with a much more advantageous (i.e. smaller) investment share.* Japan's investment share rose from close to 30 per cent in 1960 through a record 36.4 per cent in 1973 to 32 per cent in 1979, but its GDP growth was almost twice as strong as in the USSR (recently revised from 8.4 per cent to 7.9 per cent, as the result of a changed price base, as against the Soviet 4.25 per cent for 1960–79). The American ratio of roughly 18 per cent of GDP (with slight variations from year to year) is, as previously remarked, on the low side; in the OECD total the investment share would rise by about 1.5 percentage points if the US were excluded. It is a paradox that the increase in Soviet consumption has resulted in a declining share of consumption in the GNP, namely from 62 per cent in 1950 to 55–6 per cent in 1980. This is a testimonial to Soviet inefficiency and also to the expanding armament programmes.

At this point we must refer to a complication that cuts across Western estimates of Soviet national security and investment outlays. The military effort distorts Soviet data on capital formation. Since the published Soviet defence budget excludes three-quarters of actual national security outlays, they must be included in other categories in (and also outside) the government budget. The 'science' allocation is an obvious and not too covert place. In minor ways defence affects general administration, health and educational appropriations, a number of unexplained budget residues *and* the investment statistics. The CIA estimated that in 1970 new fixed investments amounting to 82.3 billion roubles at established prices of that year (additions to livestock excluded) were inflated by 5 billion roubles of military procurement, i.e., 6 per cent of the total. In particular, investment in construction is believed to have contained 1.5 out of 57 billion roubles, or almost 3 per cent; machinery and equipment 3.5 out of 25.3 billion roubles, or 16 per cent.[4] If these estimates come close to the mark and if, as we are tempted to assume, military procurements hidden in investment statistics increased as capital formation levelled off, then investment levels are now more overstated than ten years ago.[5]

Soviet foreign economic relations and their consequences

In every very large economy, foreign commercial and financial affairs are, inevitably, small in relation to its total volume. In the USSR an inward orientation has been strengthened by additional circumstances. East-West tension has brought forth the longest commercial war in modern history. In the USSR's economic system, transactions with foreigners not under Soviet control irritate planners, administrators and managers; they also disturb a taut economy which has trouble enough fulfilling its domestic plan targets. Last but not least, largesse in international affairs is not exactly a Soviet characteristic.

Within this limited scope, Soviet foreign relations have undergone remarkable ups and downs. Before the Second World War, the Eastern part of East-West trade was only the USSR, and practically all Westerners viewed it with misgivings and suspicion. Soviet trade began to recover moderately from the disasters of war and revolution under the NEP of the 1920s. Then, to support the power-building under the first five-year plan, the government went on a buying spree for Western equipment and knowhow. It paid for its acquisitions by selling scarce commodities (grain at a time of starvation!) at the unfavourable terms of trade of the Great Depression. The West became hysterical about 'The Red Trade Menace' (the title of H. R. Knickerbocker's bestseller of 1931) and accused the Soviets of dumping. After this hurtful experience Soviet trade authorities retrenched for several years; autarky was temporarily embraced as a principle – and this did not please the West either. On the eve of the Second World War the USSR stepped up its purchases of strategic goods, and, while the Molotov-Ribbentrop Pact lasted, Stalin tried to mollify Hitler by supplying him with vital commodities. When the Nazis, in their desire to appropriate the source itself of those shipments, invaded the USSR, Moscow became eligible for Lend-Lease goods. Goods in the pipeline continued to flow to the Soviet Union for a while after the war, supplemented by ample takings from friend and foe in territories which the Red Army had occupied. All these free imports significantly increased the national income of the war-torn USSR.

After the Allied victory, Western hopes for an intense East-West trade soared, but, despite Soviet prodding, faded rapidly as the Cold War unfolded. The American Admiral Richardson then predicted that, as the result of US export controls, the Soviet economy would soon be 'standing still like an unwound clock'. Few in the US government entertained such naive notions; the administration recognized that the embargo would be of considerable nuisance to the USSR but not more than that, particularly in the long run.

In the past three decades, Soviet trade has increased from the low levels of 1950 by an average annual 9.1 per cent in real terms, i.e. more rapidly than the corresponding American rate of 6.5 per cent and the rate for world trade of 7.7 per cent (between 1950 and 1973 world trade increased by an annual 8.3 per cent until, under the impact of the 'oil crunch', it slowed down; Soviet trade, in turn, benefited from the higher oil prices). The share of foreign trade (total trade turnover divided by two) in the Soviet GNP increased from 1.7 per cent in 1950 to 5.2 per cent in 1980 (US trade as a share of American GNP rose in those three decades from 3.4 to 9.2 per cent, world trade in relation to the planetary product from 7 to 14.8 per cent).

The Western embargo policy began to crumble in the 1960s, first in Western Europe, then, during the detente episode, also in the US. America waxed so bullish about the trade prospects that Europeans had ludicrous fears that the US might 'preempt' the Eastern markets; in reality American East-West trade remained modest, and likewise American credits to the East. Controls are now again reinforced after a fashion. Whatever the changeable political climate, the share of the advanced West in Soviet foreign trade doubled between 1955 (15 per cent) and 1980 (33.6 per cent); in the mid-1970s imports from the West rose to no less than 35.6 per cent of all Soviet imports, fuelled by ample credits, which were even cheap because of the declining value of the dollar.

The USSR has always been eager to acquire up-to-date equipment; at the same time, it has felt constrained to purchase Western grain. As an exporter, the country profited from high prices for raw materials, including precious metals. The favourable terms of trade are particularly important for a nation that, after a century of industrial development, is unable to sell advanced manufactured articles to the West (they constitute only 4 per cent of Soviet hard currency earnings). Politics aside, this incompetence is an essential factor that hampers the long-term development of East-West trade. The trouble has many aspects: Soviet inability to manufacture civilian articles that might interest Western markets, or even to recognize exportable goods among those produced in the USSR; difficulties in servicing sold goods; bureaucratic rigidity; incomprehension of the requirements of actual or potential Western customers. While these deficiencies are peculiar to the Soviet domestic set-up, it must be recognized that in dealing with 'capitalists' the USSR's foreign trade representatives have always tried hard to conform to Western standards and behaviour, if only because – despite a foreign trade monopoly – they lack clout in the West.

It is different in East-East relations. Communist regimes that displeased Moscow (Yugoslavia, Albania, the PRC, etc.) got a taste of the Cold War, Soviet version. Sino-Soviet trade absorbed in 1955 22 per cent of the USSR's exports and imports; it was 0.3 per cent in 1980. The abrupt recall of Soviet technicians from the PRC remains unforgotten. Up to the Hungarian and Polish revolts in 1956, the USSR exploited the nations of its orbit mercilessly (and Czechoslovakia exploited Albania shamelessly, defrauding the Tirana government in marketing its chrome ores abroad). Later the Kremlin had to apologize and to change its tune in regard to remaining associates. Since then it is difficult to ascertain who exploits whom in intra-communist commerce. Known price concessions on one side (e.g., discounts the USSR granted its Comecon associates on petroleum deliveries in the first years after the oil crunch) may have been offset by undisclosed concessions in compensatory deals. The East Europeans in particular have always fretted about the poor quality of Soviet equipment (which would have been unsaleable in the West), but then their shipments to the USSR have similar deficiencies. In general it can be said that the Soviet connection is disadvantageous for the orbit nations less because of losses incurred in specific transactions than because of their – enforced or subservient – imitation of the Soviet economic model (a bankrupt Poland currently offering a pathetic example). Economic relations between the USSR and the Third World began (aside from minor deals) in 1954–5 when Khrushchev added projects of economic and military aid to a continuous Leninist-Stalinist strategy of fishing in troubled political waters. The US viewed the 'aggressive program of economic diplomacy' as a 'grave danger'.[6] The danger of less developed countries becoming members of the Soviet bloc appeared the greater as the USSR concentrated its aid on a small number of likely converts. After more than a quarter of a century, the threat appears less impressive. During this period the USSR gained and lost partners in the Third World, gaining and losing money in the process. While commercial relations, aid contracts included, created some goodwill and some bad feelings for the Soviet Union, neither determined the allegiance of the underdeveloped countries in the long term; they changed their affiliation according to the international power game, as they perceived their interests at a given moment, unless they were simply forced in one way or the other. Egypt did not break with Moscow, and Afghanistan was not swallowed by the Soviets, because of trade and contracts.

It is useful to differentiate between Soviet aid and trade and between civilian and military goods and services. In 1980 exports to all kinds of less developed countries absorbed 13.2 per cent of all Soviet exports, 11.2 per cent of all imports, i.e., they amounted to 10,072 and 7,667 million dollars respectively. In 1979, only $575 million of the exports consisted of economic aid deliveries.[7] *This means that economic aid represented less than half of one-thousandth of the Soviet GNP.* Few of the deliveries were grants; the bulk was on credit. The Third World spokesmen, anxious to obtain aid to the extent of 1 per cent or 0.75 per cent of the GNP cf the advanced nations, chafe at Soviet performance; the Kremlin's parsimony reduces the pressure they can exert on the West. Willy Brandt, lobbying for larger Soviet economic aid, was allegedly told in Moscow in the spring of 1981 that 'inevitable military expenditures' limit Soviet capabilities for more aid (see *Frankfurter Allgemeine Zeitung*, 29 May 1981).

Soviet military aid, on the other hand, has been ample. In 1979 agreements were concluded to the tune of $8,365 million; deliveries were estimated at $6,615 million. This gives the USSR – to use a fashionable expression – 'approximate parity' with the US (American arms exports in 1979 were $6,665 million). It is quite advantageous for the USSR to sell arms. In so far as the equipment is obsolescent (it constituted in earlier years a large, now only a small, portion of its deliveries), it gets rid of undesired inventories at a good price. In so far as it supplies Third World countries with newly produced arms, as is currently the rule, it either uses temporarily under-utilized armament plants or – and this is more to the point – it maintains an industrial reserve capacity for use in an emergency. This reserve capacity, now employed to supply less developed countries as well as communist allies in Eastern Europe and elsewhere, must add a considerable potential to industries working for the USSR's military and space establishment. It is true that, as Edward A. Hewitt observes: 'These [i.e., the export arms] are high quality products in a high priority industry, and significant increases in production must have a telling effect on the remainder of the system.'[8] In the Kremlin's view, the reserve potential alone must justify the additional allocation of labour and capital to the armament industry. And if there is a field in Soviet manufacturing with a comparative advantage in the outside world, it is arms production. Other Warsaw Pact governments seem to pay good prices for Soviet arms; the Third World pays not only well but in hard currency, something it would not do for Soviet civilian articles. The hard currency earnings from arms exports to the Third World probably exceeded $2 billion in 1979. In addition to economic advantages, arms exports allow the USSR to influence the political power game in strategically important regions, to make countries accustomed to Soviet equipment and dependent upon spare parts and complementary supplies, to penetrate Third World military establishments and to keep military technicians in contested areas.

An element of security in Soviet international trade – and also in seaborne domestic trade – is provided by the Soviet merchant fleet. It is hardly necessary to add that commercial tonnage plays a potential role in military operations and an actual role in Intelligence gathering. The size of the Soviet merchant fleet grew from 3.3 million deadweight tons at the end of 1959 to 19.29 million tons late in 1981. This is practically as much as the American tonnage (which stood by the end of 1981 at 21.17 million tons, not counting ships operating only on the Great Lakes), except that the US, for good economic reasons, owns large numbers of ships flying flags of convenience. Both the Soviet merchant fleet and other carriers (such as the railroads with container traffic over the Siberian land bridge) add to the USSR's hard currency revenues.[9]

To sum up the foreign economic relations section: since a rational division of labour bestows advantages on all who participate in it, the Soviet Union has benefited from its commercial relations with the West, chiefly by acquiring advanced technology (embodied in equipment or through licence), but also through the imports of foodstuffs to relieve domestic tensions. That the advantages have not been greater had two reasons: first, the Soviet regime and its policies antagonize foreign partners; second, the Soviet economy has not been efficient in absorbing Western technology. (Here one should remember that easy access to advanced knowhow abroad tends to bring on poor imitations, while foreign embargoes often force an economy to develop its own powers of innovation.)

East-East relations were, on the whole, mutually disadvantageous. Political benefits that the USSR derived from international economic intercourse were largely the result not of Soviet economic effectiveness but of its superpower status (combined with its availability as an alternative to American ties for some smaller countries). In the field of arms exports to the 'Third World', however, the Soviet economy is effective; such exports allow the USSR to influence the power game in contested areas, to earn hard currency for imports from the West, and to maintain a reserve potential in armament industries for use in any strategic emergency.

The Soviet output record and its impact on world opinion

The productive forces of the USSR, directed according to the regime's priorities, produce in the various branches of the economy, often with shortfalls, sometimes with windfalls, the goods and services for public and personal consumption and reinvestment which combine to create the national product – with some modification in volume and structure through foreign economic transactions. American economists, rectifying official Soviet statistics and applying Western concepts, recalculate the GNP totals by adding up estimates of the value added originating in agriculture, industry, etc. The results are harmonized with a similar reckoning of the values believed to have entered final consumption and capital formation. They show, as does the net material income (NMI) series that the USSR publishes in line with Marxist concepts, the slowdown of the Soviet product in recent decades that we mentioned in the context of its two main causations, an inefficient system and decelerating capital formation.

Table 2

Average annual GNP growth rates (USSR, US, world) in per cent

	1950–5	1956–60	1961–5	1966–70	1971–5	1976–80	1950–80
USSR	5.8	6.0	4.9	5.4	3.6	2.6	4.7
US	4.2	2.3	4.6	3.1	2.3	3.5	4.0
World	5.2	4.3	5.0	5.0	4.2	3.6	4.6
World less US	5.6	5.2	5.2	5.8	4.8	3.7	5.1
Non-communist world	4.9	3.9	5.3	4.8	3.4	3.5	4.3
Same less US	5.7	5.3	5.8	6.1	4.0	3.6	5.1

Source: Block (1981).

We will begin with the growth rates (table 2) and then return to the magnitudes in an international context. Soviet growth was rapid in the 1950s, first because after a war economies recover rapidly, then because of a policy of heavy investments. In the 1960s, with Khrushchev's economic policy in trouble, the system's friction mounting, and arms outlays reducing capital formation, growth slowed down, with a minor pickup in the second half of the decade. The growth rate continued to decline in the 1970s. During these thirty years the American economy expanded at a rate (4 per cent) below the world average (modest investment an important reason). Soviet growth (4.7 per cent) was close to average world economic growth (4.6 per cent) and slightly above the rate of the non-communist world (4.3 per cent); when we deduct the US GNP, with its great weight, from the output of either the entire world or the non-communist world, the USSR remains below average (5.1 per cent in both cases). In the second half of the 1970s the Soviet economy's rate dropped even below the rates of the US (3.5 per cent) and of the rest of the world (3.6–3.7 per cent).

All these rates refer to medium-term periods, quinquennia or decades. In the two years 1979 and 1980 Soviet GNP growth was on average a mere 1.1 per cent as compared with a planetary rate of 2.5 per cent or, since the American GNP increased also as little as 1 per cent, of 3 per cent without the US. In 1981 and 1982 Soviet growth was on average 1.6 per cent. It is not yet clear whether the slump is a temporary aberration, a deepening of the system's malfunctioning, or the result of additional military efforts, and we will come back to the issue in Part Two.

Viewed with international relations in mind, the rates just mentioned greatly impressed the world in the days of Khrushchev's stewardship, particularly since the Soviet-American differential was considered a continuation of the 1930s, with the USSR expanding, the US depressed. Some governments with neutralist propensities (Brazil to a degree) pondered whether their foreign associations should not take account of the USSR's fast approaching primacy; the Soviet economic model won esteem. The American public became quite disturbed and the US government embarked on growth-promoting policies.

Today there is nothing left of the Soviet prestige gain in growthmanship, from the point of view both of economic power and model supremacy. But the repute lost in this field was recouped in the strategic-military field. The USSR's obvious weakness during the 1962 crisis over Cuba – at a time when the Sino-Soviet split worsened – was redressed by many years of systematic arms build-up (and American setbacks in Vietnam and elsewhere). Whatever the exact strategic balance at this moment (the proof of the military is always in the fighting!), the world is under the impression that militarily the USSR and the US are in 'approximate parity', with the Soviets possibly somewhat superior.

Soviet and US growth: 1913–80

On the eve of the First World War, the Swedish geopolitician Rudolf Kjellén wrote a book on the Great Powers. Speaking of the future, he recognized three 'planetary powers', the United States, Russia and China. He was uncertain of England and unsure about a Central Europe under the hegemony of Germany (his pet power). Comparing the two first-named nations, he called the United States 'economically a great power without equal, but militarily weak'; while Russia, 'judging by the statistics, appears as the greatest military power in the world, but without a corresponding economic flowering'.[10] The USSR's economy is still not exactly flowering, while its military strength cannot be doubted. The US continues economically without equal, and while before 1914 it had contented itself with naval power, it is now militarily a superpower.

In 1913 the Russian-American population ratio was 162.4:100, the GNP ratio something like 40:100. At that time, Russia had close to 9 per cent of the world's population, the US 5.5 per cent; their

138

respective share in the planetary product was about 9 and 23 per cent. In 1980 the Soviet-American demographic ratio was 116.6:100, with respective shares in mankind of 5.9 and 5.1 per cent; the GNP ratio was roughly 50:100 or, as a share in the planetary product, 11.4 and 22.7 per cent. In the decades in between, the Soviet-US GNP ratio declined steeply on two occasions: during the defeat and revolution in Russia at the end of the First World War, and during the German invasion of the 1940s. Twice the USSR recovered (on the eve of the Second World War the ratio was probably slightly above 40:100), and during the past ten years the economic balance as measured by the GNPs of the two countries has not changed perceptibly. The population ratio has remained stable since 1950. The present Soviet-American economic and demographic ratio at a period of uneasy but as yet unbroken peace is as close to 'normal' as history ever gets. We will return to the international comparison later in a broader context including the Eastern and Western alliance systems.

Inputs: labour, capital, land

We now return to the productive forces that, in limited obedience to the regime's priorities, managed to supply the military, capital and consumer goods and services by way of inputs of labour, capital and land. A production function, accounting for the quantity and quality of the inputs, can easily convey the notion that economic development moves with mathematical logic or according to divine predestination. The elements that enter such equations (and several equations offer themselves with different weighting proportions) may at a given moment be hard to change (in contrast to political moods and political agents). But all of them can be influenced not only by accidental happenings – which have to be accepted – but also by measures of economic policy. Past developments might have been different (example: did Khrushchev really have to reduce the workweek exactly during years of particularly small entries into the labour force?), and extrapolations into the future may operate with erroneous assumptions (e.g., the presumption that the Soviet system is simply unable to shift the large number of auxiliary workers into more productive jobs).

This leads us to that part of the production function that measures the contribution of labour. The weight that labour services bestow upon the input total is derived from their costs as incorporated in the national product; the Office of Economic Research (OER) of the CIA estimated a weight of about 0.56 (as against 0.41 for capital services, and 0.3 for land) for one unit of input. Labour inputs change from year to year in accordance with the man-hours of employment; changes in the quality of the labour from variations in skill, age, sex or ethnic composition are accounted for (precariously) in that portion of productivity that can be directly imputed to labour. The formula is rigid, the ends are loose.

During the interwar period the USSR's natural population increase was (for that era) low (1928–37 about 1 per cent), understandably in view of the nation's convulsions. But there had been unemployment up to 1928 and much underemployment, particularly in rural areas, where more than 80 per cent of the Soviets still lived. Abram Bergson calculated that in the period 1938–40 employment in terms of man-years increased by an annual 3.7 per cent.[11] After the war there was the usual comeback of the birth rate and a decline in the death rate; the natural increase of the population peaked in 1958 with 1.81 per cent. This, however, was the time when, as an after-effect of the war casualties, the number of entrants into the labour force was at a low and total employment began to stagnate (population of working age in 1958 was 119.6 million; in 1963, 121.2 million).[12] At that very time, Khrushchev reduced the workweek and, while this may have had a beneficial influence on labour productivity, the labour input as measured by man-hours dipped until 1961; it was back at the 1958 level only in 1963.

From 1960 on, the population of working age rose as a result of the postwar baby boom; the annual increments (entrants less retirement or death) peaked in 1978 with 2.8 million. From then on it has again been on the decline, to 1.6 million in 1980 and 1.1 million in 1981. This is the result of a fall in the natural increase of the population from its 1.8 per cent peak in 1958 to 0.8 per cent in 1980. *Labour supply has become a key problem.* The input of man-hours in the entire economy, which had risen from an annual average 1.3 per cent in the late 1950s to 1.5 per cent in 1961–5 and 2 per cent in 1966–70, declined to 1.7 per cent in 1971–5 and to 1.3 per cent in 1976–80, with a levelling-off from year to year below 1 per cent in 1980.

The annual capital inputs of an economy consist of the services derived from the capital stock on hand. Soviet economics, aside from operating with insufficient depreciation rates, considers capital charges as un-Marxist. Western economists must therefore make their own assumptions on depreciation and on a return on capital. There are additional problems: the capital input should include the services attributable to inventories, but in the Soviet case the figures are uncertain. If published, they would probably include military stocks. In fact, as mentioned above, the investment series and perhaps also the capital stock series are defence-affected; whether these series, when purged of military ingredients, would show a different growth rate is beyond our knowledge. Thus we must accept the estimates of Soviet capital costs with reservation and resignation. But while we harbour doubts about the decimals, the trend appears true to life. Capital inputs (less inventories) increased on average during the 1950s by 9.4 per cent, in the late 1960s by 8.1 per cent, in the first half of the 1970s by 7.9 per cent, in its second half by 6.5 per cent. We will return to this series in discussing productivity and capital productivity in particular.

The services of 'land' (whoever owns it) have a rather small share in total inputs (about 3 per cent). It is therefore possible to neglect differences in measuring the 'economic rent' and its change over time in this context. The rent increases when diminishing returns in exploiting land raise the real price of the products obtained.

Two developments have affected land rent in the USSR. There has been the necessity to expand agricultural production by extending or improving the land under crops through heavy inputs of labour and capital. These endeavours upped the cost on marginal soils (marginal for reason of quality or location) and correspondingly the economic rent on better acreage. Khrushchev started crop production on 'virgin lands' in the eastern regions of the country with an immediate increase in output but at enormous cost. Later, some of the lands had to be taken out of cultivation because of soil erosion and weed infestation. The Brezhnev administration, in turn, promoted soil amelioration through irrigation and similar measures. These advances and fallbacks are accounted for in a land input growing in the annual average by 2.4 per cent in the 1950s and by 0.6 per cent in the first half of the 1960s, declining by 0.3 per cent in its second half, increasing again in 1971–5 and remaining unchanged in 1976–80.

The second development is the operation of the law of diminishing returns in forestry, and above all in the extraction of minerals and similar resources. No doubt the Soviet Union, with its large expanse, has plenty of material resources but – after creaming off the best of them in past decades – much of what is available now is located far away in hostile climes or is of poor quality, and sometimes the two disadvantages are combined, as in the case of Siberian coal. Their extraction requires large investments in plant and equipment and in infrastructure; labour dislikes the jobs and the location; Soviet industry is ill-prepared to supply the advanced technology that the exploitation of such deposits requires; and innovative management is not exactly a Soviet forte. The USSR has its own energy squeeze, and other raw materials (iron ore, for example) are equally in short supply.

Poor productivity, a systematic problem

Productivity and the sources of growth are a knotty subject even in this country, after much investigation of a theoretical and statistical nature; they are by far more problematic in the case of the Soviet economy. And yet, while the details are murky, the picture as a whole is pretty clear. In comparison with other advanced nations Soviet productivity is low; over the decades productivity gains have always been minor, and sometimes there have been productivity losses instead of advances.

Earlier Soviet economic growth has been achieved with massive inputs. Labour inputs were heavy in the 1930s and they comprised large numbers of peasants unprepared for work in modern industries. It should be recognized that the Soviet regime has done a creditable job in improving the education and also the health of the masses. An illuminating CIA report draws attention to the employment even now of 'many older workers from peasant households with little formal training. About 22 per cent of the Soviet labor force has less than eight years of education, and less than 10 per cent has finished college.'[13] The same report substantiates 'impressive results' in education since the 1950s, notwithstanding a policy zigzagging between the goals of supplying labour in a rush or providing skills for long-range upgrading. The report arrives at a striking result: if educational improvements are deducted from factor productivity (using the weights arrived at by different scholars), the latter shrinks in the annual average of the 1960s (when GNP rose by an average 5 per cent) from 0.7 per cent to 0.1 or 0.2 per cent, in the years 1971–7 (GNP growth 3.8 per cent) – with educational advances declining (from 0.5 or 0.6 to 0.4 or 0.5 per cent) – from a negative 0.3 to minus 0.7 or 0.8 per cent.

Compare these figures with Denison's findings for the US. In the average of the years 1948–73, the American national income rose by 3.65 per cent, education by 0.41 per cent, and output per unit of inputs, not counting advances in education, by 1.52 per cent.[14] There lies the difference between an economy growing – at least until recently – at a goodly pace but practically only due to increases in inputs and with no productivity increase to speak of except in education, and another economy growing moderately, also with strong educational progress, but with still other sources of productivity growth advancing altogether more rapidly than inputs.

What explains the low and slow productivity of the Soviet economy? There may be national traits. The 'Russian soul' is expected to explain many things and may be invoked in this case (e.g., in regard to a Russian gigantomania). The USSR has vestiges of an underdeveloped country, and yet even the Tsarist Russia of the decades before 1914 was not what we call an LDC; its cultural achievements were outstanding, its industries booming, its infrastructure extensive. It was only less developed in comparison with the US or Western Europe. At any rate, more than half a century has elapsed since the Soviet state started its Great Leap into the modern industrial age; the country should be developed by now. What has hampered the enormous efforts and sacrifices of the Soviet people from being more productive is Stalin's '*sui generis* war economy'.

This has been the subject of copious literature. The analysis shows in detail how efficiency suffers in a command economy with autocrats at the top and a bureaucracy dominating the entire economy, not without plenty of infighting. Key factors include the all-pervading secretiveness; a price system that distorts scarcity relations; managerial incentives that reward plan-fulfilment irrespective of whether the plan makes sense and regardless of a wasteful use of labour, capital, land and material resources; managers reluctant to undertake innovations because they interfere with fulfilment of taut output goals; uncertainties in the flow of supplies (particularly of spare parts) in time and quality; the requirement to keep repairing obsolescent equipment; the temptation to start investments as empire-building ploys irrespective of whether they can be realized ('dispersion of funds' is still increasing despite decades of exhortation); a desire of enterprises to hoard labour, materials and machines irrespective of their under-utiliz-ation; and a tendency to oversize projects and organizations (Brezhnev: 'big is better') – a gigantomania that contrasts with the millions of agricultural dwarf holdings and miniature workshops in the 'second economy'.

The ineffective use of resources can be easily illustrated by a whole array of facts and figures. Suffice it to point out that, compared with American performance, the USSR applies in the production of each unit of GNP 2.75 times as much labour, invests twice as much capital, and uses 2.2 times as much land per unit of agricultural product. (The labour comparison includes civilian and military manpower, employed and unemployed.) In the USSR unemployment is not mentioned; it is probably small, and it needs repeating that in the eyes of Soviet workers stability in employment is regarded as a favourable feature of their society. They probably have not missed the opportunity to strike (whatever the legal situation), at least up to now, but such attitudes may change overnight.

The camps East and West

In its own alliance system the Soviet Union has an exceedingly dominant position. In terms of population figures, the Poles, by far the largest member of the Warsaw Pact, are 13.4 per cent as numerous as the Soviets, the Romanians 8.4 per cent, the East Germans 6.3, Czechoslovakians 5.8, the Hungarians 4 and the Bulgarians 3.3 per cent. The 1980 GNP ratios are similar: Poland 9.8 per cent of the Soviet GNP, East Germany 7.8 per cent, Romania 7, Czechoslovakia 6.6, Hungary 3.1 and Bulgaria 2.3 per cent. If the six East European nations were combined (but their animosities towards each other rule this out) they would represent 41.2 per cent of the Soviet population, 36.6 per cent of the Soviet GNP. The US role in its alliance is quite different, politically, demographically (each of the four major European NATO members has a population one-quarter that of the US), and economically (the US share in NATO's 1980 output was 51.7 per cent).

Disregarding the internal structure of each alliance system, NATO is considerably superior to the Warsaw Pact members, both demographically and economically. The population ratio has been unchanged since 1950 (birth rates are low everywhere); it is now

155:100 in favour of NATO. The NATO:Warsaw Pact GNP ratio was 379:100 in 1950; it is now 284:100, the decline chiefly attributable to the below-average economic growth of the US.

The East-West gap widens further when we add the other associates of the two superpowers, knowing full well that, when the chips are down, the nations that actually unite around their protagonist may differ from those with formal links, and that further changes are likely during protracted conflicts, whether these be diplomatic, economic or military. Let us include on the American side Australia and New Zealand, Japan and the Republics of China and Korea, on the Soviet side Cuba, Mongolia, Vietnam, Kampuchea and Laos (North Korea seems to be sitting on the fence in the Sino-Soviet rift). These additions raise the GNP gap between West and East to 347:100 and at the same time slow down the decline of the ratio over time (the ratio had been 386:100 in 1950), because the American partners in Asia belong to the fastest growing economies in the world. The West-East population ratio rises to 172:100.

Part Two: the Outlook for a Decade or Two

Adverse trends and possible offsets

The USSR has entered a period of faltering economic growth and irritating shortages. They are due to developments lowering both the quantity of available inputs, and also input productivity. Before discussing them, let us remember that history does not move of necessity, that 'fated' courses can be changed through countervailing measures or simply by happenstance, and that any system, whatever its overall efficiency, has ups as well as downs, elasticities as well as rigidities.

The adverse trends hindering present Soviet economic performance and threatening future growth can be summarized as follows:

● Labour as a factor of production will level off quantitatively as an after-effect of low birth rates in the past decade and a half; labour quality is also likely to suffer. Offsetting measures would require decisions transcending pure economics.

● Capital inputs have been and will continue to be modest because military demands have encroached upon capital formation and are likely to continue to do so. Moreover, the productivity of the investments is poor and transfers of Western capital funds and technology may fall off. Here again, any significant improvements would have to go beyond economics.

● Land inputs will be under the law of diminishing returns in extracting agricultural as well as industrial materials; bad weather may also take its toll. This negative statement would be mitigated by an unusually able implementation of technological and organizational advances, by unexpectedly good atmospheric conditions, or by lucky strikes.

● Net availabilities of resources from abroad may fall off because, politics apart, in relations with the West the terms of trade and finance will not be as favourable as in the 1970s. The Soviet orbit is likely to remain a burden, though the USSR will try hard to lighten the weight without losing control.

Productivity is not only a quality inherent in the labour force, the capital stock on hand, or in the land, it is, in addition, the result of general economic, social and political conditions. The case of Poland in the years 1979–81 shows how drastically the 'quality of life' can deteriorate, with the economy sliding downhill.

Disregarding the possibility of major social dissension and also major foreign conflicts, it is only prudent to assume that Soviet institutions, with some modifications here and there, will grind on. To be sure, the Soviet-type economy is less resourceful than an advanced market economy. Nevertheless, with its thousands of organizations, millions of economic agents and myriads of decisions in its first and also its second economy, its adaptability should not be underrated. The regime's instrumentarium is multiple enough to provide some relief in bottleneck situations without radical departures from customary institutions and policies.

It would be unwise, therefore, to anticipate a weakening of the country's status as a very great power, at least for the remnant of this century. Moreover, since power is relative, even a gain in strength is thinkable, for instance through disarray in the West or a Sino-Soviet rapprochement, improbable though such happenings may appear. Long-term trends will in any case alter the power weights of the nations of the world to the disadvantage of *both* the

US and the USSR *and* their major allies, in the wake of demographic developments now clearly visible.

Labour stringencies and their causes

The labour stringencies now worrying the Soviets can best be viewed in a broad demographic context. Soviet birth rates are low and death rates are creeping up. The rate of natural increase is currently 0.9 per cent per annum; it may possibly decline to 0.5 per cent towards the end of the century. The Soviet population, 265.5 million in mid-1980, would then number around 300 million, perhaps less rather than more. With 223.64 million Americans in 1980 and an expected 265 million by the year 2000, the Soviet-US demographic ratio would move from 116.6:100 in 1980 to roughly 113:100 at the end of the century. By then there may be 1.3 billion Chinese and 1 billion Indians (in 1980 1.03 and 0.68 billion, respectively).

There exists a North-South issue within the USSR (and in a more figurative sense, because of greater dispersion, also in the US and in other Western countries). While the rate of natural increase recedes in all parts of the Soviet Union, the decline is by far steeper in the Slav metropolis than in the colonized southeastern regions with non-Slav nationalities. Data for 1960, 1980 and (medium projection) for 2000 show the following trends: natural increase in the entire USSR from 17.8 to 9.4 to 5.5 per cent; in the RSFSR from 15.8 to 6.1 to 1.5 per cent; in Kazakhstan (by now with a Slav majority) from 30.6 to 17.6 to 10 per cent; in Uzbek SSR from 33.8 to 28.7 to 21.1 per cent. The share of three economic regions, Kazakhstan, Central Asia and Transcaucasus, in the Soviet population rose from 13.9 per cent in 1950 to 15.9 per cent in 1960 and 21.1 per cent in 1980; it may reach 27.4 per cent by 2000. In 1970 these regions supplied 18.4 per cent of all eighteen-year-old males – i.e, presumed inductees; the ratio is climbing past 20.6 per cent in 1980 and may reach 33 per cent by 2000.[15]

Muslims are numerous throughout the regions mentioned, though they can be found also in other parts of the USSR. Their share in the Soviet population rose from close to 11 per cent on the eve of the Second World War (an estimated 20.7 million Muslims) to almost 16 per cent (40 million) in 1975; it may be 30 per cent (90 million) by the turn of the century. Even if this forecast were on the high side, its implications are all-embracing and include the labour outlook, as will be shown presently.

Future birth rates will not affect the expected labour supply, all persons reaching working age as late as 1998 are already alive (we are excluding any calamitous increase in death rates from whatever cause). With 'working age' or 'able-bodied' defined as ranging from sixteen to fifty-nine for men, fifty-four for women (the range should perhaps be moved to somewhat higher ages), this broad age group expanded dynamically as a result of the usual postwar baby boom until 1973 (in that year the group increased by 1.85 per cent): then the rate declined to 1 per cent in 1980. During the four quinquennia of the 1980s and 1990s the working-age population will increase annually first by 0.3 and 0.34 per cent and then by 0.44 and 1 per cent respectively.

The civilian labour force is smaller than the working-age population. It excludes by definition armed forces personnel and, furthermore, millions who abstain from employment because they are students or disabled persons or housewives or members of the leisure class; their number exceeds that of elderly workers or working youngsters. What enters the production function, however, is not the labour force but the hours they spend at work. Man-hour statistics are precarious. Their average annual fluctuation has been, perhaps fortuitously, close to the change in the able-bodied population. Let us, therefore, use the percentages at the end of the preceding paragraph as an index for the prospective stringency in man-hours available (but this is an index which disregards major policy measures to add to the future labour supply or to reduce future demand for labour).

The stringency is and will be greater in specific vocations and locations. Mining, for instance, attracts workers in the USSR as little as elsewhere, despite extra pay. Regions with icy or burning climates are, of course, shunned; even bonuses cannot keep workers there for more than a few years. The constant turnover entails costs for travel and adaptation at the expense of productivity.

The USSR's southern nationality problem has vocational and locational aspects. Just as the Slav population sticks to the central portion of the country and preferably its large cities, the minorities native to Kazakhstan, Central Asia, and to some extent also the Transcaucasus are reluctant to leave their sunbelt, their traditional lifestyle, their linguistic surroundings and rural pursuits for the industrial districts farther to the north. The following figures highlight the implications for the labour market: in 1971–5 the three southern regions already supplied 32 per cent of the *increment* of able-bodied persons in the USSR. Between 1981 and 1995 their increments will be larger (125 per cent) than those of the nation as a whole, all the other regions providing increments much below those of previous years.

Measures to increase the labour supply

What remedies offer themselves? We have to start from the truism that, while commodities can be allocated, though with plenty of evasion, it would be hopelessly ineffective and costly to commandeer many millions of workers, to tell each of them what to do, and to keep him or her on the job. Therefore the Soviet labour scene has never conformed to the model of a command economy, not even under Stalin (except for the war years). On the supply side (to use a fashionable term) the labour market has been by and large free. There is, of course, compulsory military service. The workweek is regulated, as everywhere; inconveniently, the hours are even stipulated in the constitution (Brezhnev's own of 1977). There are, furthermore, quite a few peculiar institutions: workers are often pressed into 'voluntary' efforts; persons avoiding employment can be punished as 'parasites', unless they belong to the official leisure elite; there are labour camps, and so forth. In general, however, Soviets choose their places of employment and change them at will; in fact, they change them disconcertingly often. Such a spectacle would gladden the heart of a libertarian except that the demand side, in the shape of the government apparatus, state-owned enterprises and even so-called collective farms, is warped by bureaucratically planned targets, administrative prices, including wages, ordained incentives, and regulations for hiring and firing.

If under such conditions demographic developments level off the expansion of the working-age groups, the regime may practise supply-side economics by making it attractive to join the labour force; it may invite guest workers from abroad; extend workhours; demobilize soldiers; transfer bureaucrats to factories or farms; force individuals against their will to do specific jobs; or conversely utilize labour more rationally by turning the economy from planning and administering to a freer play of demand and supply.

More recourse to female labour does not promise a way out of Soviet scarcities because half of the labour force is already female. The slight decline of women's share in the labour force (from 51.2 per cent in 1960 to 49.6 per cent in 1980) reflects nothing but the redressed population balance after the war (ratio of women to men 54.8 per cent in 1950 and 53.3 per cent in 1980; the American ratio in 1980, 51.3 per cent). Still, a participation rate of 50 per cent instead of 49.6 per cent would add 0.6 million women to the workforce. In so far as female labour is deemed less productive or more inclined to work part-time (more women at work would lower overall productivity marginally), further normalization of the sex balance, i.e. more male labour, ought to improve average productivity in a minor way. In view of the low number of eighteen-year-old males, the armed forces may use more female personnel, but inevitably at the expense of civilian activities. Incidentally, the labour supply would suffer if the new measures to bolster the Slav birth rate (partially paid leave for working mothers, short workweek for them, etc.) were to succeed – but the effects will be minor because money alone (with little to buy) is not sufficient to stimulate interest in large families.

As in other countries, the senior citizenry increases as a percentage of the Soviet population. Income incentives and propaganda may draw elderly and likewise handicapped persons into employment. Since the best-qualified among them – numbering several millions – are already at work (many of them probably in the second economy), a higher participation rate would lower average productivity. The same applies if youngsters were to be turned from further education to jobs.

In past decades Western industrialized countries have accepted vast numbers of guest workers from backward areas, with beneficial as well as adverse effects. While foreign economic relations will be dealt with later, we may mention that immigration is an unlikely cure for Soviet labour deficiencies. East European governments, recently also the Vietnamese, are occasionally induced to send small contingents of their citizens temporarily to Soviet construction sites – a mere stopgap measure. Turkic herdsmen fled from Xinjiang over the Soviet border, adding to the USSR's Asian population. In general, foreigners steer clear of the communist commonwealth; Soviets, on the other hand, are eager to leave the country, and small numbers of them are from time to time allowed to do so.

What distinguishes the intra-Soviet North-South problem from that of the Western world is not only its national instead of international character, but a different behaviour of the less developed population. While Mexican or Turkish peasants are anxious to move to American or European cities, the traditionalist Soviet Asians prefer to stay put, even at the price of rural underemployment. Washington, Bonn, Berne or Paris, with a recession looming, are currently eager to stave off immigrants; Moscow wants to convince the Asians in its South that they ought to move North. If set into motion, this would cause in the industrial centres the usual problems of where to house the migrants, how to train them, how to overcome language barriers, and in what spirit to bring up the children. Productivity loss and human friction would be inevitable. The alternative – topical also in the West (but as a transnational issue) – is the location of new industries in Asian areas away from infrastructure in existence in the North, and with the further need to recruit unskilled and perhaps even unwilling labour.

In two ways the Soviet regime could add substantially to the supply of civilian man-hours, but both measures presuppose difficult decisions: they are a longer workweek and demobilization.

Khrushchev had reduced the workweek in 1956 from forty-eight to forty-six hours and then around 1960 to forty-one hours. Each workhour added now – after the required amendment of the constitution! – would increase the man-hour total by 2.4 per cent. In purely arithmetical terms the demographic shortfall during the present five-year plan could be offset at one strike (if a word odious to the government is permitted) by restoring half the workhours eliminated two decades ago. But life is not an arithmetical calculation. Extending the workweek would be most unpopular, particularly in a country where shopping and commuting are time-consuming and strenuous. The measure could be enacted only in an atmosphere of national emergency by a leadership capable of inspiring the populace. The same would be true of so-called voluntary overtime work on a larger scale. Even if the policy should not antagonize the workers, it would lower their productivity. In so far as they would be paid for additional hours, the workweek would speed up an endemic inflation.

In contrast to the productivity loss incurred by a longer workweek, demobilization would raise overall labour productivity. Since there is little prospect of the bear dwelling with the eagle, the dragon and other heraldic beasts, only a fraction of the armed forces personnel could possibly be discharged. Their total of close to 5 million men represents about 3.5 per cent of the civilian labour force; it is easy to calculate the one-time increment of the workforce by a discharge of 100,000 men or multiples thereof.

The problem would be complicated if the scarcity of eighteen-year-old Slavs and a desire to forestall what is called the 'yellowing' of the armed forces[16] were to lead to an extended military service for Slavs; this would worsen the imbalance between the regions within the civilian labour force. At any rate, discharge of soldiers is dependent on reduced international tensions and a Soviet willingness to compromise in foreign relations. If such a course were decided upon, the threat from abroad could not easily be used to rally the population in favour of longer workhours (but let us not underrate Agitprop).

Measures to reduce the demand for labour
Demobilization would increase the supply of civilian labour by curtailing the government's demand for military manpower. The system could also greatly reduce its demand for civilian manpower if it could improve its productivity. As mentioned above, it takes the USSR 2.75 times as much labour to produce one unit of GNP as the US; the corresponding ratio for the USSR versus Japan is 1.9 to one. Between 1960 and 1980 Japan's labour force grew in the annual average by only 1.2 per cent and its GNP nevertheless by 7.7 per cent; the corresponding rates for the USSR are 1.4 and 4.1 per cent. Thus there ought to be ample opportunity in the Soviet Union to produce a given output with less labour (and capital!) and to achieve economic growth despite a slow increase in the labour force.

The problem is how to make the enterprises cost-conscious and how to prevent the controlling administrations from interfering with managements once they are cost-conscious. Then, in regard to labour, enterprises would desist from hoarding labour as they now do in order to cope with sudden plan changes or 'storming' plan datelines, or the temporary transfer of employees for harvest work and to avoid the diseconomies of a high labour turnover. Enterprises would then shift attention in planning investments and factory organization from prestigious plants and machinery to equipments and arrangements for the humbler task of curtailing auxiliary work. The struggle to mechanize auxiliary activities had been going on for a very long time with very meagre results; a new endeavour is currently under way. In industry almost half of all employees are auxiliaries; this is less than the 55 per cent in 1959, but since in the meantime employment increased by close to 70 per cent, the number of auxiliary workers increased from 12 to 16–17 million.[17] In machine-building, with a fast-growing output almost half consisting of armaments, the ratio of basic to auxiliary workers is even worse. If the share of auxiliary employment in industry could be reduced by five percentage points, 2 million workers would become available, i.e., about 40 per cent of the manpower in military service. But this presupposes training of unskilled or half-skilled workers as well as investments in the right type of equipment. Given the Soviet industrial mentality, one could imagine a future factory with gigantic robots (in the USSR planners have just discovered that the robot age has begun in the West) and, milling around them, multitudes of workers with handcarts.

The labour force in Soviet agriculture is 8.3 times as large as that in America[18] but its output is only four-fifths that of the US, and this despite far larger investments in the USSR. Natural endowment plays a role, but the extraordinary difference is in the main due to organization and management. The age and sex structure of Soviet agricultural labour is also unfavourable. In the USSR young men try to escape rural life by moving to industrial cities; older men and women remain on the farms. In 1950 half of the Soviet labour force was still in agriculture; the share declined to 22.7 per cent by 1980. In absolute numbers the reduction was by one-third. But the US gets along with 3.2 per cent of its labour force in agriculture. Sovietologists expect the share to fall to 17–18 per cent by 1990; this would release 6 million workers in the course of the 1980s but also cause a further downward trend in the quality of farm labour – unless Soviet agriculture were radically restructured.

The foregoing considerations dealt chiefly with the number of persons in the future labour force and their workhours, though they touched occasionally upon the individuals' productivity. This latter feature blends different trends with what appears a downward trend overall. To be sure, entrants into the labour force will be better educated than future retirees with their instruction of years long past, except that schooling may be curtailed and pensioners called back, adding quantity at the cost of quality. The main depressant of productivity will be the larger number of minority entrants with educational and language impediments.

Social intangibles would lower overall productivity if the Soviet body politic were to manifest something akin to the Polish syndrome of the early 1980s. These are unpredictable eventualities. In addition, the Soviet population is afflicted by phenomena that seem to characterize an overregulated autocracy or, possibly, today's stage of the industrial society everywhere (though there may be as yet undiscovered causations). Environmental and professional diseases reduce the labour supply; so does rampant alcoholism; wrongdoings of all sorts from job shirking to serious crime have their cost in labour (not to mention materials). For the US we have Denison's estimate of the productivity-lowering effects of dishonesty and crime;[19] similar research does not exist for the USSR. The growth-depressing impact of all these negative phenomena must be substantial, but it has persisted for a long time and, in the absence of domestic disturbances, we need not conclude that it will worsen in the years ahead.

To sum up: past changes in the birth rate will curtail the growth of the Soviet working-age population at least until the late 1990s. The labour force will level off correspondingly unless remedial action is taken. Since the country's system squanders labour throughout, labour-saving measures could be taken on a very broad front. Some might be implemented with moderate efforts; many would require new outlays for equipment and training; most of them would run counter to engrained habits. If, minor relief apart, the system should prove as incapable of reform as heretofore, the regime would have to discharge soldiers or extend workhours. How would the population react? Willingly if the leadership (by policies resulting in further international tension) could convince the nation that it was in grave danger from foreign foes. This policy would, of course, rule out demobilization. Otherwise the masses would resent the return to longer workhours; and the Kremlin, in turn, would have to resort to old-fashioned repression dressed up with old-fashioned ideology. Andropov or, later on, a younger man in the mould of Suslov would be the right leader for either option.

Capital stock levelling off

The second largest force moving a nation's product, as represented in the production function, is the capital input. It is the capital stock's contribution to the annual output, and it must be replaced by constant additions to the stock in the form of investments. A declining rate of new fixed investments will after several years lower the quantity of the capital stock and also its quality – mere repairs keep obsolescent capital in service, reduce capital input and thus diminish economic growth. This is what has happened in the Soviet economy during the past twenty years. New fixed investment in plant and equipment – disregarding military procurement posing as capital investment (and without deflation for rouble depreciation) – grew by 11.6 per cent in the annual average of the 1950s (with a peak of 16 per cent in 1958), by roughly 6.5 per cent in the 1960s and the first half of the 1970s, and by only 3.5 per cent in their second half. The original average rate for the 1981–6 plan ranged from 2.1 to 3 per cent. But, to quote Finance Minister Garbuzov speaking to the Supreme Soviet on 17 November 1981: 'The plan for 1982 and for subsequent years of the Five-Year Plan envisages maintaining the volume of capital investments largely at the level of actual fulfilment in 1980.' In other words, Soviet investment policy was decided in favour of zero growth. Up to now the GNP increased continuously at rates below those for investments, but from now on, according to Gosplan chief Baybakov in his statement at the same opportunity: 'For the first time in the practice of national economic planning, increased preferential growth of national income compared with the growth of capital investments is planned.' Actually, in 1981–2 the national product grew by 1.8 and 1.5 per cent, investment by 3.8 and 2 per cent, i.e. the traditional pattern continued, though at rates close to zero.

Measures to improve capital productivity or increase investment

As in the case of labour, the question arises: what remedies offer themselves to alleviate capital stringencies? They might entail either less demand for capital (per unit of output) or an additional supply of investment funds. The leadership emphasizes currently the first alternative. Baybakov's new investment-output relation shows not only that the priority of guns and butter over economic growth continues, but that he nourishes the planner's eternal hope of gains in capital productivity offsetting shortfalls in investment volume.

Efforts to reduce the amount of capital required per unit of output have been unending. Enterprises are constantly exhorted to use their 'hidden resources', i.e., equipment and materials hoarded for unplanned events. Excessive use of materials and energy is deplored, together with the idleness of machinery in disrepair or simply for lack of supplies, and above all the 'dispersion' of capital funds. This often-used term refers to the widespread practice of enterprises and administrations beginning new projects before completing the ones under way or before ascertaining that equipment, materials and labour will arrive on time. More than twenty years ago Khrushchev gave Kosygin powers to reverse the 'dispersion' of funds. Kosygin had some success, but it was shortlived. Soviet statistics on unfinished investments show that the backlog in enterprises (collective farms are omitted) increased in the twenty-five years from 1955 to 1980 by an average annual 8.3 per cent, namely from 15 to 112.4 billion roubles. The latter amount equals roughly all investments of the Soviet economy outside the collective farms. Delays in capital construction occur under any system (it is sufficient to cite the special case of nuclear energy production in the US) but nothing comparable in size could be found in Western market economies.

While the leaders have called for a redress of shortcomings and wrongdoings throughout the decades, their admonitions have changed in style. Khrushchev's folksy expression was 'kick them in the pants'. Brezhnev displayed more decorum. Occasionally he browbeat his subjects (as in a severe statement on 27 November 1978); more recently he was merely mournful, at least in public. His recurrent use of the word 'complex' indicated that he was perplexed (a condition not limited to leaders in communist countries). If Coolidge called business America's business, Brezhnev's slogan for the USSR was 'The Economy must be economic.' In a 1981 speech he urged that: 'the whole economic mechanism must be brought into line with this requirement . . . we have still not managed to rid ourselves of the kind of indicators which . . . encourage squandering'.[20] The new plans 'envisage a considerable increase in bringing capital projects into operation, with a smaller growth in capital investments [smaller is zero!]. Nonfulfilment of plan tasks is sometimes covered up by alterations to the plan in the direction of reducing it.' Brezhnev was against such falsification:

Some may say that many of the issues raised have been reflected
. . . in the well-known Resolution on the Improvement of the
National Economic Mechanism. Indeed, that is so. But after all,
more than two years have passed and the Resolution is being
implemented slowly and halfheartedly.

What can we expect of these attempts at reform – or rather, since
the word reform has acquired a bad odour in the USSR after the
failure of Kosygin's reform of 1965, at 'improvements of the
economic mechanism'? Our main doubts arise from a failure to
recognize that 'the indicators which encourage squandering' are
part and parcel of the ideas and theories underlying the Soviet
system. Brezhnev's stance resembled that of a political figure in the
West who would wish to fight stagflation by ridding the economy of
market prices. Furthermore, the plaintive tone of his pronounce-
ment does not bode well for success. In Soviet practice it takes a
rousing campaign and dire threats to get some results; after a while
these peter out anyhow. Finally, in this world all changes are bought
at a price; adverse side-effects offset the benefits – often to a large
extent. This will be true for Andropov, as it was for his
predecessors.

If capital productivity during a plan period stipulating zero
growth for investments does not improve more than marginally,
might it be possible to add to capital formation at the expense of
public or personal consumption in order to fill particularly urgent
investment needs? Pent-up requirements exist to an extent surpass-
ing a volume of capital formation that, even with no further growth,
is very large indeed. The question is whether the directors of the
economy will be able to enforce investment priorities in favour of
the industries that are in urgent need of modern equipment and of
labour-saving devices (to free auxiliary manpower), to break series
of specific bottlenecks (a general overhaul of the railroad system
would have been economically preferable to the construction of a
costly Baikal-Amur mainline, which of course is not without
strategic value) and to strengthen the extractive activities in
agriculture and industry.

An arms-limitation policy would release not only labour for
civilian purposes but above all equipment, materials and organizational skills. With military procurement rising faster than the
accelerating national security expenditures as a whole, even a
decline in expansion, a mere delay in the time-schedule of strategic

programmes, would alleviate the investment stringency. Many small steps have a cumulative effect. The prospects of obtaining investment funds from saving at the expense of personal consumption are poor – unless there is a credible national emergency. Voices denouncing 'consumerism and petit bourgeois property consciousness' preach to the winds. In *Pravda* of 9 November 1981, a writer – who by Soviet standards probably leads a comfortable life – exposes 'The myth of the so-called "consumer society" . . . a mentality . . . killing that which is sacred in the human soul', namely, a delight in 'spirituality' (not to be confused with a penchant for spirituosity). The leaders know that this approach is quixotic.

Resources could only be shifted from consumption to investments if the weather were balmy and crops abundant for several years. The additional agricultural product could be used to satisfy a lively consumer demand (particularly lively as long as state store-prices are subsidized) and to absorb the excessive cash reserves in the pockets of the population; then hard currency and gold could be used to pay not for foreign foodstuffs but for Western capital goods. Curtailment of the output of consumer goods other than foodstuffs in anything but a national emergency would adversely affect the popular mood, and have an inflationary result. Soviet consumers are in need of 'supply-side economics'.

Diminishing returns on land

Land, in a literal sense the basis of all primary output and construction, plays a minor role in the production function (it is calculated at about 3 per cent of all input value). The USSR, as the largest country in the world, has plenty of real estate ranging in quality from excellent to poor, with economic rents correspondingly high or low or even zero. But in important respects its natural endowment is inferior to other large economies.

Soviet agriculture operates in a climatic and geological setting less productive than its American counterpart; this natural disadvantage is greatly worsened by the inefficiency of the Soviet system. To quote Brezhnev:

The experience of many years shows that weather unfavourable for agriculture occurs in our country virtually every other year. Hence it must be regarded not as the exception, but as a fairly normal and natural phenomenon of our climate. A number of practical conclusions are to be drawn from this.[21]

This, however, is more easily said than done. Meanwhile, the USSR has to import huge amounts of grain, chiefly for feed, and other foodstuffs (in 1981 to the tune of $12 billion!). These purchases are not meant as a systematic division of labour using comparative cost advantages, as was Tsarist Russia's practice of exporting grain in exchange for manufactured goods. The present Soviet quest for American grain is an expedient, which goes against the grain of the Kremlin. It creates political and strategic dependencies that the regime detests (the current American discussion on whether to hurt the farmers here or the consumers there will remain unforgotten in the USSR); moreover, grain preempts foreign exchange earnings that the Soviets would rather spend in Western markets for capital equipment (and these markets are less subject to Washington's decisions). Thus in years to come the USSR will renew its efforts to balance its domestic food balance through further investments on its capital-gobbling farms, perhaps through organizational changes within ideological limits, possibly – with due attention to popular moods – by raising the subsidized prices of meat and dairy products towards their cost prices. Unavoidable imports of grain will be financed through exports of industrial raw materials, one of which is gold – since Soviet manufactured goods do not sell in the West, with the important exception of arms.

There is, of course, no lack of industrial raw materials in the vast Soviet expanse, but their exploration, exploitation and distribution is, in general, costly – and it would be costly even if the economic system knew how to produce and use materials more efficiently. Among the raw materials which form the bulk of Soviet exports to the non-communist West there are two – or rather one group and one single product – that experienced a particularly strong price rise, namely, energy products and gold. Their world markets were bound up, at one time or another, with market controls. As an exporter of energy products the USSR profited greatly from the OPEC oligopoly; as an exporter of gold the Soviets got rid of the American monopsony that had fixed the international price at a very low level.

The natural energy endowment of the USSR cannot be compared with that of the chief OPEC members. The latter, and above all the Arab producers, continue to produce and ship their oil at extremely low cost prices. To these costs are then added two different types of economic rent: a land rent responding to a greatly increased world demand for energy products and a monopoly rent levied by an astutely directed cartel. In the USSR either the quality of the fuels or their location (or both) leave much to be desired. As a result, the rent component of its export prices is by far smaller than that of the OPEC members and, since Soviet costs are rising with the shift of output to the North and East (while the power of the cartel is no longer what it used to be), Soviet profits from exports are shrinking. The only potential windfall in energy sales might be in the prices the USSR charges the countries of its orbit – a topic to which we will return presently.

As long as the US enforced a price of $35 per troy ounce of gold, the Soviets may have spent more resources producing gold than they received selling it on the world market. Since then the gold price rose to astronomical heights; in 1980, after going beyond $800, it was even expected to crash through the $1,000 barrier. Platinum prices were dragged along with corresponding profits for Soviet exports. Current gold prices hover around $450, and although Soviet costs may be higher than those of South Africa, exports remain highly advantageous.

Foreign trade and capital flows

Since foreign economic relations concern surpluses and shortfalls in commodities and funds, i.e., in residues, their prediction is far more hazardous than forecasts for aggregate inputs and outputs. If this writer knew the exact gold price in a near future, he would turn his attention to more profitable pursuits than Sovietological fortune-telling. But it does seem certain that, without drastic change in international politics, foreign economic relations will not offer the USSR in years to come the very favourable circumstances of the 1970s. This does not mean that the Soviets will not find buyers for their wares, that they will not be able to purchase what they can afford (some Western trade controls notwithstanding) and that, the Kremlin willing, they could not meet obligations on time by dipping into their considerable gold hoards.

Assuming away any as yet unexpected windfall in the goods and services which the USSR offers, we can detect only one (not too likely) opportunity for lucre, namely, making the satellite countries pay world market prices for energy products and other Soviet goods. Ever since the oil crunch, Soviet client-states have been granted concessionary energy prices, which are only now being phased out. According to a recent calculation,[22] the six smaller Warsaw Pact countries – once exploited by the Kremlin – in turn exploited the USSR to the tune of about $100 billion between 1972 and 1981. If this analysis were correct, the Soviets would still have a windfall reserve that they could realize in years to come by ending their discounts. However, Eastern Europe (not to mention countries like Vietnam or Cuba) would not pay the USSR in freely exchangeable currencies but in their own and frequently undesirable products, or ask for loans. They may be able to increase their own prices; otherwise the additional cost would further destabilize greatly weakened satellite economies.

In its relations with the West, the USSR will be able to cater to a demand for raw materials, some semi-fabricated goods and armaments that will remain lively – though fluctuating with the business cycle and politics in general. The scenario of a USSR shifting from net exports to net imports of oil and oil products remains entirely improbable. Soviet energy products will continue to flow to the West, with the probable aid (in technology and funds) of OECD Europe and Japan, and even the US. But while the level of future prices and exchanges is hard to predict, particularly in a time of inflation, the terms of trade are not likely to yield the lucre of the 1970s. Soviet costs will be high, and the prices for Soviet imports will rise more or less in step with those for Soviet exports.

This latter statement may also apply to gold. Moreover the USSR profits from better prices for gold only inasmuch as it sells. The Kremlin could not unload gold on a rather fragile market without depressing the price, even conceding that its agents in the West, the gnomes of Zurich and other emporia, are astute brokers.

I will not endorse statistical extrapolations for the USSR's future foreign trade, nor could I attempt them. Such calculations have had very mixed results. In my musings I start from the proposition that the Soviet Union (disregarding the mid-1930s) has never been autarkic in principle but rather that, in practice, the system discourages easy relations with clients or suppliers abroad. Within these constraints Moscow tries to satisfy its urgent import requirements (political urgency – need for grain, for example – sometimes defeating economic desirability, e.g. for modern Western equipment), exporting whatever is in surplus and proves exportable. In other words, the Kremlin exports in order to meet obligations abroad rather than to keep export industries employed and profitable. Like any great power, the USSR wishes to avoid a vulnerability to foreign embargoes on its imports and exports, both for economic and prestige reasons. Even though history, and in particular Soviet history, shows that embargoes are very rarely effective (sometimes they are introduced for no other reason than to show one's displeasure), it must be Kremlin policy to thwart foreign trade control by lowering the threshold of its strategic vulnerability. For this reason we should not expect in years to come an expansion of real Soviet trade as fast as in the past two decades (between 1960 and 1980 the ratio of Soviet merchandise trade to GNP increased from about 2.8 to 5.2 to 100, as against a change from 3.6 to 9.2 per cent in the US). Such a strategy appears at least reasonable in future relations between East and West. If at the same time the USSR can combine useful foreign transactions with stratagems to make countries in Western Europe or the Third World dependent upon itself, it will certainly pursue such a course, assuming that such countries are not in turn intent upon avoiding vulnerabilities vis-à-vis the USSR.

In sum: the USSR will try hard to reduce its need to import grain in order to escape political pressures and to shift funds to the acquisition of Western machinery and other desirables. Whether such a policy succeeds will depend on weather conditions and, above all, on Soviet progress in agricultural organization and technology. On the export side, the USSR will continue its effort to develop its energy and other (e.g. timber) resources with the help of Western firms. This serves its economic interests, makes Western capital a potential captive of the Kremlin, and creates supply vulnerabilities in Western countries, while enabling the USSR in case of conflict to use its energy product within the Soviet bloc itself.

This likely scenario of a more moderate expansion of Soviet trade with preferential treatment of its own empire would, of course, undergo fluctuations depending on the world business outlook, and the degree of tension and unrest in the world. Both aspects will in any case influence the USSR's lucrative arms trade with less developed countries. Just as in the past the oil crunch benefited the Soviet Union not only through higher energy prices but also by making petrodollars available for OPEC purchases of arms (and some other goods) in the Soviet bloc, OPEC's future clout and success or failure will have a corresponding influence on the bloc's economic outlook.

I do not develop a scenario for highly turbulent East-West relations – whether they involve the Middle East or Europe or some other region. In such a case, even short of armed conflict between the great powers, governments would forcefully intervene in international trade and finance (this might include a Western attempt to embargo the purchase of Soviet gold); prices would be regulated; the demand for important goods subjected to priorities. With all economies converting to an emergency status, the Stalinist 'war economy *sui generis*' would command a headstart – to what advantage would depend on the character and length of the confrontation.

Future output and its structure

The downward productivity trends have affected the output rates and will continue to do so. But while an input-induced slowdown beginning around 1980 was expected, the slump came earlier than expected. The weather could not be blamed for it. To be sure, it was unfavourable in 1979 and in the next three years, and climatic conditions affect not only agriculture but to a lesser degree also construction and other activities carried out in the open air (or depending on agricultural materials). Nonetheless, farm output registered in 1971–5 a negative 0.4 per cent in the annual average; in 1976–80 it increased slightly by an annual average of 1 per cent. Comparing the first and second half of the 1970s, it was output in construction that dipped from 5.6 to 2.4 per cent and in industry from 5.9 to 3.6 per cent. In toto the GNP rate declined in the two quinquennia from 3.6 to 2.6 per cent, and in the last two years of the quinquennium even to 0.8 and 1.4 per cent. In 1981, despite a bad crop, there was a minor relief, with a GNP increase estimated at 1.8 per cent; but the estimate for 1982 is again a low 1.5 per cent.

When plan targets for the second half of the 1970s became known (and actually until 1978), Western observers of the Soviet scene expected a higher growth in 1976–80 than in 1971–5; the forecasts favoured a GNP growth of 4 per cent and more. Models offering a baseline case deemed 'reasonable', as well as alternative scenarios, showed little difference in these variations. A Soviet performance significantly below the preceding plan period 1971–5 was not anticipated. Nor are the reasons for the slump of recent years even now clearly understood. International tension following the invasion of Afghanistan and in the course of the Polish unrest has probably deflected resources from civilian sectors to the national security apparatus. Administrative and managerial flops may have bulged so that an inefficient economy fell below its usual level. The USSR, publishing fewer facts and figures than before, of course did its level best to obscure the situation. Sovietologists may draw some comfort from the fact that their colleagues forecasting the future of the US and other Western economies had also to feast on crow. Extrapolations rest everywhere on definitions and theories that may no longer conform to real life (example: how do we define money in the America of today); they use assumptions that prove wrong, while relevant assumptions are overlooked. Modern models are very sophisticated and elegant; you cannot live without them, but life with a model is not a bed of roses either.

Predictions of things to come are period pieces; the spirit of the times pervades them. Ten or twelve years ago they used to be upbeat; even the 1970s, a decade of malaise, had years (e.g. 1976) when rose-coloured glasses became sporadically fashionable. Currently, forecasters and their models are depressed. In 1977 reputable extrapolations for the US GNP foresaw for the second half of the 1970s an average annual GNP growth of 5.2 per cent. The actual rate was only 3.5 per cent. SOVMOD, the comprehensive model for the USSR developed since 1974 by Wharton Econometric Forecasting Associates (WEFA), University of Pennsylvania, and the Stanford Research Institute (SRI), came out in 1975–6 in its second-generation edition (SOVMOD II) with a baseline GNP rate of 4.7 per cent (alternatives 4.5 and 4.6 per cent). In a presentation early in 1978, SOVMOD III increased the rate to 4.8 per cent.[23] Actual growth, as mentioned above, was 2.6 per cent.

For the 1980s the Wharton model for the United States predicts an average annual GNP growth of 2.9 per cent in the first half, 2.7 per cent in the second half, and 2.8 per cent for the entire decade. There are projections of a similar range for the EEC. My hunch is that current projections are on the low side. SOVMOD IV[24] uses rates averaging 3.1 per cent up to the year 2000 (disregarding minute variations in the second decimal served up by the obedient computer). SOVSIM, CIA's econometric model, envisaged in a forecast published in 1977[25] a baseline rate of 3–3.5 per cent for 1981–5, with a best case 0.25 per cent higher and a worst case of 2–2.5 per cent. Forecasts in late 1982 operated with an average annual rate of 1–2 per cent. In other words, these extrapolations continue into the 1980s and 1990s the average rate of the 1970s (3.1 per cent), just as the forecasts early in the past quinquennium continued the 4.5 per cent growth rate of 1965–75.

An overall growth of slightly more than 3 per cent would still give the USSR an edge over the US and Western Europe – in the event that all these rates should materialize. The rate of 3.1 per cent implies that the malfunctioning and the dislocations of the most recent years (in transportation, primary materials output, etc.) will be straightened out and that climatic conditions will be neither worse nor better than in the very mediocre 1970s. If military allocations should continue along the path of the 1960s and 1970s, their share in the GNP would move up by 1990 to 16 per cent, a heavy burden, though not much different from the current 14 per cent or so. Since – in the absence of outright mobilization – the numbers of the armed forces personnel will not change greatly, arms procurement must exceed the 4–5 per cent growth rate significantly. The official five-year plan for machine-building and metal-working provides indeed an average annual growth of 7 per cent (originally 'no less than' 7 per cent) – an increase that does not account for considerable net machinery imports. While this is in line with Baybakov's promise of 'serious attention to retooling of all sectors of the economy',[26] it is in odd contrast to a zero growth in new fixed investment. This restraint in investment, of course, calls for correspondingly higher outlays for capital repairs, but patching up old equipment is not retooling. *The growth in machinery output must be indicative of the USSR's weapons policy.*

Zero growth in new fixed investment may be enforced for a short period; it would certainly be followed by years of intense demand for capital formation. Let us assume that in the 1980s as a whole total investment (including capital repairs and inventory changes) will move up by the annual 3.1 per cent which WEFA-SRI posited for the GNP – a new experience for the USSR, where investment always grew faster than overall production. Let us further assume that military expenditures will continue their 4.5 per cent annual rise, as throughout the 1960s and 1970 (according to the CIA). Let us finally disregard the impact of foreign economic relations on growth and structure of the GNP. Then – and this is simply an arithmetical finding – consumption would increase in the annual average by 2.7

per cent as a whole and by 1.8 per cent per head of the population. This would be a rather mediocre performance. Percentages by themselves do not tell the whole story; they have to be viewed against the background of shopping difficulties and the surplus cash reserves. People have rebelled at higher levels of per capita consumption, while other nations have remained quiet during many years of hardship. Currently Soviet dissatisfaction may be effectively deflected against a Poland considered ungrateful for all the USSR has done for it over the years.

The future of the system

The first alternative lacks drama. It looks as follows: international tension more or less as heretofore; and the regime, pointing to dangers from abroad, is able to persuade the nation that sacrifices are inevitable. The Soviet orbit remains quiet, if only from emotional exhaustion and awareness of Western do-nothingness. Productivity, as calculated the Western way, remains deficient, but small improvements here and there, overcoming the current bottlenecks to a degree, and a strenuous effort to increase inputs, above all on the labour front, increase the average GNP growth rates to 3 per cent or even somewhat more.[27] The regime mobilizes organizations and populace through 'socialist' campaigns as in past decades, but since their successes are bought with a lot of confusion and waste, the current administration, with a more sober approach, may spurn such brouhaha, mindful of Khrushchevian days. As a result of a more authoritarian style plus nationalist propaganda plus native passivity, all is quiet on the domestic front. Under such conditions the present political and economic system might toddle on for a lengthy time with minor adjustments in trouble spots. Trouble there would be, but the Soviet economy has been in trouble for two-thirds of a century and the Stalinist economic structure for fifty-five years. One might even quip that a nation fond of the bottle knows how to handle bottlenecks.

This first political-economic scenario does not prevent the regime from trimming in important respects. There may be periods of harsher foreign policy and more authoritarian rule but also – if the regime is temporarily less self-assured – periods during which the Kremlin tries to arrange itself with the outside world and on the domestic scene, as did Stalin's successors immediately after the death of the tyrant. It should be understood that neither alternative presupposes a greatly increased international tension nor, if the second approach is chosen, a headlong Soviet retreat. The Soviet Union will continue to act as a Great Power in the classical sense – barring conditions as in 1920! – and the West would probably be only too happy to arrive at a fairly moderate compromise.

Other alternatives may be strongly reformist or even revolutionary. In a number of cases the group in power has radically changed the economic system because it felt that without a thorough reorganization the state would not survive (Japan in the Meiji period). Or an opposition group evicted the representatives of the *ancien régime* and changed institutions that it held responsible for a time of troubles in state and economy. The opposition may speak for economic forces that are already in place but lack sufficient political recognition (the Third Estate in the France of 1789), or for a utopian ideology (Russia in October 1917). One day the Soviet order may be swept away under similar circumstances. This, however, is unforeseeable, and we are not at that point.

In fact, why should the USSR at the present time do more than tinker with its system? Ideology, a power as strong as religion in other cases, supports the existing system. The bureaucracy and the military thrive upon it. The managerial class is attuned to it (and knows how to circumvent it, whenever profitable). The elite has no reason to be critical, a few idealists excepted. The second economy and its official protectors exploit official inefficiencies. The masses appreciate their job security. The desire for more creature comforts has not yet taken on rebellious urgency nor has it been reinforced by demands for liberty or democracy. The danger of upsetting the applecart by introducing completely unaccustomed modes of management and administration is appreciated. The systems in other countries are not particularly attractive. Any drastic change would be particularly shunned at a time when a succession at the top has just taken place and the international scene is disturbing.

There are various other scenarios neither radical nor merely cosmetic. One such alternative would be a modernized version of Lenin's New Economic Policy (NEP), i.e. a retreat to a quasi-capitalist market economy, with the ruling elite still controlling the 'dominating heights' in industry, transportation and finance. There is, of course, quite a difference. Lenin, in an utterly shattered economy and at the end of his rope, permitted the still numerous representatives of a previous order to recapture some of their functions after only three years of Bolshevism. Are there potential NEP-men in today's USSR? Peasants or former peasants would probably be willing to manage private or semi-private farms. The second economy would provide entrepreneurs reminiscent of the rough businessmen of the nineteenth century, though they would be hedged in by modern labour legislation, the Party (or parties) and, perhaps, revitalized trade unions. A new middle class and also a new elite would develop and they might later storm the bureaucracy's 'dominating heights'. This would be the extreme version of such a scenario; a micro-NEP is thinkable, with modest free-enterprise features as in Hungary, Poland or East Germany.

A further scenario would be Titoist with a touch of Polish Solidarity: enterprises run by worker committees, though under government controls, and farms, either private (as in Yugoslavia and Poland) or semi-collective but with considerable autonomy. This order would clash with the decided aversion of the Soviet leadership (from Lenin to our time) against 'anarcho-syndicalism'; it would also – after a short period of enthusiasm – lead to badly run economic units and to centrifugal regionalism. Only a touch of worker participation is thinkable under strong centralistic controls.

Let me mention still another scenario, but one that is unlikely in the present century: a computerized economy with a shadow price system run by a handful of econometricians from an office of the Kremlin full of sophisticated equipment bought from Western firms on credit.

If I had to choose one of these scenarios on the grounds of likelihood, I would opt, with the next several years in mind, for the present system muddling through with cosmetic reforms and with periods of either greater harshness or greater willingness to make concessions. In the longer run I would not count on a Western-type democracy. I would rather expect strong-man rule over a rather inefficient economy. This could come about in the wake of the recent succession or by a palace revolution or after another time of troubles.

Table 3

Estimated Soviet GNP at factor cost, 1950–80, by sector of origin and by end use

(in billions of 1970 roubles)

	1950	1955	1960	1965	1970	1975	1976	1977	1978	1979	1980
Gross national product	115.4	153.1	205.1	260.6	338.2	406.3	423.8	438.4	452.2	455.8	462.2
By origin: of which											
Agriculture	33.6	41.0	50.0	56.4	69.4	62.6	67.9	69.9	71.1	67.2	64.4
Industry	20.2	33.4	53.2	73.1	99.2	132.4	137.3	142.9	147.9	152.3	157.5
Construction	6.2	10.7	17.9	23.0	30.1	38.9	40.1	41.0	42.0	42.4	43.4
Transportation	4.4	7.5	12.5	18.5	26.5	36.5	38.1	39.4	41.4	42.3	43.7
Services, etc.[a]	51.0	60.5	71.5	89.6	113.0	135.9	140.4	145.2	149.8	151.6	153.2
By end use: of which											
Consumption	73.6	97.4	125.8	153.3	195.9	235.1	241.7	250.9	257.7	264.9	270.7
New fixed investment	13.7	25.2	41.2	56.7	77.0	96.8	104.4	109.6	113.0	114.6	117.2
Capital repair	3.3	4.6	7.5	11.1	14.9	23.0	24.5	26.0	27.7	28.5	29.8
Remainder[b]	24.8	25.9	30.9	39.5	50.4	51.4	53.2	51.9	53.8	47.8	44.5

[a] Includes trade, communications, and unallocated items.
[b] Remainder includes defence, R&D, administration, inventory changes, the foreign trade balance (a minus item), and statistical discrepancy.

Source: Data derived and updated from Rush V. Greenslade's calculations published as 'The Real Gross National Product of the USSR, 1950–1975', in *Soviet Economy in a New Perspective* (1976). See also Appendix tables in Block, 'Soviet Economic Performance in a Global Context', in *Soviet Economy in a Time of Change*, vol. 1 (1979). For the latest data see USSR: *Measures of Economic Growth and Development 1950–1980* (Washington, DC: Joint Economic Committee, 8 December 1982).

169

Table 4

GNP for important countries and groupings, 1950–80; population and per capita GNP 1980

(GNP in billion 1980 dollars – per capita GNP in 1980 dollars – mid-year population in millions)

	GNP 1950	GNP 1955	GNP 1960	GNP 1965	GNP 1970	GNP 1975	GNP 1980	Population 1980	Per capita GNP 1980
Warsaw Pact total	457.12	601.28	795.71	997.35	1,269.34	1,535.40	1,745.47	375.00	4,655
USSR	323.12	427.97	573.48	728.55	945.44	1,125.44	1,280.14	265.50	4,822
Non-Soviet Warsaw Pact	134.00	173.31	222.23	268.81	323.90	409.95	465.32	109.50	4,250
Other Soviet associates[a]	16.45	20.32	25.61	32.18	39.62	30.79	35.80	74.21	482
PRC (mainland China)	84.99	142.74	173.03	219.66	311.30	436.82	591.65	1,032.06	573
NATO total:	1,622.84	2,040.21	2,419.14	3,051.65	3,687.44	4,214.23	4,951.90	578.50	8,560
of which: US	958.99	1,176.21	1,318.62	1,652.39	1,925.05	2,159.11	2,556.71	227.64	11,231
NATO-Europe	602.37	784.64	1,004.01	1,271.97	1,601.74	1,850.56	2,158.31	326.87	6,603
Pacific allies[b]	149.46	215.35	303.96	463.03	752.22	948.20	1,204.19	192.28	6,263
of which: Japan	91.90	143.65	216.48	349.18	595.16	746.41	955.31	117.03	8,163

[a] 'Other Soviet associates' are Cuba, Mongolia and Vietnam, which in turn has a hold over Kampuchea and Laos.
[b] 'Pacific allies' refers to Japan, Australia, New Zealand and the Republics of China and Korea.

Source: Block (1981). This report explains the statistical procedures used to arrive at the figures in the table. The author prefers the above estimates to recently revised series in CIA's Handbook of Economic Statistics 1982.

Table 5

Estimated rates of growth of Soviet GNP and its subdivisions, 1950–80, with an international comparison

(Average annual or annual rates in per cent)

	1950–5	1955–60	1960–5	1965–70	1970–5	1975	1976	1977	1978	1979	1980
Gross national product	5.8	6.0	4.9	5.4	3.7	1.8	4.3	3.4	3.2	0.8	1.4
By origin: of which											
Agriculture	4.1	4.1	2.4	4.2	-2.1	-8.8	8.5	2.9	1.7	-5.8	-4.4
Industry	10.6	9.8	6.6	6.3	6.0	5.9	3.7	4.1	3.5	3.0	3.4
Construction	11.5	10.9	5.1	5.5	5.3	5.0	3.1	2.2	2.4	0.9	2.5
Transportation	11.3	10.8	8.2	7.5	6.6	6.2	4.4	3.4	5.1	2.3	3.3
Services, etc.	3.5	3.4	4.6	4.8	3.8	3.3	3.3	3.4	3.2	1.2	1.1
By end use: of which											
Consumption	5.8	5.3	4.0	5.0	3.7	3.9	2.8	3.8	2.7	2.8	2.2
New fixed investment	13.0	10.4	6.6	6.3	4.7	3.2	7.8	5.0	3.1	1.4	2.3
Capital repair	6.9	10.3	8.2	6.1	9.1	8.9	6.5	6.1	6.5	2.9	4.6
Population	1.7	1.8	1.5	1.0	0.9	0.9	0.9	0.9	0.9	0.8	0.8
Per capita consumption	4.0	3.4	2.5	4.0	2.7	2.9	1.9	2.9	1.8	1.9	1.4
Warsaw Pact total	5.6	5.8	4.6	4.9	3.9	2.4	4.3	3.4	3.2	1.0	1.1
Of which: non-Soviet Pact	5.3	5.1	3.9	3.8	4.8	4.1	4.3	3.4	3.3	1.7	0.2
NATO total:	4.7	3.5	4.8	3.9	2.7	-0.8	5.5	3.8	3.9	2.8	0.5
Of which: US	4.2	2.3	4.6	3.1	2.3	-1.0	5.6	5.1	4.4	2.3	-0.2
NATO-Europe	5.4	5.1	4.8	4.7	2.9	-0.9	5.2	2.5	3.2	3.4	1.4
Japan	9.3	8.5	10.0	11.3	4.6	7.0	-0.2	8.2	11.6	7.1	5.0

Sources: As for tables 3 and 4.

Table 6

Total population, working-age population and labour force in the USSR

(mid-year data in millions)

	1950	1955	1960	1965	1970	1975	1980
Population	180.1	196.2	214.3	230.9	242.8	254.4	265.5
Working-age population	103.3	114.7	119.5	124.1	131.7	144.4	155.5
Labour force	97.6	104.9	110.1	116.5	125.6	135.8	146.1
By sex: male	n/a	n/a	53.2	56.4	61.3	67.4	73.6
female	n/a	n/a	56.9	60.1	64.3	68.4	72.4
By occupation:							
Agriculture	50.2	49.4	45.4	40.0	37.5	34.9	32.2
Industry	15.3	19.0	22.6	27.5	31.6	34.1	36.9
Others, incl.							
armed forces	32.1	36.5	42.1	49.0	56.5	66.8	77.0

Source: Stephen Rapawy, 'Estimates and Projections of the Labor Force and Civilian Employment', in *The USSR 1950 to 1990* (1976), tables 1, 9, 10. See also Murray Feshbach, 'Population and Labor Force', Appendix table I, in Bergson and Levine (eds) (1983).

Table 7

Soviet foreign trade and its geographic distribution, 1955–80

(in millions of current dollars)

	1955[a]	1960	1965	1970	1975	1976	1977	1978	1979	1980
Exports										
Total	3,247	5,558	8,166	12,787	33,401	37,269	45,227	52,395	64,913	76,470
Communist countries	2,723	4,209	5,554	8,359	20,271	21,890	26,009	31,244	36,152	41,463
of which: Eastern Europe	1,792	3,071	4,548	6,752	16,494	17,432	20,762	24,910	28,380	32,216
PRC	748	816	191	25	129	239	161	241	268	294
Western world	704	1,348	2,612	4,428	13,130	15,378	19,219	21,151	28,761	35,006
of which: developed	544	996	1,473	2,414	8,382	10,269	12,226	12,932	19,586	24,427
less developed	112	353	1,139	2,014	4,748	5,109	6,993	8,219	9,175	10,579
Imports										
Total	3,061	5,623	8,050	11,720	37,070	38,212	40,926	50,795	57,961	68,477
Communist countries	2,418	3,977	5,605	7,630	19,415	20,088	23,354	30,495	32,801	36,424
of which: Eastern Europe	1,663	2,792	4,668	6,627	15,723	16,261	18,839	24,661	26,751	29,407
PRC	644	847	225	22	150	179	177	257	241	230
Western world	642	1,645	2,444	4,089	17,654	18,123	17,573	20,300	25,160	32,053
of which: developed	431	1,098	1,620	2,814	13,473	14,360	13,416	16,228	19,718	24,211
less developed	210	547	824	1,275	4,181	3,763	4,157	4,072	5,442	7,842

[a] In 1955 Eastern Europe included not only the six smaller Warsaw Pact members but also Albania; for that year Cuba was part of the less developed Western world.

Sources: For 1955: *Annual Economic Indicators for the USSR* (1964), p. 104. For 1960–80: *Handbook of Economic Statistics 1981* (1981), table 58.

173

Notes

1 Seweryn Bialer, 'Politics and Priorities', in Bergson and Levine (eds) (1983), forthcoming.

2 ibid.

3 Earl R. Brubaker discussed the problem in an article, 'The Opportunity Costs of Soviet Military Conscripts', in *Soviet Economic Prospects for the Seventies* (1973), pp. 163–74.

4 *USSR: Toward a Reconciliation of Marxist and Western Measures of National Income* (1978), p. 13.

5 Furthermore, the share of investments in the Soviet GNP may be slightly lower than indicated, perhaps by one percentage point. If the capital stock data of the Soviets are derived from their investment statistics (and not from an unrelated survey of enterprise assets), then capital stock values would also be exaggerated. This, in turn, would overstate the services derived from the stocks and thus the estimate of capital inputs entering Western computations of the Soviet production function. It would, finally, lead to a modest undervaluation of Soviet output per unit of inputs, i.e., productivity both in relation to the capital in operation and to all factors of production combined.

6 Quoted from *Dimensions of Soviet Economic Power* (1962), pp. 416 and xvi.

7 See *Handbook of Economic Statistics* and *Communist Aid Activities in Non-Communist Less Developed Countries, 1979 and 1954–79* (1980).

8 Edward Hewett, 'Foreign Economic Relations', in Bergson and Levine (eds) (1983).

9 See the article by William Carr on 'The Soviet Merchant Fleet', in *Soviet Economy in a Time of Change*, vol. 2 (1979), pp. 663–77.

10 Quoted in my article in *Soviet Economy in a New Perspective* (1976), p. 246, after the German translation of Kjellén (1916), pp. 204 and 161.

11 Bergson, *Productivity* (1978), p. 122.

12 Murray Feshbach and Stephen Rapawy, 'Soviet Population and Manpower Trends and Policies', in *Soviet Economy in a New Perspective* (1976).

13 *USSR: Trends and Prospects in Educational Attainments 1959–85* (1979), p. iii.

14 Denison (1979), table 8–1, p. 104.

15 The US has a rich literature on Soviet population and labour force, with Murray Feshbach's research leading the field. I have drawn on facts and figures in the following papers: Murray Feshbach and Stephen Rapawy, 'Soviet Population and Manpower Trends and Policies', in *Soviet Economy in a New Perspective* (1976), pp. 113–54. Murray Feshbach, 'Prospects for Outmigration from Central Asia and Kazakhstan in the Next Decade', and Stephen Rapawy, 'Regional Employment Trends in the USSR: 1950 to 1975', both in *Soviet Economy in a Time of Change*, vol. 1 (1979), pp. 656–709 and 600–17 respectively. Three papers by Murray Feshbach: *Employment Trends and Policies in the USSR* (1978); *Population and Labor Force*, prepared for the Airlie House meeting on 'The Soviet Economy: Toward the Year 2000' and, like all contributions for this conference, some of them referred to in other notes, published in Bergson and Levine (1983); *Demography and*

Appendix I: Notes

Soviet Society: Social and Cultural Aspects (1981). See also Christopher Davis and Murray Feshbach, *Rising Infant Mortality in the USSR in the 1970s* (1980), and *Estimates and Projections of the Labor Force and Civilian Employment in the USSR 1950 to 1990* (1976); Godfrey S. Baldwin, *Population Projections by Age and Sex* (1976); S. E. Wimbush and D. Ponomareff, *Alternatives for Mobilizing Soviet Central Asian Labor: Outmigration and Regional Development* (1979); Jeremy Azrael, 'Mass Expectations and Regime Performance', in Bialer (ed.) (1981).

16 Murray Feshbach in *Soviet Economy in a Time of Change*, vol. 1 (1979), p. 690.

17 Murray Feshbach and Stephen Rapawy in *Soviet Economy in a New Perspective* (1976), p. 140.

18 See article by Douglas B. Diamond and W. Lee Davis, 'Comparative Growth in Output and Productivity in the US and USSR', in *Soviet Economy in a Time of Change*, vol. 2 (1979).

19 Denison (1979), pp. 73-4.

20 Brezhnev's speech of 16 November 1981 at the CPSU Central Committee plenum.

21 ibid.

22 Vaňous and Marrese (1980), table 4. The Soviet loss is arrived at with world opportunity prices in mind; the orbit may pay high prices for Soviet armaments.

23 For SOVMOD II see Green, Klein and Levine (1975), and the article by Green, Guill, Levine and Miovic, 'An Evaluation of the Tenth Five-Year Plan Using the WEFA-SRI Econometric Model of the Soviet Union', in *Soviet Economy in a New Perspective* (1976), pp. 301–31. SOVMOD III quoted from Green (1980), table 2.

24 Quoted from Daniel L. Bond and Herbert S. Levine, 'An Overview', in Bergson and Levine (eds) (1983).

25 Quoted from *Soviet Economic Problems and Prospects* (1977), p. 17.

26 The original plan goals of the current five-year plan were published on 5 March 1981 as 'The Basic Guidelines for the Economic and Social Development of the USSR for 1981–5 and for the Period Through 1990'. Most of them were scaled down in the statement of Gosplan chief Baybakov on 17 November 1981, machine-building an exception.

27 The average annual GNP increase of slightly over 3 per cent in the baseline case of WEFA-SRI rests precariously on the assumption that total factor productivity would rise by a yearly 0.74 per cent in 1981–5 and 0.95 per cent in the following ten years. WEFA-SRI presents a Scenario A with a more sombre outlook resulting from a productivity rate of only 0.2 per cent. It yields a GNP growth of 2.1 instead of 3.1 per cent, and an annual increase in per capita consumption of 0.5 instead of 1.2 per cent. Bond and Levine consider this 'a "crisis scenario" for the domestic economy' ('An Overview', in Bergson and Levine (eds) (1983), forthcoming). With such a standstill in welfare the regime would indeed have arrived at a moment of truth. Productivity calculations are, unfortunately, fragile. CIA arrives for the 1970s at an annual GNP growth of 3.2 per cent with a factor productivity of minus 0.6–0.7 per cent. (*Handbook of Economic Statistics 1981* (1981), table 43.) Abram Bergson's hypothetical rates of growth require for a 3.3 per cent GNP growth in the 1980s a productivity growth of 1 per cent. If the latter were zero, GNP would increase by only 2.3 per cent (Bergson, *Soviet Economic Prospects Revisited* (1978), table 2). Whatever the exact figures, the Soviet regime is faced with and will continue to face very grave decisions, with opportunities for improvements and occasions for errors.

The Evolution of Soviet Military Power Since 1965

by W. Seth Carus

Strategic- and Theatre-nuclear Forces

Intercontinental (land-based) ballistic missiles (ICBMS)

The most important weapons in the Soviet Union's arsenal of offensive strategic-nuclear forces are the land-based intercontinental ballistic missiles. Though the Soviet Union developed an ICBM of sorts by 1956, long before the United States, technical and industrial problems delayed the large-scale deployment of ICBMs for several years. By 1965, at a time when the United States already had 854 ICBMS, the Soviet Union only had a total of 224, many of a design already obsolescent. Throughout the late 1960s, the Soviet Union devoted considerable efforts to the improvement of the ICBM force, and by 1970 it had acquired a total of more than 1,400 ICBMS of five different types. After this vast expansion, the Soviet Union slowed the rate of deployment, and in 1975 the ICBM force stood at just under 1,600. By then, however, a new generation of ICBMs had been introduced – the SS-17, SS-18 and SS-19s – all with multiple-warhead systems and good accuracy potential.

The overall size of the ICBM force declined during the late 1970s from just under 1,600 to just under 1,400. This decline obviously reflected a Soviet decision to increase the strength of the sub-marine-based ballistic missile force at the expense of the ICBMs, in anticipation of an overall SALT ceiling.

The decline in numbers had been more than offset by the significantly greater throw-weight of the new generation of missiles. Since the new ICBMs can launch heavier payloads, they can carry more warheads (of large yields) than the older missiles removed from service. The SS-17, which is deployed in silos originally built for the SS-11, has a payload (or 'throw-weight') of 6,000 pounds as compared to less than 2,000 pounds for the SS-11; it can carry four

900-kiloton warheads as compared with only one 1- to 2-megaton warhead for the ss-11. (There is also a second version of the ss-17, with only one 5-megaton warhead, but probably it has not been deployed operationally.) With a throw-weight more than double that of the largest American ICBM (the obsolete Titan II), the ss-18 is easily the largest and most powerful ICBM in the world. It has appeared in several versions, including two versions with single warheads (of 18 to 25 megatons), and one with a multiple-warhead system for eight or ten warheads (of up to 2 megatons each). It is the latter version that generated especial concern in the United States, since the megaton yield and accuracy of the individual warheads, and the large number of warheads on these missiles, would make it theoretically possible for the Soviet Union to attack and destroy most American ICBM silos using only the ss-18 force.

The ss-19, the third of the new-generation missiles in service, has been deployed in two versions, one with a single 5-megaton warhead and the other with six 550-kiloton warheads (most now in service are of the multiple-warhead version). Like the ss-17, the ss-19s have been put into modified ss-11 silos; unlike the ss-17 (or ss-18) the ss-19 still uses the 'hot launch' technique (whereby the missile's boost engine is ignited inside the silo – which means that extensive repairs would be needed before a new missile could be placed into the silo). With the 'cold launch' technique of the ss-17s and ss-18s, on the other hand, the boost engine is ignited only after the missile is ejected from the silo. This makes it much easier to reload the silo (and it is believed that the Soviet Union has stocks of additional ss-17s and ss-18s).

The effectiveness of ballistic missiles is a function of the energy yields of the warhead(s) and of the accuracy with which they can be delivered. Originally, the Soviet Union relied upon large missiles fitted with single, large-yield warheads, since accuracies were very low (e.g., the 5-megaton ss-7, whose median inaccuracy was of the order of 3 kilometres). The Soviet Union has made considerable progress in improving the accuracy of ICBMs but the original large-payload configurations have been retained. As a result, the hard-target effectiveness of the Soviet ICBM force (i.e. its ability to attack targets protected to withstand nuclear attack) is high, since the new-generation missiles can deliver several very powerful warheads with great accuracy (300 metres and less median inaccuracy).

Before the new-generation of ss-17s and ss-19s were placed in the silos that formerly housed the ss-11s, their passive protection was upgraded to improve survivability against blast and other effects of nuclear detonations. It is believed that Soviet ICBMs now have protection equivalent to that of the best-protected American missiles (up to 2,200 pounds psi). Since the ICBMs of the United States are fitted with very small (albeit accurate) warheads, the new passive defences of the Soviet ICBMs have considerably reduced their vulnerability to a counterforce attack.

Submarine-launched ballistic missiles (SLBM)

During the early 1960s, while the American SLBM force was growing rapidly, Soviet SLBMs were primitive, and carried on equally primitive Golf and Hotel submarines, each with three SS-N-4 or SS-N-5 missiles. The Golfs are diesel-electric submarines, and though the Hotels were nuclear-powered, they were in no sense comparable to the American Polaris SSBNs, being greatly inferior in endurance, survivability and navigation accuracy. It was only in the late 1960s that the Soviet Union began to produce the Yankee-class submarines with a Polaris configuration. Thirty-four Yankees were built, each with sixteen SS-N-6 missiles. The rapid production of the Yankee type enabled the Soviets to increase their SLBM force from 120 short-ranged and surface-launched SS-N-4 and SS-N-5 missiles in 1965 to a force of 757 SLBMs in 1975, with only about eighty of the older missiles remaining in service. Even before the Soviets ended production of the Yankee class, they had started producing a new, larger SSBN, the Delta. This class remains in production, though it has appeared in three different versions: first as the Delta I with twelve SS-N-8s (eighteen or nineteen of these were built), then as the Delta II with sixteen SS-N-8s (of which only four were built), and currently as the Delta III with sixteen of the larger SS-N-18s (of which thirteen are operational, with more under construction). During 1980 the Soviets launched the first of a new class of SSBN, the Typhoon. Though not yet operational, it is the largest submarine in the world, and will carry twenty of the new SS-N-20.

During the last seven years the Soviets built thirty new SSBNs, and by 1980 they had more than 940 SLBMs. This massive construction effort has enabled the Soviets not only to expand the number of available SLBMs, but also to deploy newer missiles with longer ranges and a greater number of warheads. Thus, while in 1975 the ss-n-6 with a maximum range of 3,000 kilometres predominated, by 1980 almost half the missiles were ss-n-8 or ss-n-18 types with ranges of up to 9,100 kilometres. In order to stay within the limits defined by the SALT negotiations (62 boats, 950 SLBMS) the Soviet Union has had to remove some SSBNs from service: all the Hotels have been converted to other uses (though the older Golfs, not covered by SALT limits, remain), and many of the Yankees are being converted from SSBNs to attack submarines. Currently, only twenty-nine or thirty Yankee SSBNs remain operational, including one armed with sixteen of the experimental ss-n-17. As additional Delta III and Typhoon types enter service, more Yankees will be converted, and with this, the overall capability of the Soviet SLBM force (and the attack-submarine fleet) will continue to expand.

Manned bombers

Along with the Strategic Rocket Force and the Soviet navy's SLBMS, the Soviet Union also operates a small strategic bombing force. During the late 1940s and early 1950s the Soviet Union built several hundred strategic bombers, mostly Tu-4s copied from the American B-29. In 1955 the Soviet Union stage-managed a major deception operation which convinced the United States that it was building large numbers of two new classes of bomber (the jet-powered Mya-4 and the turbo-prop Tu-95), but in fact only small numbers (under 200) were ever produced. As a result, in 1965 the Soviet Union only had a small force of strategic bombers and those were of very restricted capability. During the 1960s and early 1970s, the Soviets concentrated their efforts on ICBM and SLBM production, and built no new strategic bombers. It was not until 1975 that a new bomber with a strategic capability began to enter service. This aircraft, the supersonic Backfire, has stirred much controversy in the United States, because it was not included in the terms of the SALT negotiations as a strategic weapon even though it evidently had sufficient range to function as an intercontinental weapon. Even with the Backfires, the bomber force provides only a small portion of Soviet strategic nuclear capabilities, and this is the one area where the Soviet Union is still inferior to the United States. The Soviet Union, however, is developing a new class of bombers, which appear to be similar in design to the American B-1. Currently known in the West by the codename Ram-P, this new aircraft would give the Soviet Union a supersonic bomber comparable to the best American system if and when it became operational.

Strategic air defences

Unlike the United States, the Soviet Union devotes considerable resources to defences against air attack. The Soviet Union has the world's most complete air-defence system, which includes an enormous number (12,000±) of surface-to-air missiles (SAMS), as well as some 2,600 manned interceptors. While the number of SAMS has increased since 1965, the numerical change is not substantial. Far more important has been the qualitative upgrading as older missile systems, the SA-2 and SA-1, are being replaced by newer weapons. Among these the SA-X-10 is the most advanced, and reputedly it has a (limited) ability to intercept cruise missiles – very exacting targets indeed. In contrast to the slow growth of the SAM force, the number of interceptors has decreased dramatically, from 3,800 in 1965 to only 2,500 in 1981. Along with the numerical decline, there has been a very major qualitative improvement, since the new aircraft types, especially the MiG-23s and MiG-25s, are far superior to the MiG-17s, MiG-19s and Yak-25s that they have replaced.

The Soviet Union has also upgraded its air defence command and control system. Additional radars have been added, including some advanced over-the-horizon 'backscatter' radars. These are supplemented by several early warning satellites. The Soviets also have about ten Tu-126 Moss airborne early-warning aircraft, similar to – but considerably less capable than – the American E-3A AWACS. Because of the proximity of the Soviet Union to potential conflict areas in Europe, the Middle East or China, these defences also serve to protect the Soviet Union in the event of a conventional or even a limited nuclear conflict.

Soviet anti-ballistic missile defences are still now limited by treaty to a small network comprising thirty-two ABM-1 Galosh missile launchers deployed around Moscow. This system is too small, and presumably too ineffective, to have any impact on the strategic nuclear balance. During the past few years the Soviet Union has removed from service another thirty-two ABM-1 launchers, but it is presumed that they will be replaced during the next few years by a new system using the SH-4 long-range and SH-8 short-range missiles. In addition, the Soviet Union has made a considerable effort to develop advanced directed-energy weapons, including lasers and particle-beam devices for use against ballistic missiles. For the present, however, neither the United States nor the Soviet Union has an operational capability in this area; nor is it considered likely that either country will have such a capability until late in the 1980s at the earliest.

Theatre-nuclear forces
The Soviet Union has supplemented its strategic-nuclear forces (aimed primarily at the United States) with a substantial theatre-nuclear force, directed at Western Europe and China. During the 1950s, theatre-nuclear forces had a much higher production (but not development) priority than intercontinental nuclear forces. Medium-range (Tu-16) bombers able to reach Western Europe were built in large numbers (900+), while only a few strategic bombers ever entered service. Similarly, some 600 medium-range ballistic missiles (MRBMS) and intermediate range ballistic missiles (IRBMS) were built, but only a handful of ICBMs. By 1965 the Soviets had a force of several hundred IRBMS and MRBMS, all but a handful of which were aimed at Western Europe, as well as almost 900 medium bombers.

After 1965 Soviet priorities changed, and the production of theatre-nuclear weapons sharply declined. While considerable efforts were devoted to the improvement of intercontinental forces, the only new theatre-range weapons procured before 1975 were a small number of Tu-22 bombers (a supersonic aircraft but of small value). This phase ended in the mid-1970s with the introduction of two new weapons: the Backfire bomber and the SS-20 missile. The Backfire has been produced in small numbers, but the same is not true for the SS-20. The SS-20 is a mobile missile with a 5,000-kilometre range and carries three warheads. By the middle of 1981 some 250 SS-20 launchers were in service, each launcher being given two missiles. Deployment is proceeding at a rapid pace, and by the end of 1981 the Soviets had about 270 operational SS-20 launchers with a total of about 550 missiles and 1,650 warheads.

Most Soviet theatre-nuclear weapons are deployed for use against NATO. Of the 700 SS-4 and SS-5 missiles operational during most of the 1960s, all but about seventy were aimed at targets in Western Europe. The same was not true of the bomber force. Since it is easier to redeploy aircraft, it was always possible to use the same bombers against China or NATO. Many SS-20s are now being deployed along the Chinese border, and the Soviets now have about 110 missiles of all types deployed east of the Urals.

The Soviets have other weapons that can now fire or carry nuclear weapons. There are a large number of short-range ballistic missiles of the Frog-7 (70-kilometre range), Scud (300-kilometre range) and SS-12 Scaleboard (900-kilometre range) types. These older systems, first deployed in the middle of the 1960s, are now being replaced by three new missiles: respectively the SS-21, SS-22 and SS-X-23. Little is publicly known of any of these systems. Some artillery pieces can also fire nuclear weapons. More important are the strike aircraft of the Soviet air force, in particular the new Su-24 Fencer and MiG-27 Flogger strike aircraft, but all tactical strike aircraft are now nuclear-capable. Finally, some older SLBMS, especially SS-N-5 missiles deployed on Golf and Hotel submarines, could easily be used against targets in Western Europe.

Table 8

Strategic nuclear weapons delivery systems

	1965	1970	1975	1980
ICBM				
ss-7	?	190	190	0
ss-8	?	19	19	0
ss-9	0	228	288	0
ss-11	0	970	960	580
ss-13	0	20	60	60
ss-17	0	0	10	150
ss-18	0	0	10	308
ss-19	0	0	60	300
Total	224	1,427	1,597	1,398
SLBM				
ss-n-4	?	27	21	0
ss-n-5	?	54	60	60
ss-n-6	0	208	544	469
ss-n-8	0	0	132	302
ss-nx-17	0	0	0	12
ss-n-18	0	0	0	160
Total	120	289	757	1,003
Bombers				
Tu-95 Bear	110	100	100	110
Mya-4 Bison	35	40	35	45
Total	145	140	135	155

Sources: For 1970 and 1975, Collins and Cordesman (1978), pp. 48 and 54. *MB 1980–81* (1980), p. 9, supplemented by the 1981–2 version of the same work, and *Soviet Military Power* (1981), especially pp. 53–60, provide 1980 data. Information for 1965 drawn from Collins (1976).

Table 9

Theatre and strategic bombers

Type	Year in service	Maximum range (km)	Payload (kg)	Missiles
Tu-16 Badger A, B, C, G	1955	6,400	9,000	2 AS-1 Kennel or 1 AS-2 Kipper or 1 AS-5 Kelt or 1 AS-6 Kingfish
Tu-95 Bear-B	1956	12,800	11,350	1 AS-3 Kangaroo
Mya-4 Bison-A	1956	11,200	4,540	—
Tu-22 Blinder-B	1962	2,250	10,000	1 AS-4 Kitchen
Backfire-B	1974	8,000	9,450	1 AS-4 Kitchen

Sources: MB 1980–81 (1980), pp. 89–91; MB 1975–6 (1975), p. 71.

Table 10

Ballistic missile submarines

Class	Year in service	Number built + building	Displacement dived (tons)	Missiles
Nuclear-powered				
Typhoon	?	0+1	25,000	20 ss-n-20
Delta III	1978	13	11,750	16 ss-n-18
Delta II	1973	4	11,750	16-ss-n-8
Delta I	1972	18	9,300	12 ss-n-8
Yankee	1968	34	9,300	16 ss-n-6
Hotel III	1962	8	5,600	6 ss-n-8
Hotel II	?	1	5,600	3 ss-n-5
Diesel-electric				
Golf I	1958	20	2,850	3 ss-n-4
Golf II	1967	(13)[a]	2,800	3 ss-n-5

[a] Figures in parentheses are conversions, not new construction.

Sources: The basic sources are: *Understanding Soviet Naval Developments*, especially the fourth edition (1981) and the second edition (1975); *Soviet Military Power* (1981), pp. 39–51; *Jane's Fighting Ships* for various years; Collins and Cordesman, (1978), pp. 160–61, 165; Breyer (1970); various issues of *MB*; and Collins (1976), p. 44; Couhat (1980). There are major discrepancies between the various sources, and whenever possible official American information was relied upon.

Table II

Strategic ballistic missiles

Missile	Year in service	Maximum range (km)	Throw-weight (kg)	Warheads	Yield	Median inaccuracy (CEP) (m)
ICBM						
SS-7	1961	11,000	500	1	5 MT	3,600
SS-8	1963	11,000	1,200	1	5 MT	3,600
SS-9 — mod 1	1965	12,000	5,500–6,800	1	18 MT	1,700
mod 2	1966	12,000	5,500–6,800	1	20+ MT	1,700
SS-11 — mod 1	1966	11,500	700–900	1	1–2 MT	1,500
mod 3	1973	11,500	700–900	3	100–300 KT	?
SS-13	1968	10,000	450	1	1 MT	1,500
SS-17 — mod 1	1975	10,000	2,700	4	900 KT	300–600
mod 2	1977	11,000	1,650	1	6 MT	450
SS-18 — mod 1	1974	12,000	7,600	1	24 MT	400
mod 2	1975	11,000	7,600	8–10	2 MT	400
mod 3	1975	16,000	7,600	1	20 MT	200
mod 4	1982	9,000	7,600	10	500 KT	300
SS-19 — mod 1	1975	9,600	3,400	6	550 KT	300–450
mod 2	1979	10,000	3,400	1	5 MT	200
mod 3	1982	10,000	3,600	6	550 KT	300
SLBM						
SS-n-4	1961	480	?	1	1–2 MT	1,800
SS-N-5	1964	1,400	?	1	1–2 MT	1,800
SS-N-6 — mod 1	1968	2,400	700	1	1–2 MT	1,800
mod 2	1973	3,000	700	1	1–2 MT	?
mod 3	1975		700	2	? KT	?
SS-N-8 — mod 1	1972	7,800	700	1	1–2 MT	1,500
mod 2	?	9,100	700	1	? MT	?
SS-NX-17	1977	3,900	1,500	1	? MT	?
SS-N-18 — mod 1	1978	6,500	2,200	3	200 KT	1,350
mod 2	?	8,000	2,200	1	450 KT	1,350
mod 3	?	6,500	2,200	7	200 KT	600
SS-N-20	1982–3	8,300	?	12	? KT	?

Sources: Soviet Military Power (1981); *Flight International* 119 (1981), pp. 1610, 1615 and 1619; *MB 1980–81* (1980), pp. 89–91; *MB 1981–2* (1981), p. 79; Luttwak (1976), pp. 25 and 36.

Table 12

Strategic defence forces

	1965	1970	1975	1980
ABM Launchers				
ABM-1B/Galosh	0	64	64	32
SAM Systems				
Batteries	–	–	1,650	1,200
Launchers	8,900	9,800	9,500	10,000
Missiles	10,700	10,700	11,800	12,000
Radars	–	–	5,000	7,000
Aircraft				
MiG-17	–	1,000	150	0
MiG-19	–	350	200	0
MiG-23	–	0	0	600
MiG-25	–	0	200	330
Su-9/11	–	750	700	430
Su-15	–	400	850	800
Tu-28	–	150	150	135
Yak-25	–	200	0	0
Yak-28	–	350	350	320
Total	3,800	3,200	2,600	2,600

Sources: Collins and Cordesman (1978), pp. 28 and 100, for 1970 and 1975, except for the number of radars, which comes from *MB 1975–6* (1975), p. 8. Figures for 1965 from Collins (1976), p. 44. Information for 1980 from *MB 1980–81* (1980), p. 10.

Table 13

Air defence aircraft

Designation	Year in service	Speed (Mach)	Combat radius (km)	Missiles
Su-9 Fishpot-B	1959	1.8	500	4 AA-1 Alkali
Su-11 Fishpot-C	1967	1.8	500	2 AA-3 Anab or 2 AA-2 Atoll
Su-15 Flagon-A	1967	2.3	725	2 AA-3 Anab
Tu-28P	1961	1.75	1,450	4 AA-5 Ash
Yak-25F Flashlight-A	1955	0.9	965	none
Yak-28P Firebar	1966	1.1	925	2 AA-3 Anab
MiG-17PF Fresco-D	1952	0.98	580	4 AA-1 Alkali
MiG-19PM Farmer-D	1955	1.28	450	4 AA-1 Alkali
MiG-23S Flogger-B	1971	2.3	960	2 AA-7 Apex and 2 AA-8 Aphid or 4 AA-2 Atoll
MiG-25 Foxbat-A	1971	2.8	1,100	4 AA-6 Acrid or AA-3 Arab

Sources: Polmar (1976); Krivinyi (1977); Berman (1978); *MB 1980–81* (1980); *Soviet Military Power* (1981), pp. 31–7; *Jane's All the World's Aircraft 1980–1981* (1980).

Table 14

Theatre-nuclear weapons delivery systems

	1965	1970	1979	1980
Missile launchers				
ss-4	608	600	496	320
ss-5	101	100	87	35
ss-20	0	0	0	225
	709	700	583	580
Aircraft				
Backfire	0	0	25	70
Tu-16 Badger	775	500	475	310
Tu-22 Blinder	105	175	170	125
	880	675	670	505

Sources: Missile totals for 1965 and 1975 come from Collins (1976), p. 44, with all his IRBMs counted as ss-5s and his MRBMs being counted as ss-4s. Total for 1970 is from *MB 1970–71* (1970), p. 6, but the breakdown is estimated. The 1980 figures come from *Soviet Military Power* (1981), p. 6, but may actually apply to 1981. According to production data on p. 12 of the latter source, from 1976 to 1980 the Soviets built 450 IRBMs, which can refer only to the ss-20. Allowing for two missiles per launcher, total number of launchers through the end of 1980 would be 225. Aircraft totals from Collins and Cordesman (1978), p. 139, for 1970 and 1975; Berman (1978), p. 25, for 1965; and *MB 1980–81* (1980), p. 10, for 1980. *Soviet Military Power* (1981), p. 63, which reports 600 Tu-16 and Tu-22, appears to include aircraft converted to tankers or used for reconnaissance or electronic warfare activities. Backfire figure for 1980 from *Soviet Military Power* (1981), p. 63.

Table 15

Theatre ballistic missiles

Missile	Year in service	Maximum range (km)	Warheads	Yield
SS-4	1959	1,900	1	1 MT
SS-5	1961	4,100	1	1 MT
SS-12 Scaleboard	?	700–800	1	1 MT
SS-20	1977	5,600	3	150 KT
SS-21	1978	120	1	?
SS-22	1979	1,000	1	500 KT
SS-23	1980	350	1	?
Scud B	?	280	1	?
Frog 7	1967	60	1	?

Sources: As for table 11.

Army

The manpower reductions during the late 1950s resulted in a reduction in the number of army divisions from about 175 to about 150. By 1965 the Soviets were thought to have about 147 divisions. During the subsequent fifteen years new divisions have been formed, and by 1981 it was estimated that more than 180 divisions were in existence. Virtually all of the newly created units have been motorized rifle divisions; there appears to have been no change in the number of tank or airborne divisions.

Soviet divisions are rated according to the extent to which they are fully mobilized. Category I divisions are those manned with 75 to 100 per cent of wartime manpower strength. Category II divisions are at 50 to 75 per cent of wartime strength, and Category III divisions have less than 50 per cent. In 1965 most divisions were in Category I or II, and only about thirty-five divisions were in Category III. As the number of divisions has increased this distribution has changed. It is estimated that by 1981 almost 100 divisions were in Category III, an increase of sixty-five divisions. By contrast there were only an estimated eighty-three Category I and II divisions in 1981, which might actually indicate a decrease in the number of Category I and II divisions during the past fifteen years (assuming that the publicly available information from 1965 is accurate, which may not be the case).

The increasing number of divisions has made it possible for the Soviets to expand their forces deployed against China without reducing the number of units stationed in other areas. In 1965 the Soviets had only seventeen divisions stationed in the Far East. By 1970, this total had increased to thirty. Further expansion occurred through the mid-1970s, and there are now more than forty-five divisions deployed against China. Fully half of these are Category III divisions, and only fifteen are Category I. In addition, there are only six tank divisions: the rest are motorized rifle divisions. These forces are not comparable to those facing NATO, but they certainly pose a serious threat to the Chinese.

The Soviets have thirty divisions in Eastern Europe, all Category

I units, equally divided between tank and motorized rifle divisions. This represents only a small increase over the twenty-six Category I divisions deployed there in 1965. It is commonly believed that these divisions have been given more men and equipment than Soviet divisions deployed elsewhere. Since they also have the most modern equipment and the best-quality manpower, these forces are the main striking force of the Soviet army. This is confirmed by the simple fact that two-thirds of the Soviet Union's forty-five Category I divisions are deployed in Eastern Europe, along with almost a third of their forty-seven tank divisons.

Supporting the forces in Eastern Europe are some eighty divisions in the north European and Urals regions of the Soviet Union. More than a third of these units are now tank divisions, but fully 75 per cent are Category III units and only 5 per cent Category I. The primary role of these divisions is reinforcement of the European theatre. According to published information (of uncertain reliability), it appears that the number of divisions in this area declined gradually during the late 1960s and early 1970s, but that in the late 1970s two new divisions were added every year. While most of the thirty divisions added by the Soviets since 1967 were placed in the Far East, facing the Chinese, during the last few years most new units have been added in Europe.

Finally, there are currently about twenty-five divisions along the southern border facing Turkey, Iran and Afghanistan. Most of these units are motorized rifle divisions, though there are two airborne and two tank divisions. Only about 20 per cent of the divisions are Category I, and fully 60 per cent are Category III. There has been little change in the disposition of forces in this region, though it appears that a few divisions may have been added since 1965.

The Soviets have increased the average strength of their divisions during the past fifteen years. In 1965 a tank division had only 8,500 men and 316 tanks. By 1980 each tank division had 11,000 men and 335 tanks. The number of artillery pieces in each division has been increased; new BMP infantry fighting vehicles have replaced older BTR-50 armoured personnel carriers; and air defence capabilities have been greatly expanded by the introduction of ZSU-23-4 self-propelled radar-guided anti-aircraft guns and SA-6, SA-7, SA-8, SA-9, SA-11 and SA-13 surface-to-air missile systems. The quality of the tanks is also much greater, as T-64 and T-72 medium tanks have replaced older T-62s. The infantry component of the divisions was substantially strengthened by the addition of a mechanized infantry battalion to each of the division's three tank regiments.

The same trends can be seen in the motorized rifle divisions. In 1965 this type of division had only 10,000 men and 175 tanks. Today they have 13,000 men and, in some cases, 266 tanks. In addition to the larger number of tanks, these divisions also have increased their artillery strength, from 54 to 110 pieces, and have started to receive the new BTR-70 wheeled armoured personnel carrier to replace the older BTR-60. They have anti-aircraft weapons like those in the tank division, replacing older radar-guided guns that had to be mounted in static positions. Equally important, the motorized rifle divisions have many more anti-tank missile launchers and, like the tank divisions, they have received some of the new generation of anti-tank missiles now in service.

Perhaps the most impressive development has been the mechanization of Soviet airborne divisions. The Soviets have developed a version of the BMP, the BMD, specifically designed for use by airborne troops. By the late 1970s a total of 346 BMDs were assigned to each airborne division, along with about 160 other armoured fighting vehicles of various types. These divisions remain weak in artillery, but have a ground mobility unmatched by the airborne forces of any other country in the world.

The Soviets have also made substantial improvements in their non-divisional support forces. Air assault brigades have been added, a reflection of the increased Soviet reliance upon helicopters. Though under the control of Frontal Aviation (see pp. 206–13), and not the army, the number of tactical helicopters has been greatly expanded. They now have some 3,500 helicopters, compared with only about 2,000 five years ago. Most impressive has been the addition of 950 Mi-24 Hind assault helicopters, each armed with rockets, anti-tank missiles and an automatic cannon. They can also transport up to eight infantrymen. More recent versions mount a Gatling-type gun and the new AT-6 Spiral anti-tank missile.

During the past decade, the Soviet army has paid increasing attention to its logistics system. Previously largely dependent upon rail for the bulk of its rear-echelon transport, the Soviet army has added large numbers of trucks to its inventory. Other improvements have included the increased use of palletized supplies to cut down on the handling of materials, and the adoption of modern pipelaying equipment to ensure that petroleum supplies are available to combat units even after an advance deep into enemy territory.

As has already been noted, the Soviet Union has greatly expanded its tactical air defences. In 1965 it relied primarily on SA-2 and SA-3 surface-to-air missiles and a variety of radar-guided anti-aircraft guns for tactical air defence. While including numerous weapons, the 1965 defences would have been incapable of stopping determined air attacks by modern strike aircraft. That weakness no longer exists. During the past fifteen years the Soviet Union has introduced six new surface-to-air missile systems. The SA-7 hand-held missile is deployed in units down to the platoon level. Every tank and infantry regiment has four ZSU-23-4 radar-guided anti-aircraft guns and the SA-9 short-range missile. The SA-9 is already being replaced by the newer SA-13 in first-line units. In the early 1970s the Soviet army also began to replace radar-guided, towed 57mm anti-aircraft guns (at the divisional level) by SA-6 and SA-8 missile systems. Finally, starting in 1967 the Soviet army began to deploy the SA-4 mobile area-defence missile. Most important of all, it has now integrated these various weapons into a mutually supporting network in which each system protects against a particular kind of attack, often forcing enemy aircraft to adopt tactics that make the aircraft more vulnerable to other weapons or decrease its net potential, or both. Additionally, the sheer multiplicity of weapons types makes it difficult for an attacker to develop a comprehensive range of electronic countermeasures, thus helping to ensure that at least some of the overall defence will remain unaffected.

The Soviet army is beginning to replace older anti-tank missiles with newer types. While it is a simple system and easy to build, the well-known AT-3 Sagger is manually controlled, and thus requires considerable skill by the user; constant practice is needed to maintain proficiency. The newer anti-tank missiles appear to have automatic control systems, which are more sophisticated and costly, but only require that the operator keep the target in the cross-hair of the sight. In addition, it appears that many AT-3 Saggers are being modified to take the new guidance system. The newest missiles are the AT-4 Spigot and the AT-5 Spandrel. The AT-4 is an infantry weapon fired from a tripod and the AT-5 is fired from a quintuple launcher mounted on an armoured car. These 2,000-metre-range missiles are very similar to the Franco-German Milan, and there are suspicions that the Soviets adapted stolen plans of the Western system in building the AT-4 and AT-5.

The Soviet army's modernization and expansion programmes reflect an enormous arms production effort. Until 1979 the Soviet Union produced three different types of tank at the same time (T-55, T-64 and T-72). By 1980 only two types of tank were in production: the T-72, 2,500 of which were built in that year, and the older but more sophisticated T-64, of which 500 were built. A small number of prototype T-82s were also produced. The Soviets also build numerous other types of armoured fighting vehicles: more than 26,000 during the years 1976 to 1980. Production in such enormous quantities has enabled the Soviet army to rearm with modern weaponry at a pace that no Western country can match. By giving high priority to units in Eastern Europe and along the China border, the Soviet army can completely re-equip front-line units in a period of only a few years.

Table 16

Army divisions, by type and region

	1965	1970	1975	1980
Types				
Tank	50	46	47	47
Motorized rifle	90	104	114	126
Airborne	7	7	8	7
	147	157	169	180
Category				
I and II	112	101	104	83
III	35	56	65	97
	147	157	169	180
Region				
Eastern Europe	26	31	31	30
Central USSR	82	68	69	79
Southern USSR	22	28	26	25
Far East	17	30	43	46
	147	157	169	180

Sources: 1965 information from Collins (1976), p. 44, and *MB 1965–6* (1965), pp. 4 and 5. The 1970 and 1975 breakdowns from Collins and Cordesman (1978), p. 126, *MB 1970–71* (1970), pp. 7–8, and *MB 1975–6* (1975), p. 9. 1980 data from *MB 1980–81* (1980), pp. 10–11, *MB 1981–2* (1981), p. 12, and especially *Soviet Military Power* (1981), pp. 6–7 and 27–8.

Table 17

Divisional strength

	1965	1970	1975	1980
Tank division				
Men	8,500	9,000	9,500	11,000
Medium tanks	316	316	325	335
Armoured fighting vehicles	?	?	244	?
Artillery	48	72	78	?
Motorized rifle division				
Men	10,000	11,000	12,000	13,000
Medium tanks	175	188	215	266
Armoured fighting vehicles	180	180	470	470
Artillery	54	72	90	90
Airborne division				
Men	?	7,000	7,000	7,000
Armoured fighting vehicles	?	45	100	370
Artillery	?	?	54	36

Sources: Collins and Cordesman (1978), p. 286, for 1965, 1970 and 1975 tank and motorized rifle divisions. 1975 data is supplemented by *Opposing Forces Europe* (1978), especially pp. A–12, A–13, and A–29. Although dating from 1978, this manual is believed to give a reasonably current image. It was supplemented by *Soviet Military Power* (1981), p. 28, and *MB 1980–81* (1980), p. vii.

Table 18

Army weapons and equipment

	1965	1970	1975	1980
Tanks	30,500	41,000	45,000	55,000
Artillery	–	16,000	17,000	20,000
Mortars	–	–	8,000	7,200
Armoured fighting vehicles	35,000	30,000	38,750	62,000
Anti-tank missile launchers	–	4,500	6,000	–

Sources: Collins (1976), p. 44, for 1965; Collins and Cordesman (1978), pp. 121–2 for 1970 and 1975, supplemented by *MB 1975–6* (1975), p. 9; and *MB 1980–81* (1980), p. 10, supplemented by *Soviet Military Power* (1981), pp. 2 and 28, and *MB 1981–2*, (1981) p. 12.

Table 19

Tanks

Type	Year in service	Weight (tons)	Gun (mm)	Rounds carried	Road speed (kph)	Cruising range (km)
T-10	1953	50	122	30	42	250
T-54	1949	36	100	34	48	400
T-55	1961	36	100	43	50	500
T-62	1961	36.5	115	40	48	500
T-64	1974?	35	125	28?	50	?
T-72	1975?	41	125	40	60	500

Sources: Foss (1976); *Jane's Weapons Systems 1977*; Isby (1981); *Soviet Military Power* (1981).

Table 20
Light armoured vehicles

Vehicle	Year in service	Weight (tons)	Road speed (kph)	Range (km)	Crew passengers	Machine guns	Other weapons
Armoured personnel carriers							
BMD	1971	9	60	?	3/3–6	1	73mm gun; AT-3 Sagger anti-tank missile
BMP	1967	12.5	55	300	3/8	1	73mm gun; AT-3 Sagger anti-tank missile
BTR-60P	1961	10	80	500	2/14	2	
BTR-50P	1957	14	44	260	2/20	1	
BTR-152	1950	8.9	75	650	2/17	1	
Armoured cars							
BRDM-2	1966	7	100	750	2/2	2	Versions with SA-9, AT-3, and AT-5
BRDM-1	1959	5.6	80	500	2/3	1	Versions with AT-1 and AT-2
Light tanks and assault guns							
ASU-85	1962	14	44	250	4/0	–	85mm gun
ASU-57	1957	5.4	45	250	3/0	–	57mm gun
PT-76	1955	14	40	260	4/0	–	76mm gun

Sources: As for table 19.

199

Table 21
Artillery

Designation	Year in service	Calibre (mm)	Range (m)	Rate of fire (rpm)	Notes
S-23	?	180	30,000	1	Can fire nuclear shell
D-20	1955	152	18,500	5	
M-1973	1973	152	18,500	6-7	Self-propelled
D-1	1943	152	12,200	4	Obsolescent
M-46	1954	130	27,000	5	
M-1974	1974	122	15,300	?	Self-propelled
D-30	1963	122	15,300	8	
D-74	1955	122	24,000	6	
M-30	1938	122	12,000	5-6	‡ Obsolescent

Sources: As for table 19, as well as Hofmann (1977), pp. 1057–1061.

Multiple rocket launchers

Designation	Year in service	Calibre (mm)	Tubes	Maximum range (m)	Reload times (minutes)	Notes
BM-14	1954	140	17	9,810	3–4	Older models had 16 tubes; some versions truck-mounted
BM-21	1964	122	40	20,500	10	Truck-mounted, standard divisional weapon
BM-24	1954	240	12	10,200	3–4	Truck-mounted
BMD-20	1954	200	4	20,000	6–10	Truck-mounted
BM-25	1957	250	6	30,000	10–20	Truck-mounted

Sources: As for table 21, as well as Foss (1981).

Table 23
Mortars

Designation	Year in service	Calibre (mm)	Maximum range (m)	Rate of fire (rpm)	Notes
M-240	1953	240	9,700	1	Can fire nuclear and chemical ammunition
M-160	1953	160	8,040	3	Can fire chemical and possibly nuclear ammunition
M-43	1943	120	5,700	9	
M-37	1943	82	3,040	25	

Sources: As for table 21.

Table 24
Anti-tank guns

Designation	Year in service	Calibre (mm)	Effective range (m)	Armour penetration (mm) at 500m	Rate of fire (rpm)	Notes
Artillery						
T-12	1965	100	1,000	406	10	
SD-44	1954	85	1,000	130	10–15	Obsolescent
CH-26	1956	57	500	140	20–25	Obsolescent
Recoilless weapons						
B-11	1956	107	1,000	380	6	Obsolescent
B-10	1950	82	400	240	5–6	Obsolescent
SPG-9	1968	73	1,000	330	–	
RPG-2	1949	40	150	180	–	Obsolescent
RPG-7	1962	40	500	330	4–6	
RPG-16	1980?	58	500–800	375	4–6	RPG-7 replacement
RPG-18	1980	64	200	375	–	Copy of US LAW

Sources: As for table 21, with Backofen (1980), pp. 16–21.

Table 25

Anti-tank guided missiles

Designation	Year in service	Minimum-maximum range (m)	Armour penetration (mm) at 500m	Notes
AT-1 Snapper	1959	600–2,300	350	Triple launcher on BRDM armoured car; quadruple jeep launcher. Obsolete.
AT-2 Swatter	1962	500–2,500	400	Quadruple launcher on BRDM armoured car
AT-2 Swatter B	1973	?–3,500	?	Quadruple launcher on BRDM 2 armoured car
AT-3 Sagger	1965	500–3,000	480	Portable and vehicle-mounted versions
AT-4 Spigot	1975	?–2,000	500	Portable
AT-5 Spandrel	1977	?–4,000	?	Quintuple launcher on armoured car
AT-6 Spiral	1977	?–10,000?	?	Mounted on Mi-24 helicopters

Sources: As for table 19, with *Flight International* 119 (1981), p. 1652.

Table 26

Land-based surface-to-air missiles

Missile	Year in service	Slant range (km)	Altitude Minimum (m)	Altitude Maximum (km)
SA-1 Guild	1954	32	?	?
SA-2 Guideline	1958	45	1,500	25
SA-3 Goa	1961	35	300	15
SA-4 Ganef	1964	70	1,000	25
SA-5 Gammon	1967	250	?	27
SA-6 Gainful	1967	35	30	13
SA-7 Grail	1967	3.6	25	1.5
SA-8 Gecko	1975	12	50	10
SA-9 Gaskin	1968?	7	20	5
SA-10	?	50	300	?
SA-11	1979	25	30	15
SA-12	?	100	100	32
SA-13	1980?	7	?	10

Sources: As for table 19, with *Flight International* 120 (1981), pp. 725–42.

Table 27

Anti-aircraft guns

Designation	Year in service	Calibre (mm)	Tactical range (m)	Rate of fire (rpm)	Fire control	Notes
s-60	1950	57	6,000	120	Radar or optical	Now being replaced by sa-8 and sa-6
zsu-57-2	1957	57	4,000	2×120	Optical	Mounted on т-54 chassis
zu-23-2	?	23	2,500	2×1,000	Optical	
zsu-23-4	1965	23	3,000	4×1,000	Radar or optical	Mounted on light amphibious armoured vehicle
zpu-4	?	14.5	1,400	4×600	Optical	Obsolete

Sources: As for table 21.

Air force

The Soviet Union has five different air forces. The PVO Strany, the
strategic air defence force, is a separate service, while the Naval Air
Service is under the control of the navy. The air force itself is
divided into three parts: Long-Range Air Force, Frontal Aviation
and Military Transport Aviation. Only Frontal Aviation and
Military Transport Aviation are discussed in this section. Frontal
Aviation provides air support for the Soviet army. Its units are
placed directly under the control of the ground forces. Currently it
controls not only ground attack aircraft and air superiority fighters
for use in the battle zones, but also helicopters and short-range
transport aircraft. Military Transport Aviation now has only
longer-range aircraft and some helicopters.

In 1965 Frontal Aviation had about 3,250 tactical aircraft,
including 2,800 fighters and ground attack aircraft and 450 reconnaissance aircraft. Most of these aircraft were first-generation
types, including MiG-17 fighters and Il-28 light bombers built
during the 1950s. These planes could carry limited weapons
payloads over short distances. This same weakness was shared by
the newer second-generation aircraft then in service: the MiG-21
Fishbed interceptors, Su-7 Fitter A ground attack planes, and the
Yak-28 light bombers. As a result, in 1965 Frontal Aviation had
only a limited ground attack capability, at the same time relying
upon counter-air aircraft inferior to those available in the West.
This qualitative gap was not rectified during the later 1960s, though
Frontal Aviation grew to about 3,700 aircraft in 1970.

During the 1970s the Soviet Union succeeded in radically
strengthening Frontal Aviation by increasing the number of operational tactical aircraft and by replacing older aircraft with newer,
more capable types. By 1972 Frontal Aviation had about 4,200
aircraft, and by 1975 there were 4,500, including 750 reconnaissance
planes. During the early 1970s the Soviets built just under 1,100
tactical aircraft a year. This production rate increased to 1,300 at the
end of the decade. About half of these newly built aircraft were
assigned to Frontal Aviation, and by 1980 all of the air superiority
fighters and three-quarters of the ground attack aircraft used by
Frontal Aviation were less than ten years old. During the early and

middle 1970s most of the remaining first-generation fighters were removed from service, and by the late 1970s even more modern second-generation aircraft were being replaced. By 1980 Frontal Aviation had about 4,800 tactical combat aircraft, including almost 800 reconnaissance and electronic warfare types.

Frontal Aviation received three completely new types of aircraft during the 1970s, along with much improved versions of two older types of aircraft. The most numerous aircraft now in service with Frontal Aviation is the Flogger, which is produced in both MiG-23 and MiG-27 versions. The MiG-23 Flogger B, introduced in 1971, is an all-weather air superiority aircraft which carries six AA-7 and AA-8 air-to-air missiles. An improved version, the Flogger G, is now in service. The MiG-27 Flogger D is an all-weather ground attack aircraft capable of carrying a payload of up to 3.5 tons out to 550 kilometres. The MiG-27 is optimized for ground attack; it has a laser target designator and a modern attack computer. The Flogger D has been superseded by the Flogger J, which has more advanced electronics. By 1981 the Soviets had a total of 1,400 Floggers of all types.

The second completely new type of aircraft introduced during the 1970s was the MiG-25 Foxbat. This plane has been produced in three versions. The Foxbat A is a high-altitude interceptor used only for strategic air defence, and is probably produced only in limited numbers. Frontal Aviation has two versions, the Foxbat B and the Foxbat D, exclusively for unarmed reconnaissance missions. There are now about 160 Foxbats in Frontal Aviation.

The third new type of aircraft introduced for service in Frontal Aviation is the Su-24 Fencer A. This ground attack aircraft was clearly copied from the American F-111. It can carry a payload of 8 tons to a distance of some 550 kilometres, relying upon a sophisticated variety of electronics for navigation and attack computations. The plane the Su-24 replaces, the Yak-28 Brewer, can carry only 2 tons of ordnance to a distance of about 700 kilometres. The Soviets now have 400 Su-24 Fencers.

In addition to totally new designs, the Soviets extensively modified the older MiG-21 and Su-7 designs to produce considerably improved aircraft. Throughout the 1970s the Soviets continued to build MiG-21 Fishbed fighters, but in versions with enhanced ground attack capabilities able to operate in all weathers. There are still about 1,300 MiG-21s in Soviet service. More radical changes were made to the Su-7 Fitter A. The new Su-17 Fitter c, introduced in 1972, is a swing-wing version of the Su-7 with about double the ordnance payload and a much longer range. The Su-17 has been produced in at least three versions. During the late 1970s the Su-17 has slowly replaced the Su-7, and there are now only 200 Su-7 Fitter As still in service, compared with 650 Su-17s.

All the new aircraft have significantly greater capabilities than the aircraft they replace. Some of the improvements are obvious, such as greater ordnance payloads and longer ranges. The sophistication of the electronics used has also increased significantly. Most Soviet aircraft now have attack computers, advanced navigation aids and other advanced technology items. While still behind the West in this respect, the gap is considerably smaller than it was a decade ago, and seems to be closing.

The Soviet Union has also deployed a whole new generation of aircraft-launched missiles of which not a great deal is known. New air-to-ground missiles are believed to include the AS-7 Kerry, a weapon with a 10-kilometre range and radio-command guidance, used on the Su-24 Fencer; the AS-X-9, an anti-radiation missile for use against radars and the like with an estimated 80- to 90-kilometre range; and the AS-X-10, believed to be a television-guided version of the AS-X-9. Older air-to-air missiles are now being replaced by the AA-6 Acrid (used on the MiG-25 Foxbat) and the AA-7 Apex and AA-8 Aphid missiles (both used on the MiG-23). The AT-6 Spiral, now carried by the Mi-24 Hind attack helicopter, has a range of five kilometres and is controlled by radio-command guidance.

Equally important, Frontal Aviation has made impressive strides during the past decade in developing a range of conventional ordnance comparable to that used in the West. Ground attack ordnance is now believed to include cluster bombs, laser-guided bombs, and fuel air explosives, though some of these weapons may only be under development at the present. It is also believed that the Soviets have improved the quality of their air-delivered bombs, which previously had unreliable fuses and were far less powerful than comparably sized Western bombs.

The Soviets have developed a strategic airlift capability during the 1970s. Previously, they had a substantial force of light and medium transports, primarily An-12 Cubs with a 20-ton payload but only a 1,200-km range. In 1967 the An-22 Cock was introduced, similar in size to the American C-5A Galaxy, and able to carry an

80-ton payload, 3,500 km. During the mid-1970s the Soviets also introduced the Il-76 Candid, similar in size to the American c-141 Starlifter, able to transport 40 tons out to 4,300 km. It appears that older An-12 Cubs are now being withdrawn from service as additional Il-76s are built. The Soviet strategic airlift force is still weaker than that of the United States, but because the Soviet Union is nearer to most likely trouble spots, their planes would have to fly shorter distances, and it is possible that they could rely upon short-range An-12s.

Soviet tactical airlift capabilities have expanded, primarily due to the increased production of tactical airlift helicopters. Currently the Soviets operate some 5,200 helicopters, about 3,500 of which are assigned to Frontal Aviation, to support the army. While many of these helicopters are inferior to comparable Western types, the more modern types are of higher quality. Between 1976 and 1980 the Soviets built some 4,300 helicopters of all types, or about 850 per year. About a quarter of the new helicopters were Mi-24 Hinds (discussed under the army), but many improved versions of the older Mi-8 Hip were also built. Current production is estimated at about 750 a year, but production rates varied considerably during the late 1970s (from 600 to 1,400 per year).

Frontal Aviation is organized into sixteen armies, four of which are deployed in Eastern Europe and twelve of which are assigned to military districts in the Soviet Union. In early 1980 it was estimated that the Soviets had 112 air regiments and seven independent squadrons. As of 1977 there were 1,625 combat aircraft positioned in Eastern Europe, most assigned to the 16th Air Army stationed in East Germany. Another 1,725 tactical aircraft were located in European areas of the Soviet Union. Facing Turkey and the Middle East the Soviets had about 475 aircraft. In the Far East there were about 1,300 combat aircraft. These totals appear to include not only fixed-wing combat aircraft but also helicopter gunships.

There have been some important shifts in the distribution of combat aircraft. In 1970 there were only about 2,850 combat aircraft stationed in Europe (including those in Eastern Europe, European Soviet Union and Southern Soviet Union), as compared with about 3,500 in 1975 and 3,800 in 1977. Part of this increase has resulted from the introduction of large numbers of Mi-24 attack helicopters, but much of it resulted from the introduction of modern attack aircraft. There has also been a substantial increase in the numbers of combat aircraft assigned to the Far East. In 1975 it was estimated that there were 900 combat aircraft in Soviet Asia. By 1977 one estimate put the figure at 1,300. In 1980 it was estimated that there were about 1,200 Frontal Aviation aircraft along the Sino-Soviet border.

Table 28

Air force

	1965	1970	1975	1980
Frontal aviation				
Combat aircraft	3,200	3,700	4,500	4,800
Helicopters	0	0	?	3,500
Transports	0	0	?	250
Military transport aviation				
Strategic	0	10	60	175
Tactical	750	795	800	425

Sources: Berman (1978), p. 29, for 1965 and 1970 information on Frontal Aviation. 1975 data from Alfred L. Monks, 'Air Forces', pp. 130–53, in Jones (ed.) (1978), supplemented by *MB 1975–6* (1975), p. 10. *MB 1980–81* (1980), p. 12, *MB 1981–2* (1981), p. 14, and *Soviet Military Power* (1981), pp. 31–7, provide 1980 information. It should be noted that all aircraft inventory figures are extremely unreliable, and should be used with great caution. The basic primer on the Soviet air forces is Norby (1978).

Table 29

Tactical combat aircraft

Design generation and aircraft	Year in service	Ordnance load (tons)	Combat radius (km)	Maximum speed (Mach)
First (1946–55)				
Il-28	1950	2.2	1,100	0.8
MiG-17 Fresco	1953	0.5	580	0.96
MiG-19 Farmer	1955	0.5	450	1.35
Second (1956–65)				
MiG Fishbed D	1963	1.0	600	2.0
Su-7 Fitter A	1960	2.0	250–350	1.7
Yak-28 Brewer	1963	2.2	370–500	1.1
Third (1966–80)				
MiG-23 Flogger B	1971	–	900–1,200	2.3
MiG-27 Flogger D	1971	3.5	550–800	1.7
Su-17 Fitter C	1974	3.5–4.0	550–900	1.6
MiG-21 Fishbed J	1970	0.8	350–650	2.2
MiG-25 Foxbat B	1971	none	1,100	2.8
Su-24 Fencer	1974	8.0	1,800	2.3

Sources: As for table 13.

Table 30

Air-to-surface missiles

Missile	Year in service	Range (km)	Guidance	Warhead	Aircraft
AS-1 Kennel	1963	150	cruise: inertial homing: active or passive radar	900 kg HE[a]	Tu-16 Badger B
AS-2 Kipper	1965	210	cruise: inertial homing: infrared	1,000 kg HE	Tu-16 Badger C
AS-3 Kangaroo	1963	650	cruise: inertial homing: infrared	nuclear or 2,300 kg HE	Tu-95 Bear B
AS-4 Kitchen	1967	300	cruise: inertial homing: infrared	nuclear or 1,000 kg HE	Tu-22 Backfire
AS-5 Kelt	1966	320	cruise: inertial homing: active or passive radar	1,000 kg HE	Tu-16 Badger G
AS-6 Kingfish	1976	220	cruise: inertial homing: active or passive radar	200 KT nuclear or 1,000 kg HE	Tu-16 Backfire
AS-7 Kerry	?	10	radio command	100 kg HE	Su-24
AS-X-9	?	50–90	passive radar	135–200 kg HE	Su-24
AS-X-10	?	10	laser homing	100 kg HE	MiG-27; Su-17; Su-24
AS-X-11	?	50	television	200 kg HE	Su-24

[a] HE: high explosive.
Sources: Malzeyev (1978), pp. 41–5; Panyalev (1981), p. 720; *Flight International* 119 (1981), p. 1623.

Table 31
Air-to-air missiles

Missile	Speed (Mach)	Range (km)	Aircraft
AA-1 Alkali	1.5+	SAR: 6[a]	MiG-17, MiG-19, Su-11, Yak-25
AA-2 Atoll	2.5	IR: 5.7	MiG-19, MiG-21, MiG-23
AA-3 Anab	?	SAR or IR: 16+	Su-11, Su-15, Yak-28P
AA-4 Awl	?	IR: 8	MiG-25
AA-5 Ash	?	IR or SAR: 30	Tu-28D
AA-6 Acrid	4.5	SAR: 45–50 IR: 20–25	MiG-25
AA-7 Apex	3.5	SAR: 33 IR: 15	MiG-23
AA-8 Aphid	3	SAR: 15 IR: 7	MiG-23

[a] SAR: semi-active radar homing; IR: infrared homing.
Sources: Flight International 119 (1981), pp. 1646–7; Krivinyi (1977), p. 222.

Table 32
Transport aircraft

Designation	Year in service	Range with maximum payload (km)	Maximum payload (kg)	Paratroops
An-2 Colt	1949	750	1,500	14
Il-14 Crate	1954	1,750	3,300	24
Il-18 Coot	1957	3,700	13,500	80
An-12 Cub	1958	550	20,000	60
An-26 Curl	1961	980	5,500	38
An-22 Cock	1967	5,500	80,000	175
Il-76 Candid	1975	5,000	40,000	140

Sources: As for table 29.

Navy

After the Second World War the Soviets tried to build a balanced fleet of submarines and surface vessels. This plan was abandoned during the Khrushchev years. During his tenure the Soviets emphasized coastal defence, submarine warfare and anti-carrier warfare. When Brezhnev and Kosygin ousted Khrushchev, a new naval policy was adopted which relied upon surface vessels for anti-submarine attacks on American strategic submarines and also for attacks on American anti-submarine surface vessels. Currently, the Soviet navy relies upon its submarine forces for most important roles, and uses its surface vessels for supporting submarines and for showing the flag.

Most surface ships used by the Soviets in 1965 were of improved Second World War designs. Of the twenty cruisers, only three Kynda-class vessels with eight SS-N-3 anti-aircraft missiles and a twin SA-N-I anti-aircraft missile launcher qualified as a modern design. The remaining vessels relied upon guns only, except for one Sverdlov-class vessel which was modified to take a twin SA-N-2 anti-aircraft missile launcher. Of the eighty destroyers, only twenty-four carried anti-aircraft or anti-ship missiles. Most of the destroyers were of the Skory type, which was based upon a design dating from before the Second World War. More impressive was the Kotlin series. Besides about twenty gun-armed Kotlins, the Soviets also converted about eight to the SAM Kotlin version with a twin SA-N-I anti-aircraft missile launcher, and built twelve more as Kildin and Krupny destroyers armed with one or two SS-N-I anti-ship missile launchers. These vessels were supplemented by Kashins with twin SA-N-I anti-aircraft missile launchers, which were just entering service.

During the late 1960s the Soviet navy expanded its surface fleet. Two aviation cruisers were built, the Moskva (in 1967) and the Leningrad (in 1968). Armed with two twin SA-N-3 anti-aircraft missile launchers and an anti-submarine missile known as the FRAS-I fired from the SUW-N-I launcher, and carrying eighteen Ka-24 Hormone helicopters, these two vessels were the first real indication that the Soviet navy was developing its own distinctive ship design style. During this period the Soviets also built five more cruisers, four of the Kresta I type with anti-aircraft and anti-ship missiles and one more Kynda. Destroyer construction was rather limited during this period. Only two new vessels were being built every year, mostly additional Kashin guided missile destroyers.

Rapid changes took place in the Soviet navy between 1970 and 1975. Seven Kresta II cruisers were built, armed with eight SS-N-14 anti-submarine missiles in place of the SS-N-3 anti-ship missiles. The first Kara-class cruisers appeared in 1973, each armed with eight SS-N-14 missiles, two twin SA-N-3 anti-aircraft missile launchers, and two SA-N-4 anti-aircraft missile launchers. The Krivak guided missile frigates also began to enter service in large numbers. These heavily armed vessels carry four SS-N-14 missiles and two twin SA-N-4 anti-aircraft missile launchers. About ten Krivaks were in service at the beginning of 1975.

During the late 1970s additional new Kara cruisers and Krivak frigates were built. No new destroyers were built, though some older types were extensively modified. By 1980 the Soviets had seven Karas in service and had ended production of this class. By comparison, thirty Krivaks had been built, and production was expected to continue into the 1980s.

Four new ship designs made their appearance in 1980. Most impressive was the 23,000-ton nuclear-powered guided missile cruiser, the Kirov. The Kirov class is armed with twenty anti-ship cruise missiles of a new unspecified type, two twin SA-N-4 anti-aircraft missile launchers, two twin SS-N-14 anti-submarine missile launchers (with reloads), and twelve vertically launched anti-aircraft missile systems probably based on the SA-10 used for strategic air defence. Taking into account the varied missile battery, the eight 30mm Gatling guns and two 100mm dual-purpose guns, and the Ka-25 Hormone helicopters carried on board, the Kirovs are easily the most powerful surface warships in the world. Currently under construction is the first vessel of a new class of 11,000- to 13,000-ton cruisers to follow the Kara, but little is known of this new type. Sea trials were conducted for two new destroyer classes: the Sovremennyy, equipped with anti-ship and anti-aircraft missiles and intended primarily for surface warfare; and the Udaloy, armed with anti-submarine missiles and helicopters and intended for anti-submarine warfare. These two new destroyers are larger than Soviet cruisers built in the 1960s, indicating that the Soviet navy intends to rely on larger and more capable vessels than was previously the case.

In 1965 the Soviet navy had about 335 general-purpose submarines, about 265 of them diesel-electric types armed only with torpedoes. There were about forty nuclear-powered submarines and only twenty-eight diesel-electric types armed with anti-ship missiles. The Soviet navy had over fifty submarines armed with anti-ship missiles, including about twenty-five Echo I- and II-class nuclear-powered boats armed with SS-N-3 anti-ship missiles, sixteen Juliett-class diesel-electric submarines with three SS-N-3 missiles each, and twelve Whiskey-class diesel-electric attack boats converted to carry either two or four SS-N-3 missiles. In order to fire the SS-N-3 from any of the submarines it was necessary to surface, and the range of the missile far exceeded the distance at which any of these submarines could acquire targets. There were also fourteen November-class nuclear-powered attack submarines in service. The November was far inferior to American attack submarines then entering service, being far noisier and possessing inferior sonar detection equipment.

During the next few years the Soviet navy began significantly to improve its submarine fleet. More Echo II-class submarines were built, and the new Charlie-class nuclear-powered boats armed with eight SS-N-7 anti-ship missiles began to enter service in 1968. Unlike the SS-N-3, the SS-N-7 could be fired even when the launching submarine was submerged, making the Charlie into a potent threat to American carriers and other high-value surface ships. Equally important, production of the mediocre November boats was ended and in 1967 the new Victor nuclear-powered attack submarines entered service. A great many older submarines were removed from service during this period, and by 1970 the Soviets had only about 300 submarines, but including sixty nuclear-powered boats.

During the early 1970s the Soviet navy concentrated on the production of nuclear-powered ballistic missile submarines. Between 1971 and 1975 the Soviets built an estimated forty-eight nuclear-powered submarines, but only eighteen were of general-purpose types. About a dozen Victor-class submarines were built and only six Charlie-class submarines. In addition, the Soviet navy usually built about one diesel-electric submarine a year. The Soviet navy recognizes that diesel-electric boats are much less expensive than nuclear-powered submarines, and believes that they are actually more useful in shallow water coastal defence operations. Not enough diesel-electric submarines were built to compensate for the withdrawal of a substantial number of older boats, and by 1975 the Soviet navy had only about 185 diesel-electric submarines, including twenty-five armed with SS-N-3 anti-ship missiles and 160 with torpedoes only.

During the late 1970s the Soviets increased submarine production, building a total of fifty-eight between 1976 and 1980. Most of the new vessels were nuclear-powered ballistic missile submarines, but by 1980 general-purpose boats came to predominate. Two new general-purpose submarines were introduced: the Charlie II, armed with eight of the new SS-N-9 anti-ship missiles, and the Victor II, larger than the Victor I, with improved sonar detection equipment and probably armed with the new SS-N-15 and SS-N-16 anti-submarine missiles.

In 1980 the Soviet navy still had the world's largest submarine fleet, including 290 general-purpose boats and about eighty-five armed with ballistic missiles. The general-purpose submarines include 110 nuclear-powered and 180 diesel-electric types. Currently the Soviets are building four different classes of general-purpose submarines: the Oscar (nuclear-powered and armed with anti-ship cruise missiles), Alfa (nuclear-powered attack), Victor (nuclear-powered attack), and Tango (diesel-electric attack) classes. Currently, most new submarines are general-purpose types, and only a small number of ballistic missile submarines are now built each year. About eight of the twelve Soviet submarines built in 1979 were general-purpose types, mostly Victor nuclear-powered attack boats, and it is likely that the preponderance of general-purpose boats is even greater today. In addition, Yankee-class ballistic missile submarines, withdrawn from service as a result of SALT restrictions on the total number of nuclear-powered ballistic missile submarines that the Soviet Union can have, are being converted into attack boats. This concentration on general-purpose submarines has led to substantial increases in the numbers of nuclear-powered attack submarines, which previously had received a low priority.

The construction of large surface combatants and nuclear-powered submarines has made it possible for the Soviet navy to establish a global naval presence. In 1965 the Soviet navy managed only 4,200 ship-days beyond its littoral seas. By 1970 it generated almost 44,000 ship-days, and in 1975 exceeded 57,000 ship-days. In 1979 it managed only 47,000 ship-days, but even this reduced total exceeded that of the United States navy. The Soviet navy has paid considerable attention to developing logistics capabilities to support these deployments and, while still far behind the United States in underway replenishment of naval vessels, it has made substantial improvements in the past decade. Equally impressive has been the development of command and control capabilities using satellite communications. Another impressive array of photographic, radar and electronics Intelligence satellites, along with a fleet of more than 50 specialized Intelligence collection vessels, give the Soviet navy a global naval Intelligence capability.

The Soviet navy continues to emphasize coastal defence. For this reason it operates some 500 small combatants of various types, many of modern construction, deployed along the Soviet Union's lengthy coastline. There has been a slight reduction in the number of such vessels during the past fifteen years, but the size of the average small combatants has increased substantially. The 75-ton Komar missile boats, each armed with two SS-N-2 missiles, have been replaced by 950-ton Nanuchka-class corvettes with six SS-N-9 anti-ship missiles, Matka-class hydrofoils armed with two SS-N-2CS, a new, longer-range version of the old SS-N-2, or 240-ton Osa missile boats with four SS-N-2 missiles. The Soviet navy only increased the number of small missile vessels from 140 to 145 during the 1970s, but the total tonnage of these vessels has tripled and the number of anti-ship missiles has doubled. The Soviet navy continues to develop new classes of torpedo boats, patrol craft and submarine chasers to replace older vessels. In addition, an 8,000-man coastal artillery and rocket force is equipped with guns and anti-ship missiles.

The Soviet navy controls an air force that in 1981 possessed some 1,440 aircraft. This force performs four main functions: reconnaissance and surveillance of the oceans; anti-ship strike; anti-submarine warfare; and logistics support for the navy. As the size and importance of the navy has increased in the last fifteen years, so has the number of aircraft supporting it. The Soviet navy had only about 900 aircraft in 1965, consisting mostly of Tu-16 Badger bombers and Be-6 Madge anti-submarine amphibians. By 1975 there were more than 1,200 naval aircraft, including improved versions of older aircraft and three completely new types of aircraft

(Tu-142 Bear F and Il-38 anti-submarine aircraft and Ka-25 Hormone helicopters).

During the past five years the Soviets have added several new types of naval aircraft. The best-known is the Backfire B, which was introduced in about 1976, armed with the AS-4 or AS-6 anti-ship missiles. Another new anti-ship strike aircraft is the Su-17 Fitter, operated in large numbers by the Soviet air force for ground support and used by naval aviation to support operations in the Baltic. Other new aircraft include a vertical take-off and landing strike fighter called the Yak-36 Forger. Only about thirty Forgers are currently in service, deployed on the new Kiev-class aircraft carriers. The Forger has very limited capabilities, and will probably be replaced in the next few years. The same is not true for the new Mi-14 Haze land-based anti-submarine helicopters, which are slowly replacing the obsolescent Mi-4 Hound.

Soviet naval aviation also retains in service many older types of aircraft. The 180 Ka-25 Hormones, shipboard helicopters used in anti-submarine, missile targeting and utility roles, first entered service in 1967. There are still 400 Tu-16 Badger bombers in service, though seventy have been converted into tankers and seventy now operate primarily as reconnaissance and electronic warfare aircraft. Similarly, the Soviets retain about 100 Tu-95 Bear bombers (in the Tu-142 model) for reconnaissance and anti-submarine missions.

The Soviet navy currently has eighty-six amphibious vessels, more than the United States navy has. Most of the Soviet vessels are smaller than those used by the United States. There are about fifty Polocny-class 1,000-ton medium amphibious assault landing ships, small vessels suitable only for coastal operations. Of more significance are the twenty-five Alligator- and Ropucha-class tank landing ships, mostly built during the past decade. The largest and most capable amphibious vessels are of the new 13,000-ton Ivan Rogov class of amphibious transports. Only one is now in service, but more are believed to be under construction. This is the first Soviet amphibious vessel comparable in size and function to the larger American amphibious vessels intended for trans-ocean amphibious operations.

The Soviet navy maintains a small force of naval infantry. About 10,000 strong in 1965, it currently has 12,000 men organized into five regiments (two in the Pacific and one each attached to the Baltic, Northern and Black Sea fleets). Though equipped with light

PT-76 tanks and BMP armoured personnel carriers, Soviet naval infantry is intended primarily for use in small-scale commando operations or to spearhead amphibious assaults staged by regular army troops.

Table 33
Naval vessels

	1965	1970	1975	1980
Submarines, nuclear-powered				
Cruise missile	29	35	40	50
Torpedo attack	14	24	35	55
Submarines, diesel-electric				
Cruise missile	14	28	25	20
Torpedo attack	310	210	163	160
Aircraft carriers and aviation cruisers				
Carriers	0	0	0	1
aviation cruisers	0	2	2	2
Cruisers				
Guided missile, nuclear	0	0	0	1
Guided missile	4	10	21	25
Gun	16	14	9	9
Destroyers				
Guided missile	26	29	45	36
Gun	54	48	37	30
Frigates				
Guided missile	0	0	10	28
Gun	140	111	118	140
Small Combatants				
Missile	110	140	135	145
Patrol/anti-submarine/torpedo	350+	475	445	395
Minesweepers	500	295	270	400
Others				
Amphibious	14	80	95	86
Auxiliary	?	?	750	760

Sources: As for table 10.

Table 34
Cruise missile submarines

Class	Year in service	Number built + building	Displacement dived (tons)	Speed dived (knots)	Torpedo tubes	Missiles
Nuclear-powered						
Oscar	1981	1+?	15,000	30	8	24 SS-N-19
Charlie II	1973	6	5,500	28	6	8 SS-N-7 or -9
Charlie I	1968	12	5,000	28	6	8 SS-N-7
Papa	1973	1	7,000	35	6	10 SS-N-7 or -9
Echo II	1962	29	5,800	25	8	8 SS-N-3 or -12
Echo I	1960	5	5,800	22	8	6 SS-N-3
Diesel-electric						
Juliett	1962	16	3,800	14	6	4 SS-N-3A
Whiskey/Long-Bin	1963	6	1,500	12	4	4 SS-N-3A
Whiskey/ Twin-Cylinder	1960	6	1,600	10	6	2 SS-N-3A

Sources: As for table 10.

Table 35
Torpedo attack submarines

Class	Year in service	Number built + building	Displacement dived (tons)	Dived speed (knots)	Torpedo tubes
Nuclear Powered					
Alfa	1972	5+2	3,800	42+	6
Victor II/III	1972	20?+3	5,800	31	6
Victor I	1967	16	5,200	32	6
Echo	1971	5	5,200	25	8
November	1959	14	5,000	30	10
Diesel-Electric					
Tango	1973	15+2	3,700	16	8
Bravo	1968	4	2,700	14	6
Foxtrot	1958	60	2,400	16	10
Zulu IV	1952	26	2,300	17	10
Romeo	1958	20	1,800	14	8
Whiskey	1951	235	1,350	14	6
Quebec	1954	22	540	16	4

Sources: As for table 10.

Table 36
Aircraft carriers and aviation cruisers

	Class	
	Kiev	Moskva
Year in service	1976	1967
Number built + building	3+1	2
Displacement, full load (tons)	42,000	20,000
Anti-aircraft missile launchers	2 twin SA-N-3 (72 missiles) 2 twin SA-N-4	2 twin SA-N-3 (72 missiles)
Anti-ship missile launchers	4 twin SS-N-12 (24 missiles)	–
Anti-submarine missile launchers	1 twin SUW-N-I	1 twin SUW-N-I
Aircraft:		
Ka-25 Hormone helicopters	22	18
Yak-36 Forger fixed-wing	13	0
Guns	2 twin 76mm 8 single 30mm Gatling	2 twin 57mm

Sources: As for table 10.

Table 37
Cruisers

Class	Year in service	Number built + building	Displacement full load (tons)	Missile launchers			Guns
				Anti-ship	Anti-aircraft	Anti-submarine	
Nuclear-powered							
Kirov	1980	1+1	25,000	20 SS-NX-19	12 SA-NX-6 (72–96 missiles) 2 twin SA-N-4	twin SS-N-14 (with reloads)	2 single 100mm 8 30mm Gatling
Conventional							
Kara	1973	7	10,000	–	2 twin SA-N-3 (44 missiles) 2 twin SA-N-4 (36 missiles)	2 quad SS-N-14	2 twin 76mm 4 30mm Gatling
Kresta II	1970	10	7,800	–	2 twin SA-N-3 (44 missiles)	2 quad SS-N-14	2 twin 57mm 4 30mm Gatling
Kresta I	1967	4	7,500	2 twin SS-N-3B	2 twin SA-N-1 (44 missiles)	–	2 twin 57mm
Kynda	1962	4	5,700	2 quad SS-N-3B (16 missiles)	1 twin SA-N-1 (22 missiles)	–	2 twin 76mm
Sverdlov	1951	14	17,000	–	–	–	4 triple 152mm
Chapaev	1950	5	15,000	–	–	–	4 triple 152mm

Sources: As for table 10, with Kehoe and Brower, 'The Kirov' (1981), pp. 154–9.

Table 38
Destroyers

Class	Year in service	Number built + building[a]	Displacement full load (tons)	Missile launchers		Guns
				Anti-aircraft	Anti-ship	
Kashin	1963	20	4,500	2 twin SA-N-1 (44 missiles)	–	2 twin 76mm
Modified Kashin	1973	(6)	4,750	2 twin SA-N-1 (44 missiles)	4 SS-N-2C	2 twin 76mm, 4 30mm Gatling
Kildin	1958	4	3,600	–	1 SS-N-1 (8 missiles)	4 quad 57mm
Modified Kildin	1973	(3)	3,800	–	4 SS-N-2C	2 twin 76mm
Kanin	1968	8	4,700	1 twin SA-N-1	–	2 quad 57mm
SAM Kotlin	1962	(8)	3,600	1 twin SA-N-1	–	1 twin 130mm
Modified Kotlin	1958	(12)	3,600	–	–	2 twin 130mm
Kotlin	1954	27	3,600	–	–	2 twin 130mm
Skory	1949	72	3,080	–	–	2 twin 130mm
Udaloy	1980	2+4	8,000	–	8 SS-N-14 anti-submarine	2 100mm, 4 30mm Gatling
Sovremennyy	1980	2+3	7,500	2 launchers for SA-N-7	2 quad SS-N-22	2 twin 130mm, 4 30mm Gatling

[a] All figures in parentheses are conversions, not new constructions.
Sources: As for table 10, with Kehoe and Brower, 'The Soviet Sovremennyy Class Destroyer' (1981), pp. 911–16, and 'Bal-Com 3 at Sea' (1981), p. 976.

Table 39
Frigates

| Class | Year in service | Number built + building | Displacement full load (tons) | Missile launchers | | Guns |
				Anti-aircraft	Anti-submarine	
Krivak II	1976	11	3,800	2 twin SA-N-4	1 quad SS-N-14	2 single 100mm
Krivak I	1970	21	3,800	2 twin SA-N-4	1 quad SS-N-14	2 twin 76mm
Mirka I/II	1964	20	1,150	–	–	2 twin 76mm
Peyta I/II	1960	65	1,140	–	–	2 twin 76mm
Riga	1952	64	1,320	–	–	3 single 100mm
Grisha I/III	1968	32	1,100	1 twin SA-N-4 (18 missiles)	–	twin 57mm
Koni	1977	2	2,000	1 twin SA-N-4	–	2 twin 76mm

Sources: As for table 10.

Table 40
Small combatants

Class	Year in service	Number built + building	Displacement full load (tons)	Missiles	Other weapons
Tarantul	1978	4	550	2 twin SS-N-2C	single 76mm
Nanuchka I/III	1969	23	930	2 triple SS-N-9 1 twin SA-N-4 (18 missiles)	twin 57mm or single 76mm
Poti	1961	64	580	–	twin 57mm
Sarancha	1976	1	330	2 twin SS-N-9 1 twin SA-N-4	30mm Gatling
Matka	1978	7+1	215	2 SS-N-2C	76mm; 30mm Gatling
Babochka	1977	1	440	–	2 quad torpedo tubes
Turya	1973	30	220	–	4 torpedo tubes; twin 57mm
Osa I/II	1959	120	210	4 SS-N-2	some with quad SA-N-5
Komer	1960	?	75	2 SS-N-2	–
P4	1951	?	22.5	–	2 torpedo tubes
P6/P8/P10	1951	?	75	–	2 torpedo tubes
Shershen	1963	?	160	–	4 torpedo tubes

Sources: As for table 10.

Table 41

Ship-borne anti-ship missiles

Missile	Year in service	Range (km)	Speed (Mach)	Warhead type	Notes
Anti-surface ship					
SS-N-1 Scrubber	1958	180	0.9	nuclear or HE	few still in service
SS-N-2 A/B Styx	1960	42	0.9	HE	replaces SS-N-2A and B
SS-N-2C	?	75	0.9	HE	requires mid-course guidance correction
SS-N-3 Shaddock	1962	375	1.4	nuclear or HE	
SS-N-7	1969	55	1.5	nuclear or HE	
SS-N-9 Siren	1968	110	0.8	nuclear or HE	replaces SS-N-3
SS-N-12	?	500	2.5	nuclear or HE	
SS-N-19	1980	450	?		
SS-N-21	1980	?	?		
SS-N-22	1980	?	?		improved SS-N-9
Anti-submarine					
SS-N-14 Silex	1968	45–55	subsonic	anti-submarine torpedo	possible anti-ship capability
SS-N-15	1974	35–45	?	nuclear depth charge	submarine launched
SS-N-16	1974?	120?	?	anti-submarine torpedo	version of SS-N-15
FPAS-1	1968	24	?	nuclear depth charge	launched from SUW-N-1

Sources: As for table 10, with *Flight International* 119 (1981), pp. 1627–8.

Table 42

Ship-borne surface-to-air missiles

Missile	Year in service	Guidance system	Range (km)	Notes
SA-N-1 Goa	1961	beam-rider, semi-active homing	18	version of SA-3 Goa
SA-N-2 Guideline	1961	radar command	55	version of SA-2 Guideline
SA-N-3 Goblet	1967	radar command	55	
SA-N-4	1969	radar command	15	
SA-N-5	?	optical with infra-red homing	6	version of SA-7 Grail
SA-N-6	1979	active radar homing	55	version of SA-10

Sources: As for table 26.

Table 43

Naval aviation

	1965	1970	1975	1980
Strike/bombers	400	440	410	370
Fighters/fighter-bombers	0	0	0	90
Reconnaissance/electronic warfare	140	100[a]	110	170
Anti-submarine	160	320	450	390
Tankers	–	–	100	70
Transport/training	200	200	200	340

[a] Includes some tanker aircraft.
Sources: 1970 and 1975 adapted from Collins and Cordesman (1978), pp. 156 and 173; *Understanding Soviet Naval Developments* (1975), pp. 27–8, 73–6; *MB 1975–6* (1975), p. 9; and *MB 1970–71* (1970), p. 9. 1980 from *Understanding Soviet Naval Developments* (1981), pp. 41–4, 121–30. 1965 from Jones (ed.) (1978), p. 205.

Table 44
Naval aircraft

Designation	Year in service	Maximum speed (kph)	Operational radius (km)	Armament	Notes
Strike/bombers					
Backfire-B	1975	2,125	5,320	2 AS-6 Kingfish	
Tu-22 Blinder-B	1963	1,500	1,500	1 AS-4 Kitchen	
Tu-16 Badger-A	1953	1,000	4,800	9,000 kg of bombs	
Tu-16 Badger-C	1961	1,000	4,800	1 AS-2 Kipper or 2 AS-6 Kingfish	
Tu-16 Badger-G	?	1,000	4,800	2 AS-5 Kelt or 2 AS-6 Kingfish	
Fighters/fighter-bombers					
Yak-36 Forger-A	1976	?	370	1,360 kg of ordnance, including 4 AA-2 Atoll or AA-8 Aphid	
Su-17 Fitter-C	1976	2,300	420–600	3,500 kg of ordnance, including AA-22, AA-8, AS-7 Kerry, or AS-10	
Reconnaissance/electronic warfare					
Tu-16 Badger-D -E, -F, -J	?	1,000	4,800	none	electronic and photographic Intelligence versions
Tu-142 Bear-C, -D, -E	1955	800	8,000	none	reconnaissance
Anti-submarine					
Tu-142 Bear-F	1973	800	8,000		version of Tu-95 Bear
Il-38 May	1969	645	3,000	4,000 kg	version of Il-18
Be-12 Mail	1964	600	1,300		amphibious
Be-6 Madge	1949	415	?		amphibious
Mi-14 Haze	1976	?	305	2,000 kg	helicopter
Ka-25 Hormone-A	1967	210	300	1,000 kg	helicopter
Mi-4 Hound	1953	210	230	4 depth charges	helicopter

References

Annual Economic Indicators for the USSR (Washington, DC: Joint Economic Committee report, February 1964)

Backofen, Joseph E., 'Shaped Charges Versus Armor – Part II', *Armor* 89 (September – October 1980)

Bialer, S. (ed.), *The Domestic Context of Soviet Foreign Policy* (Boulder, Colorado: Westview Press, 1981)

Baldwin, Godfrey S., *Population Projections by Age and Sex* (Washington, DC: US Department of Commerce, September 1976)

Bergson, Abram, *Productivity and the Social System – The USSR and the West* (Cambridge, Mass: Harvard University Press, 1978)

Bergson, Abram, *Soviet Economic Prospects Revisited* (paper presented at NATO Colloquium, Brussels, 1978)

Bergson, Abram, and Levine, Herbert S. (eds), *The Soviet Economy: Toward the Year 2000* (London: Allen and Unwin, 1983)

Berman, Robert P., *Soviet Air Power in Transition* (Washington, DC: Brookings Institution, 1978)

Block, Herbert, *The Planetary Product in 1980: A Creative Pause?* (Washington, DC: US Department of State, Bureau of Public Affairs, 1981)

Breyer, Siegfried, *Guide to the Soviet Navy*, trans. by W. H. Henley (Annapolis, Maryland: United States Naval Institute Press, 1970)

Collins, John M., *United States/Soviet Military Balance: A Frame of Reference for Congress* (Washington, DC: Library of Congress Congressional Research Service, for the Senate Committee on Armed Services, January 1976)

Collins, John M., and Cordesman, Anthony H., *Imbalance of Power* (San Rafael, California: Presidio Press, 1978)

Communist Aid Activities in Non-Communist Less Developed Countries, 1979 and 1954–1979 (Washington, DC: CIA, National Foreign Assessment Center, ER 80–103180, October 1980)

Couhat, Jean Labayle, *Combat Fleets of the World 1980/81* (Annapolis, Maryland: United States Naval Institute Press, 1980)

Davis, Christopher, and Feshbach, Murray, *Estimates and Projections of the Labor Force and Civilian Employment in the USSR 1950 to 1990* (Washington, DC: US Department of Commerce, September 1976)

Davis, Christopher, and Feshbach, Murray, *Rising Infant Mortality in the USSR in the 1970s* (Washington, DC: US Department of Commerce, June 1980)

Denison, Edward F., *Accounting for Slower Economic Growth – the United States in the 1970s* (Washington, DC: Brookings Institution, 1979)

Dimensions of Soviet Economic Power (Washington, DC: Joint Economic Committee report, 1962)

Feshbach, Murray, *Demography and Soviet Society: Social and Cultural*

References

Aspects (Washington DC: Kennan Institute for Advanced Russian Studies, Occasional Paper 123, February 1981)

Feshbach, Murray, *Employment Trends and Policies in the USSR* (paper prepared for CESES Seminar, Milan, August 1978)

Flight International 119 (30 May 1981); 120 (5 September 1981)

Foss, Christopher, *Artillery of the World* (New York: Charles Scribner's Sons, 1981)

Foss, Christopher, *Jane's World Armoured Fighting Vehicles* (London: Macdonald and Jane's, 1976)

Green, Donald W., *Soviet Alternative Growth and Foreign Trade in the 1980s: Alternative Projections with SOVMOD III* (paper presented at NATO Colloquium, Brussels, 1980)

Green, Donald W., Klein, Lawrence R., and Levine, Herbert S., *The SRI-WEFA Soviet Econometric Model: Phase Two Documentation* (Stanford, California: Stanford Research Institute, October 1975)

Handbook of Economic Statistics (Washington, DC: CIA, National Foreign Assessment Center, OER 80–10452)

Handbook of Economic Statistics 1981 (Washington, DC: CIA, National Foreign Assessment Center, NF HES 81–001, November 1981)

Hofmann, Kurt, 'An Analysis of Soviet Artillery Development'. *International Defense Review* 10 (No. 6, 1977)

Isby, David, *Tactics and Weapons of the Soviet Army* (New York: Jane's, 1981)

Jane's All the World's Aircraft 1980–1981 (New York: Jane's, 1980)

Jane's Fighting Ships (London: Jane's Publishing Co. Ltd, published annually)

Jane's Weapons Systems (London: Jane's Publishing Co. Ltd, published annually)

Jones, David R. (ed.), *Soviet Armed Forces Review Annual*, vol. 8 (Gulf Breeze, Florida: Academic International Press, 1978)

Kehoe, J. W., and Brower, K. S., 'Bal-Com 3 at Sea', *International Defense Review* 14 (No. 8, 1981)

Kehoe, J. W., and Brower, K. S., 'The Kirov', *International Defense Review* 14 (No. 2, 1981)

Kehoe, J. W., and Brower, K. S., 'The Soviet Sovremennyy Class Destroyer', *International Defense Review* 14 (No. 7, 1981)

Kjellén, Rudolf, *Die Grossmächte der Gegenwart* (Leipzig, Berlin, 1916)

Krivinyi, Nikolaus, *World Military Aviation* (New York: Arco, 1977)

Luttwak, Edward N., *Strategic Power: Military Capabilities and Political Utility (Washington Papers*, No. 38) (Beverly Hills, California: Sage Publications, 1976)

Malzeyev, Alexander, 'Soviet Air-launched Cruise Missiles', *International Defense Review* 11 (No. 1, 1978)

Military Balance (MB) (London: International Institute for Strategic Studies, published annually)

Norby, M. O., *Soviet Aerospace Handbook* (prepared by the US Air Force as pamphlet 200–21) (Washington, DC: Government Printing Office, 1978)

232

References

Odom, William E., 'Whither the Soviet Union', *The Washington Quarterly* 4 (No. 2, Spring 1981)

Opposing Forces Europe (Washington, DC: US Department of Army field manual, FM 30–10, 1978)

Panyalev, Georg, 'Su–24 Fencer: A Closer Look', *International Defense Review* 14 (No. 6, 1981)

Polmar, Norman, *World Combat Aircraft Directory* (Garden City, New York: Doubleday and Company, 1976)

Soviet Economic Problems and Prospects (CIA study) (Washington, DC: Joint Economic Committee report, 8 August 1977)

Soviet Economic Prospects for the Seventies (Washington, DC: Joint Economic Committee report, 27 June 1973)

Soviet Economy in a New Perspective (Washington, DC: Joint Economic Committee report, 14 October 1976)

Soviet Economy in a Time of Change (Washington, DC: Joint Economic Committee report, 2 vols., 10 October 1979)

Soviet Military Power (Washington, DC: Department of Defense, 1981)

Understanding Soviet Naval Developments (Washington, DC: US Navy, Office of the Chief of Naval Operations, 2nd edn. 1975, 4th edn. 1981)

USSR 1950 to 1990, The (Washington, DC: US Department of Commerce, Foreign Economic Report No. 10, September 1976)

USSR: Toward a Reconciliation of Marxist and Western Measures of National Income (Washington, DC: CIA, National Foreign Assessment Center, ER 78–10505 October 1978)

USSR: Trends and Prospects in Educational Attainments 1959–85 (Washington, DC: CIA, National Foreign Assessment Center, ER 79–10344, June 1979)

Van Creveld, Martin, *Supplying War: Logistics from Wallenstein to Patton* (Cambridge: Cambridge University Press, 1977)

Vaňous, Jan, and Marrese, Michael, *Implicit Subsidies in Soviet Trade with Eastern Europe* (British Columbia: The University of British Columbia Department of Economics, Discussion Paper No. 80–32, September 1980)

Wimbush, S. E., and Ponomareff, D., *Alternatives for Mobilizing Soviet Central Asian Labor: Outmigration and Regional Development* (Santa Monica, California: Rand Corporation report R-2476-AF, November 1979)

Index

Addis Ababa, 55, 57
Afghanistan, 38, 105; seizure of Kabul,
    xi; Soviet invasion, 41, 44, 45, 53–4,
    55, 57–60, 78, 81, 85–6, 106, 116,
    134, 164; resistance to Soviet army,
    82–3, 114; under Soviet control, 108;
    as client-state, 110; Soviet forces
    deployed in, 192
Africa, 46, 64
Agitprop, 23, 152
agriculture, 158; collectivization, 23;
    failures, 24–5, 163; labour force,
    153; productivity, 158–9
aid, to Third World, 134–5, 136, 162
air defences, 180–1, 194
air-to-air missiles, 213
air-to-ground missiles, 208
air-to-surface missiles, 212
aircraft, manned bombers, 179–80,
    183–4, 189; Soviet air force, 206–13;
    Soviet navy, 218–19, 228; strategic
    defence forces, 187–8;
    theatre-nuclear forces, 182
aircraft-launched missiles, 208
airpower, changing balance of, 46–7
Albania, 133
Algeria, 113
Amin, Hafizullah, 58
Andropov, Yuri, 36, 39, 70, 74, 101,
    154
Angola, 81
Ankara, 88
anti-aircraft guns and missiles, 47, 205
anti-ballistic missile launchers, 180, 187
antisemitism, 10
anti-tank weapons, 194, 202–3

appeasement, xii, 33
Arab-Israeli war (1973), 47
Arabs, 159–60
Armenians, 9, 108
arms race, 31, 123
arms trade, 134–5, 136, 162
artillery, 200
ASEAN, 100
Asia, 64, 99
Assab, 55, 57
Australia, 145
Azerbaijan, 109
Azeris, 8, 109, 110

Backfire bomber, 179, 181, 184, 189,
    219, 228
Baikal-Amur railway, 96, 157
Bajt, Alexander, 121
balance of power, restoration of, 34
Baltic Sea, 87, 219
Baltic States, independence, 4, 5, 8, 21
Baluchis, 109, 110
Bangla Desh, 99
Bashkirs, 8
Baybakov, 155, 165
Belgium, 39, 112
Bergson, Abram, 121, 140
Beria, Lavrenti Pavlovich, 9
Berlin, 10; blockade, 50
Bessarabia, 9
Bialer, Seweryn, 120, 123
biological warfare, 62
birth rate, 128, 147, 148, 150, 154
black economy, 128
Bolsheviks, 4–5, 168; Civil War, 61;
    optimism, 21–2; transnationalism, 1

235

bomber aircraft, 179–80, 183–4, 189
Bosnia, 73
Brandt, Willy, 134
Brazil, 138
Brest-Litovsk, treaty of, 21
Brezhnev, Leonid, 36, 121, 125, 144;
    agricultural policies, 141, 158–9;
    economic policies, 156–7; 1977
    constitution, 149; police control, 69;
    and Soviet living standards, 127; and
    the Soviet navy, 214
Britain, Berlin airlift, 50; economic
    control, 22; growth of per capita
    consumption, 127; industrial
    problems, 39; Korean War, 43;
    nuclear weapons, 32; and the
    Roman empire, 82; and the Russian
    Civil War, 61
British empire, 73, 81, 112–13
Budapest, 58–9
Bulgaria, 64, 65–6; as client-state, 107;
    GNP, 144; NATO defences, 48;
    population, 144; relations with
    Soviet Union, 65–6; Soviet control
    of, 78, 79
Burma, 99
Byelorussians, 7, 11, 86
Byzantine empire, 2–3

Cambodia, 26, 100
capital, as factor of production, 121,
    140–1, 146, 155–8
capital formation, 128–30, 165
Catholic church, in Poland, 79
Caucasus, 13, 108; independence, 21;
    living standards, 11; Muslims, 8
Central Intelligence Agency (CIA), 124,
    125, 130, 142, 164–5; Office of
    Economic Research, 140
central planning, 22–5, 37
Ceylon, 99
Chechens, 8
chemical warfare, 49
China, 11, 13, 38, 69, 72, 145;
    communism, 62; Cultural
    Revolution, 93; GNP, 170; lack of
    defences, 32; nuclear weapons, 32,
    35, 93–4, 98, 105–6; population
    forecasts, 147; relations with Soviet
    Union, 26, 35, 42; role in Soviet
    strategy, 89, 91–107; Soviet defences
    against, 83, 181, 182, 191, 192; and
    Soviet expansionism, 85; trade with
    Soviet Union, 133, 173

Chinese air force, 46
Chinese Communist Party, 92, 94
Christianity, 2
civil defence, 96
coastal defence, 218
Cold War, 132
collectivization, 23
Comecon, 133
Comintern, 61
command economy, 120, 121, 143–4,
    149
communism, decline of Marxism-
    Leninism in Soviet Union, 66–71; in
    Eastern Europe, 65–6; as a religion,
    37, 66; 'socialism in one country', 2;
    Soviet influence overseas, 60–5
Communist Party, and industrial
    management, 37–8
conscription, 125
Conservative Party (Britain), 112–13
consumer goods, 121, 122–3, 126–8,
    158
consumption, per capita, 126–7
cruise missiles, 180
Cuba, 27, 30, 42, 50, 111, 145, 161;
    intervention in Ethiopia, 56; 1962
    missiles crisis, 138; Soviet use of
    military forces, 77; terrorist training
    camps, 64
Cultural Revolution, China, 93
Czechoslovakia, 87, 133; as
    client-state, 107; GNP, 144;
    nationalism, 79; population, 144;
    Prague Spring, 65, 114; prewar
    Communist Party, 65; Soviet control
    of, 77–8; Soviet invasion, xi, 26, 45,
    59, 80

decolonization, 112–13
demobilization, and labour supply,
    151–2, 154
Denison, Edward F., 143, 154
detente, 69, 132
deterrence, 30, 52, 53, 83, 90, 116
dissidence, 2
Djibouti, 55
Druids, 82

east Asia, 35
East Indies, 113
economic growth, Soviet Union,
    122–3, 136–9, 142–3, 163–6; USA,
    11, 122, 137–9, 143, 145

economics, basis of Soviet power,
119–68; central planning, 22–5, 37;
costs of Soviet imperialism, 111–12,
114–16; diminishing growth rates,
68–9; economic power as substitute
for military power, 52–3; failures of
Soviet system, 11, 24–6, 36–9, 68–70
education, 142–3
Egypt, 3, 26, 134
embargoes, trade, 162
energy, resources, 159–60, 162
Engels, Friedrich, 67
Eritrea, 54, 56, 57
Estonia, independence, 4, 5, 8;
nationalism, 9, 86
Ethiopia, 111; Soviet intervention in,
44, 53–4, 55–7, 81
ethnic reaffirmation, 9–12
Europe (Eastern), decline of Soviet
ideological influence, 65–6; GNP, 144;
guest workers in Soviet Union, 150;
living standards, 127; population,
144; Soviet air force deployment in,
209; Soviet army units in, 83, 191–2;
Soviet control of, 77–8, 79–80; and
Soviet security, 107–8; trade with
Soviet Union, 133, 160–1, 173;
Western influences, 86
Europe (West), 42; American
influences, 89; American interests
in, 29; and American rearmament,
34–5; economic growth forecasts,
164; economic problems, 39;
responses to Soviet actions, 116;
Soviet attempts to weaken links with
USA, 87, 88, 100; Soviet-sponsored
terrorism, 64; Soviet theatre-nuclear
weapons, 181–2
expansionism, 72–7, 81–110

Farsis, 109
Finland, 77; independence, 4, 5, 21,
107; Winter War, 17
First World War, 17, 21, 40, 126, 139
foreign trade, 160–3, 173
France, communists, 61, 63;
decolonization, 112, 113; growth of
per capita consumption, 127;
industrial problems, 39; nuclear
weapons, 32, 98; Third Estate, 167
French army, 22
Fujian (Fukien), 102

Gansu (Kansu), 104

Garbuzov, 155
Gaul, 82
Georgians, 9
Germany (pre-1945), Communist
Party, 65; invasion of Soviet Union,
18–19; navy, 22; Nazi-Soviet pact,
65, 131; operation Margarethe,
58–9; possibility of revolution in, 21,
22; and the Roman empire, 75–6;
Second World War, 5–7, 40–1;
treaty of Brest-Litovsk, 21
Germany (East) 64, 85; as client-state,
107; free enterprise, 168; GNP, 144;
nationalism, 79; 1953 uprising, 80,
114; population, 144
Germany (West), 42; army, 49;
economic control, 22; growth of per
capita consumption, 127; industrial
problems, 39; NATO defences, 48
Gestapo, 65
gold, 159, 160, 161, 163
Gosplan, 37, 155
Greece, communists, 63; NATO
defences, 48
Greece, ancient, 73, 77
Greek Orthodox Church, 3
gross domestic product (GDP), 130
gross national product (GNP), Eastern
Europe, 144–5, 170; forecasts, 163,
164–6; foreign trade share of, 132;
growth of, 136–9, 142–3, 155;
ratio of defence budget to,
124–5; Soviet-American ratio, 115
Guangdong (Kwangtung), 102
guerrilla warfare, 103–4, 105, 106; in
Afghanistan, 110; Soviet
sponsorship, 63–4
guest workers, 39, 149, 150–1
Gustafson, Thane, 120

Han Chinese, 103, 104
Hapsburg empire, 73
Heilongjiang (Heilungkiang), 104
helicopters, 193, 206, 209, 219
Herat, 57
Hercegovina, 73
Hewitt, Edward A., 135
Hitler, Adolf, xii–xiii, 36, 40–1, 42, 131
Holland, Paul, 123
Horthy, Admiral, 58
Hungary, 87; Bolshevik uprising, 22;
as client-state, 107; free-enterprise,
168; GNP, 144; nationalism, 79; 1956
uprising, 80, 114, 127; operation

Index

Margarethe, 58–9; population, 144;
Soviet control, 80; Soviet takeover,
65; trade with Soviet Union, 133

Ibero-Caucasians, 8, 9
imperialism, economics of, 111–12,
114–16; expansion of Russian
empire, 13–14; future of Soviet
Union, 72–7, 81–110, 113–16;
Soviet, 11–12, 26–8, 29–30
India, 105; British Raj, 81; population
forecasts, 147; Soviet influence, 99,
101
Indochina, 26, 43
Indonesia, 100, 113
industry, Central Asian dilemma, 39;
central planning, 22–5; declining
investment, 68–9, 121
inflation, 125, 151
Inner Mongolia, 100, 104
inputs, factors of production, 121–2,
139–42
intelligentsia, 66, 67–8
intercontinental ballistic missiles
(ICBMS), 176–8, 181, 183, 186
investment, 121; and capital stock
formation, 129–31, 155–8; future
prospects, 165–6
Iran, 38, 72, 83; Soviet forces deployed
against, 192; Soviet strategy, 108–10
Iranian peoples, 8, 9
Iraq, Soviet relations with, 3–4; and
Soviet strategy, 109
Iraqi Communist Party, 4
Islam, militant revival, 8, 9; Muslims in
Soviet Union, 8, 54, 108, 147–8
Israel, 44
Italy, 42; communists, 61, 63; growth
of per capita consumption, 127;
Roman empire, 82
Ivan the Terrible, 6

Japan, 19, 29, 35, 42, 69, 73, 145, 161;
economic growth, 122; GNP, 170,
171; growth of per capita
consumption, 127; investment, 130;
lack of defences, 32; Meiji Period,
167; Pearl Harbor, 41; productivity,
152; ratio of defence spending to
GNP, 124; responses to Soviet
actions, 116; Soviet-sponsored
terrorism, 64
Jews, 8; antisemitism, 10; emigration
from Soviet Union, 9; Russification,
9

Kabardians, 8
Kabul, xi, 45, 57–8, 59
Kaganovich, Lazar Moiseyevich, 9
Kalita, Ivan, 6
Kampuchea, 145
Kandahar, 57
Karelia, 13
Karmal, Barbak, 58
Kazakhs, 8
Kazakhstan, 147, 148–9
KGB, 50, 58, 59–60, 70, 111
Khalq faction, 58
Khingan mountains, 85
Khrushchev, Nikita, 156; economic
policies, 43, 68–9, 70, 122–3, 137;
reduction of workweek, 139, 140,
151; and Soviet living standards,
127; and the Soviet navy, 214; trade
with Third World, 134; 'virgin lands'
development, 141
Kiev, 18
Kirgiz, 8
Kjellén, Rudolf, 138
Knickerbocker, H. R., 131
Korea, North, 100, 145
Korea, South, 31, 45, 145
Korean War, 43, 62
Kosygin, Alexei, 127, 156, 157, 214
Kunduz, 57, 59
Kurds, 8, 109, 110
Kushka, 57
Kutuzov, Field Marshal, 6

labour, and economic growth, 142; as
factor of production, 121–2, 139–40,
142, 145; size of labour force,
147–54, 172
Labour Party (Britain), 112
land, as factor of production, 121, 122,
141–2, 146, 158–60
Lange, Oskar, 120
Laos, 26, 81, 100, 145
lasers, 181
Latin America, 64
Latvia, independence, 4, 5, 8;
nationalism, 9, 86
Lebanon, 44
Lend-Lease, 131–2
Lenin, 1–2, 27, 37, 67; Civil War, 61;
economic policies, 119–20; New
Economic Policy, 167–8; optimism,
21; transnationalism, 4–5, 10, 12
Leningrad, 18
Libya, 3

238

Lithuania, 13; independence, 4, 5, 8;
nationalism, 9, 86
living standards, 11, 27–8, 68–70,
122–3, 126–8

Malaysia, 100
Malenkov, Georgi, 122
management, Communist Party and,
37–8; Soviet failures, 15–16, 36–7
Manchuria, 19, 85, 104
Mao Tse-tung, 93, 94, 102
Margarethe, operation, 58
Mariam, Lieut.-Col. Mengistu Haile,
56
Marx, Karl, 67
Marxism-Leninism, *see* communism
merchant navy, 135
Middle East, 29, 46, 209
Mikoyan, Anastas Ivanovich, 9
military aid, to Third World, 134–5,
136
'Missile-Gap' crisis, 43
missiles, air-to-air, 213; air-to-ground,
208; air-to-surface, 212;
aircraft-launched, 208; anti-airccraft,
47; ICBMs, 176–8, 181, 183, 186;
SAMs, 180, 187, 192, 194, 204; SLBMs,
178–9, 182, 183, 185, 186; Soviet
navy, 214–18, 229–30
Moldavians, 9, 86
Molotov-Ribbentrop Pact, 131
Mongolia, 86, 99–100, 101, 102, 145
Mongols, 14, 92, 99–100
mortars, 201
Moscow, 18
multiple rocket launchers, 201
Muslims, *see* Islam
MVD, 111

Nasser, Gamal Abdel, 3
National Idea, 7–8, 12
nationalism, primacy of Russian
nationalism, 5–12, 27–8, 38–9; rise of
ethnic nationalism, 9–12; and the
Russian Revolution, 1–2; in Soviet
client-states, 79; transnationalism,
5–12, 27, 28, 113–14
NATO, 69; future prospects, 116; GNP,
145, 170, 171; ground force
imbalance with Soviets, 47–8;
nuclear weapons, 105; population,
144–5; ratio of defence spending to
GNP, 124; responses to Soviet
actions, 88, 116; role in Soviet

strategy, 89; weaknesses, 34
Nazi-Soviet pact, 65, 131
Nazis, xii–xiii, 65, 131
net material income (NMI), 136
Netherlands, 112, 113
Nevsky, Alexander, 6
New Economic Policy (NEP), 126, 131,
167–8
New Zealand, 145
Norway, NATO defences, 48;
vulnerability to Soviet attack, 85,
87–8
nuclear weapons, arms race, 31;
Chinese, 93–4, 98; and deterrence,
90; intercontinental ballistic missiles,
176–8, 181, 183, 186; long-range, 30;
rearmament, 34; Soviet, 50–3, 93–4;
Soviet reluctance to use, 40; and
Soviet war schemes, 84–5;
submarine-launched ballistic
missiles, 178–9, 182, 183, 185, 186;
theatre-nuclear forces, 181–2,
184–90; in war between China and
Soviet Union, 97–8, 105–6; and
weakness of Western conventional
forces, 88
Numeiri, 3

OECD, 127, 130, 161
Ogaden, 54, 56
oil, 159–60, 161, 162
OPEC, 159–60, 162–3
Oslo, 87–8
Ossetians, 8
Ottoman empire, 2–3, 13, 14

Pakistan, 99, 105
Palestine, 2–3
Palestine Liberation Organization
(PLO), 110
particle-beam devices, 181
Pearl Harbor, 41
peasants, collectivization, 23
Pennsylvania, University of, 164
Persian Gulf, 32, 73, 109, 110
Persians, 108–9
Peter the Great, Tsar, 6, 13
Petrov, Lieut.-Gen. V. I., 56–7
platinum, 160
Poland and the Poles, 8, 13, 17, 87;
Catholic church in, 79; as
client-state, 107; economic crisis,
146, 154, 164, 166; economic links
with Soviet Union, 77;

free-enterprise, 168; GNP, 144;
independence, 21; martial law, 80;
nationalism, 9; 1956 insurrection,
127; population, 144; prewar
Communist Party, 65; strikes, 127–8;
trade with Soviet Union, 133;
unrest, 114, 116
police, control of population, 68, 69,
70; police terror, 23, 65, 70, 86, 114,
120; secret police, 23
Politburo, 62, 64, 67, 108
political security, and Soviet
expansion, 86–8, 89
population, growth of, 127, 140; and
labour supply, 147–51, 172;
Russian-American ratio, 138–9
Portugal, 112, 113
Prague, 59
Prague Spring, 65, 114
Pravda, 5, 64, 158
production, input factors, 121–2,
139–42, 145–6
productivity, 121–2, 142–4, 146, 152,
153–4, 163, 166
propaganda, central planning, 23
public opinion, and Soviet living
standards, 126–8
PVO Strany, 206

Qinghai (Chinghai), 104

radar, 180, 187
raw materials, 141–2, 159–60, 161
regional security, and Soviet
expansion, 107–10
religion, Marxism-Leninism as, 37, 66;
Russian foreign policy and, 2–3
Ribbentrop, Joachim von, 131
Richardson, Admiral, 132
robots, 153
Roman empire, 73, 108; client-states,
78, 80; expansionism, 81, 82;
military weaknesses, 75–6; reasons
for expansion, 73; Romanization of
captured territories, 12, 76–7
Romania, 87; as client-state, 107; GNP,
144; nationalism, 9, 79; population,
144; relations with Soviet Union, 77,
78, 80; Soviet takeover, 65
Rommel, Field Marshal, 57
Ruhr, 39
Russia (pre-1917), expansionism,
13–14; gross national product, 115;
industrialization, 16; managerial

backwardness, 15–16; military
strategy, 15; military weaknesses,
14–17; revolution, 1, 167; *see also*
Soviet Union
Russian Orthodox Church, 2–3, 6, 66
Russo-Japanese war, 17
Ruthenians, 8, 9

Samarkand, 57
satellites, early warning, 180;
intelligence, 218
second economy, 167, 168
Second World War, 13, 36; causes,
40–1; defensive-offensive warfare,
18–19; living standards, 126;
restoration of Russian nationalism
in, 5–7; and Soviet economic
growth, 139; Soviet foreign trade,
131–2; Soviet preparations for, 120
secret police, 23
security, and Soviet expansion, 86–110
Shanghai, 102
Shia Muslims, 108
ships, Soviet navy, 214–30
Siberia, 13, 142
Sichuan (Szechwan), 102, 105
Singapore, 100
Skorzeny, Otto, 58
Slavs, 65
Slovaks, 65
social democracy, 65
Solidarity, 168
Somalia, 54, 55–6
South Africa, 160
southeast Asia, Soviet influence in, 99,
100
Soviet air force, 44, 46–7; Chinese
strategy, 94, 96, 97, 103; Frontal
Aviation, 206–11; Long-Range Air
Force, 206; Military Transport
Aviation, 206, 211; nuclear
weapons, 50–1; strength, 206–13
Soviet Army, air assault brigades, 193;
airborne divisions, 193, 196–7;
anti-tank missiles, 194–5;
deployment, 191–2; improvements
in, 47–50; improvements in officer
corps, 44–5; lack of infantry, 103–4;
logistics, 193–4; motorized rifle
divisions, 192, 193, 196–7; Second
World War, 5–6, 132; superiority
over Western forces, 43–4; tank
divisions, 192–3
Soviet Central Asia, 8; living

standards, 11; population, 147, 148–9; role in labour force, 39; and Russian nationalism, 38–9; under Soviet control, 108

Soviet navy, 84; and China, 101; growth of, 30, 43, 45–6; Naval Air Service, 206; strength, 214–30

Soviet Union, advent of pessimism, 28–39, 40–1, 89, 116; balance of power, 34; Chinese strategy, 89, 91–107; Civil War, 61; control of Eastern Europe, 77–8, 79–80; decline of Marxism-Leninism in, 66–71; ethnic minorities and Russian nationalism, 8–12; future expansion, xii, 72–7, 81–110; future of, 113–16; ideological influence in Eastern Europe, 65–6; ideological motivation, 2–4; imperialism, 11–12, 26–8, 29–30; intervention in Ethiopia, 44, 53–4, 55–7, 81; invasion of Afghanistan, 41, 44, 45, 53–4, 55, 57–60, 78, 81, 85–6, 106, 116, 134, 164; the minorities and Soviet imperialism, 27–8; operational confidence, 55–60; as optimistic regime, 21–5; overseas ideological influence, 60–5; population, 172, population growth, 138–9, 140, 147–8; primacy of Russian nationalism, 5–12, 27–8, 38–9; rise of ethnic nationalism, 9–12; strategic role of America, 89–91, 100; Western views of, xi–xiii

economics: capital formation, 128–30; central planning, 22–5, 37; economic basis of power, 119–73; economic failures, 11, 24–6, 36–9, 68–70; economic growth, 122–3, 136–9, 142–3, 163–6; economics of imperialism, 111–12, 114–16; forecasts of economic growth, 164–6; foreign economic relations, 131–6, 160–3; foreign trade, 173; future economic prospects, 145–68; GNP, 169–71; labour supply, 147–54, 172; living standards, 11, 27–8, 68–70, 122–3, 126–8; productivity, 142–4, 152, 163, 166; ratio of defence budget to GNP, 124–5; trade with America, 91

as a military power: bomber aircraft, 179–80; defence budget, 68–9,

123–6; defensive-offensive warfare, 18–19; growth of military power, 26, 29–31, 33, 42–55, 116; intercontinental ballistic missiles, 176–8; military optimism, 39–41; military weaknesses, 17–20; nuclear weapons, 50–3; preparedness for war, 83–5; strategic air defences, 180–1; strategic nuclear weapons, 176–90; strength, 176–205; submarine-launched ballistic missiles, 178–9; tanks, 195, 196–7; theatre-nuclear forces, 181–2, 184–90

SOVMOD, 164

SOVSIM, 164–5

Spain, 63, 108, 112

Stalin, Joseph, 1–2, 4–5, 9, 27, 63; antisemitism, 10; Berlin blockade, 50; central planning, 24; death, 68; economic policies, 120–1; foreign trade, 131; police terror, 70; and the primacy of Russian nationalism, 5–7, 10; Second World War, 19; and Soviet living standards, 126; war economy, 143–4, 149, 163; Winter War, 17; and Yugoslavia, 63, 80

Stalinism, 69, 70, 86, 114, 120, 123

Stanford Research Institute (SRI), 164, 165

'state monopoly capitalism', 120

Strategic Arms Limitation Talks (SALT), 26, 176, 179

strategic nuclear weapons, 176–90

Strategic Rocket Force, 179

strategic security, and Soviet expansion, 89–107

submarine-launched ballistic missiles (SLBM), 178–9, 182, 183, 185, 186

submarines, 45, 214, 216–17, 221–3

Sudan, 3

surface-to-air missiles (SAM), 180, 187, 192, 194, 204

Suslov, Mikhail, 154

Suvorov, Count Alexander, 6, 15

Swedes, 13

Tadzhik, 8

tanks, 15, 192–3, 195, 196–8; anti-tank weapons, 194, 202–3

Tannu-Tuva, 102

Tartars, 8, 13

Termez, 57, 59

Index

terror, police, 23, 65, 70, 86, 114, 120
terrorism, Soviet sponsorship, 63–4, 115
Thailand, 100
theatre-nuclear weapons, 181–2, 184–90
Third World, 27, 63; Soviet foreign trade, 133–4, 173; Soviet military aid, 134–5, 136, 162
Tibet, 104, 105
Tito, Marshal, 63, 80
trade, foreign, 131–6, 160–3
trade unions, in Poland, 80; support for communism in, 61, 64
Trans-Siberian railway, 96
Transcaucasus, 147, 148–9
transnationalism, 5–12, 27, 28, 113–14
Trotsky, Leon, 21
Tsars, see Russia (pre-1917)
Tudeh, 109
'Turkestan' offensive, 104, 105, 106
Turkey, 38; NATO defences, 48; Soviet forces deployed against, 83, 192, 209; and Soviet security, 108; vulnerability to Soviet attack, 87–8
Turkic peoples, 8, 9, 92, 150
Turkmen SSR, 109, 110
Turkmens, 8
Tuva, 102

Ukraine, 8; independence, 21; nationalism, 9, 86
unemployment, 123, 128, 140, 144
United Nations (UN), 77
United States of America, 69; allies, 42; arms exports, 134; arms race, 31, 123; balance of power, 34; Berlin airlift, 50; economic growth, 11, 122, 137–9, 143, 145; economic growth forecasts, 164; foreign policy failures, 26, 28–9; GNP, 170, 171; GNP ratio with Soviet Union, 115; grain exports to Soviet Union, 159; growth of per capita consumption, 127; industrial problems, 39; intercontinental ballistic missiles, 176; investment, 130; isolationism, 28, 29; Korean War, 43, 62; Lend-Lease, 131–2; likely response to Soviet attack on China, 94–5;

merchant navy, 135; military decline, 26, 29–30, 34, 43, 82; nuclear weapons, 51–3; population, 147; productivity, 152, 154; ratio of defence spending to GNP, 124; rearmament, 31, 33–4; relations with European allies, 34–5; role in Soviet strategy, 89–91, 100; Soviet attempts to weaken links with Europe, 87, 88, 100; and Soviet foreign trade, 91, 131–2; and Soviet naval power, 45–6; and Soviet presence in Afghanistan, 110; submarine-launched ballistic missiles, 178; Vietnam War, 62, 138
US air force, Strategic Air Command, 51
US army, 49
US Congress, 28, 29, 31
US navy, 30, 31
Urals, 192
Ussuri, 91
Uzbek SSR, 147
Uzbeks, 8

Vietnam, North, 27, 42, 111, 145, 161; guest workers in Soviet Union, 150; Soviet influence in, 81, 99, 100, 101
Vietnam, South, 26
Vietnam War, 43, 62, 138

Waffen SS, 7
Warsaw Pact, GNP, 144–5, 170, 171; see also Europe (Eastern)
Washington Post, 128
Western Alliance, see NATO
Wharton Econometric Forecasting Associates (WEFA), 164, 165
White Russians, Civil War, 61
Winter War (1939–40), 17
women, employment, 150

Xinjiang (Sinkiang), 104, 106, 150

Yemen, South, 27, 42, 64
Yugoslavia, as buffer state, 107; free enterprise, 168; relations with Soviet Union, 63, 80; trade with Soviet Union, 133